1994

Hemingway
Repossessed

Hemingway
Repossessed

Edited by
Kenneth Rosen

PRAEGER

Westport, Connecticut
London

Library of Congress Cataloging-in-Publication Data

Hemingway repossessed / edited by Kenneth Rosen.
    p.   cm.
    Includes bibliographical references and index.
    ISBN 0–275–94546–4 (alk. paper)
    1. Hemingway, Ernest, 1899–1961—Criticism and interpretation.
    I. Rosen, Kenneth Mark.
    PS3515.E37Z6193   1994
    813'.52—dc20   93–16260

British Library Cataloguing in Publication Data is available.

Library of Congress Catalog Card Number: 93–16260
ISBN: 0–275–94546–4

First published in 1994

Praeger Publishers, 88 Post Road West, Westport, CT 06881
An imprint of Greenwood Publishing Group, Inc.

Printed in the United States of America

The paper used in this book complies with the
Permanent Paper Standard issued by the National
Information Standards Organization (Z39.48–1984).

10 9 8 7 6 5 4 3 2 1

Copyright Acknowledgments

For Roz, who was pretty good in
there on this one.

And for Gwynne MacFadyen
who was there
when most needed.

Contents

Preface

Twenty years ago Sheldon Norman Grebstein published *Hemingway's Craft* and the naive editors of *Hemingway Notes* (the predecessor of the current journal *The Hemingway Review*) asked Robert Lewis to review the book for their spring issue. He did. His evaluation included the following:

Bunny Wilson, one of the best, a real pro, taught me how to review books. First, you check to see what the son of a bitch says about *you*, if anything. After all, just because you're in the same bottle doesn't mean you have to stick together. Each angleworm has freedom of association.

Some readers were outraged, particularly those who were not very sensitive about tone and style and not much concerned with Hemingway's iceberg view of literature, but others, particularly those who recognized themselves and who could still laugh, applauded the reviewer's courage and honesty.

The book you have in your hands is a collection of essays about Ernest Hemingway and his work that reflect the latest attempts by these individual scholars and critics, each in her or his own way, to make Hemingway their own, to make sense of the man and his fiction not only in terms of his art and his life but also in terms of *their* particular needs, *their* specific critical approaches. At least four of these pieces deal with Hemingway in good comparatist fashion, placing the works in the contexts of the visual worlds of Pablo Picasso, Juan Gris, Diego Velasquez and Paul Cezanne; several focus on the people or places of Spain as the most productive way of understanding what the author was doing, or trying to do; some of the critics here feel most comfortable concentrating, often with fanatical precision, on language and the nuances of Hemingway's details; still others attempt to know and take unto themselves one of America's most popular and yet enigmatic writers by the sheer force of their own erudition, nostalgia, or passion.

Not every critical persuasion is reflected in this book—there are no essays that take an exclusively Marxist or an exclusively feminist or an exclusively New Critical approach—but if you listen carefully you can hear echoes of most of the schools of criticism to which contemporary Hemingway studies is now heir. More important, however, is our recognition that all of these voices are raised in very individualistic attempts to apprehend, to capture and understand and even, if necessary, to make over in their own image, an author who, for about forty years, produced everything from pathetic poetry to Nobel Prize fiction.

In a bar in Collegetown in Ithaca, New York, a nineteen-year-old friend named Paul once told me that he had just that evening finished reading all of Hemingway's novels and stories (that would have been up to and including *The Old Man and the Sea*) and that he'd come to know something about himself that he'd never known before:

I *am* that guy. I mean, he is talking about *me*, the real me. The person who, inside, is really quite confused about some crucial things but who at the same time has a real sense of his need for a kind of personal integrity. Damn, that man can write! But it's really all about what *should* be, not what *is*. It's really all about goals.

Notwithstanding the time (1959) and the place, the initial possession of any fine writer is usually heady stuff; the real trick, of course, and perhaps much more difficult, is to be able to do it again with the same writer when you are in many ways a different person, when you are 29 or 49 or 69. How do you take (or get) back the self you once found in a fine poem or story or novel? How do you acquire again the knowledge of, or the control over, that private and personal world you initially encountered when you first read Hemingway?

Many of the people in this collection offer interesting answers to these questions; several simply embody an answer in the manner of the essay itself. All may be angleworms in a bottle, but, at least in Hemingway studies today, each is free to wriggle as he or she chooses.

Kenneth Rosen

I

Hemingway and Art

1

In Our Time and Picasso

Elizabeth Dewberry Vaughn

When Hemingway arrived in Paris in 1922, the realist movement in France had been in decline for two decades, while in America, recent publication of Anderson's *Winesburg, Ohio* and Lewis's *Main Street* had kept the realist tradition fully alive. Hemingway therefore inherited a set of realist assumptions, that reality can be observed objectively and that art must develop from that objective observation, and he adopted from the French, especially Cubist painters, a skepticism regarding whether complete objectivity is possible or even desirable to achieve. Parallels between Cubist painting and *In Our Time* (*IOT*) suggest that Hemingway borrowed from the Cubists, especially their founder, Picasso, a way of looking at the world as well as several more specific artistic techniques and in so doing learned how to approach his work both as a realist and as an expressionist.

Like Hemingway, Picasso remains a realist to the extent that his work depicts aspects of common life experience and opposes idealism, but Picasso also expresses his dissatisfaction with traditional realism's implicit equation of accurate representation and truth by explicitly devaluing accuracy and placing a premium on forms of representation that require interpretation. In this sense, Picasso's revolt against traditional realism may be understood as the creation of a new mode of realism. In *In Our Time* Hemingway participates simultaneously in the realist tradition and in Picasso's challenge to the assumptions about reality on which realism is based. His early realism was thus informed by a degree of acquired self-consciousness and anti-realism.

Since Hemingway's understanding of Picasso's work was first shaped by

Gertrude Stein, her pronouncements on the subject provide some insight into how Hemingway perceived it. In *Stein on Picasso* (*SOP*), Stein offers her explanation for the rise of Cubism, two tenets of which are particularly relevant here. First, she says, "the framing of life, the need that a picture exist in its frame, remain in its frame was over" (*SOP* 19). Several stories and vignettes in *In Our Time* resist closure, and "L'Envoi" introduces on the last page of the book new characters and a new setting instead of framing it conventionally. Based on Stein's teaching, Hemingway might have identified his resistance to conventional framing devices as a Cubist technique. Second, Stein maintains that "because the way of living had changed, the composition of living had extended and each thing was as important as any other thing" (*SOP* 19). In "L'Envoi" the deposed king and queen doing menial labor and living in sequestration on the palace grounds dramatically illustrate that "the way of living had changed" and that "each thing was as important as any other thing" (*SOP* 19): the narrator tells us that since the war they are "like all Greeks" (*IOT* 157). The composition of the vignette also demonstrates this equalization, for the king speaks of being isolated on the palace grounds, of trying to avoid being shot, and of drinking good whiskey, all in the same jolly tone of voice. On the basis of Stein's tutelage, Hemingway could also have identified as Cubist in nature his monoplanic style here and elsewhere in *In Our Time*, in which each fact or emotion tends to be presented as "as important as any other" (*SOP* 19).

Clearly Hemingway was trying to learn from his first artistic mentor how to write Cubist art, but other similarities between *In Our Time* and Cubist painting indicate that he also looked directly to painters he knew for instruction, particularly Picasso. Picasso defined Cubism as "an art dealing primarily with forms" (*Picasso on Art* 59), and even his earliest work communicates the significance of forms through repetition of them. Picasso's main work of 1907, *Demoiselles d'Avignon*, which is generally considered to be the first Cubist painting, depicts five geometricized nudes and a still life against a background of angular shapes. Through insistent repetition of the shapes used to depict the nudes and the background, Picasso clearly emphasizes the extent to which the painting is more concerned with forms than the objects they delineate. Picasso's 1910 portrait of Daniel-Henry Kahnweiler, in which the features of Kahnweiler are only barely distinguishable through the plethora of geometrical fragments of them, functions similarly. By definition, all of Picasso's Cubist paintings employ varieties of repetition of geometrical forms as they seek "a new expression, divested of useless realism, with a method linked only to . . . thought" (*Picasso on Art* 59–60), as Picasso put it. Apparent transpositions of all these techniques are evident in *In Our Time*.

One of Hemingway's incorporations into *In Our Time* of Picasso's repetition of geometrical forms may be his arrangement of the interchapters, where, with a few exceptions, each one paragraph unit stands alone on a page, producing the visual effect of a block of words that a paragraph within a group of paragraphs would not and thus creating with words what Picasso created with paint, geometrical forms. Hemingway's awareness of the linguistic essence of his text is thus related to Picasso's awareness of paintings as paint, and Hemingway's interest in the layout of the chapters of the first *in our time* affirms this connection by revealing his conception of that book as not only a verbal but also a visual artwork. Certainly Hemingway was familiar with visual poetry, but *In Our Time* may be the first instance in our language of visual prose.

Hemingway also adapts Picasso's technique of repeating geometrical forms in his paintings by repeating words and phrases in his text. Raymond Nelson has demonstrated how Hemingway's communication of emotional impact through the use of verbal repetition in "The End of Something" compares to Picasso's generation of "interest and impact . . . [through] repetition of four very similar figures" (64) in *Demoiselles d'Avignon*. Yet Hemingway's verbal repetitions also parallel Picasso's geometrical repetitions by forcing individual words and phrases to surrender their independence and by creating an expression whose method is linked to thought. For example, in "Soldier's Home" Krebs's "true" feelings about being home from the war are not stated in any one sentence, but Hemingway's repetition of variations of the phrase "he liked" reveals Krebs's ambivalence. Like Picasso's repeated shapes, each repetition of the phrase communicates part of the whole truth, which ultimately is evident only in the unity of all the repetitions:

He *liked* to look at them [girls] from the front porch as they walked on the other side of the street. *He liked* to watch them walking under the shade of the trees. *He liked* the round Dutch collars about their sweaters. *He liked* their silk stockings and flat shoes. *He liked* their bobbed hair and the way they walked. When he was in town *their appeal to him* was not very strong. *He did not like* them when he saw them in the Greek's ice cream parlor. *He did not want* them themselves really. (*IOT* 71, emphasis added)

As the nudes in *Demoiselles d'Avignon* surrender their solidity and spatial independence, Hemingway's repeated phrases surrender their verbal independence; no single word or phrase can be extracted from the text to communicate the truth by itself. The unifying pattern of repeated words thus becomes more significant than any individual instance of the words themselves, and words that are not part of the pattern of repetition function like the background shapes in *Demoiselles d'Avignon* and the portrait of Kahnweiler, referring and contrasting to those words that form the dominant aural patterns in the way that Picasso's backgrounds refer and contrast to the dominant visual patterns in his paintings. Similarly, as Picasso uses repetition to create a mode of expression whose method is linked to thought,

Hemingway's repetition here expresses Krebs's thought by enacting his several attempts to interest himself in the people around him as well as his ultimate failure to do so. The reader hears not so much what Krebs likes as what he tries to like, and the variation in the repetition illustrates the breakdown of his effort. Thus, as Picasso's repetition of geometrical shapes emphasizes form over object, or the extent to which objects ultimately consist of forms, and creates a distance between an object and the artistic representation of that object, Hemingway's repetition of words and phrases emphasizes the role language plays in constituting both a character's thoughts and the representation of them in fiction while it distances words from their referents.

Hemingway's use of repetition here is also comparable to Picasso's in that both lead to depictions of simultaneity. Picasso's implementation of this technique is evident in his 1910 portrait of Daniel-Henry Kahnweiler, which presents many shapes resembling eyes, many resembling noses, many resembling mouths, and so forth. Whereas in a traditional portrait the artist paints only those features that exist in a direct relationship to the person the artist is painting, here none and all of the features directly depict Kahnweiler. Kahnweiler's explanation of the Cubists' method of depicting simultaneity illuminates Picasso's implementation of this technique in this portrait:

The painter no longer has to limit himself to depicting the object as it would appear from one given viewpoint, but wherever necessary for fuller comprehension, can show it from several sides, and from above and below. (*Rise of Cubism* 11)

Rather than finding one "true" nose, one that looks exactly like Kahnweiler's from one particular angle, for example, the viewer perceives a unity through the several shapes that communicates more about the essence of Kahnweiler's nose than does any individual shape. Certainly Hemingway's use of the phrase "he liked" in "Soldier's Home" creates simultaneity within that story, where the repetition of the phrase and the differences and similarities between the repetitions reveal something about the essence of Krebs's feelings that no individual instance of the phrase can.

From *Ernest Hemingway: Selected Letters, 1917–1961* (*LTRS*), Hemingway's 18 October 1924 letter to Edmund Wilson also suggests a similarity between this Cubist method and Hemingway's vision of the book as a whole. The alternations between stories and vignettes, he says, "give the picture of the whole between examining it in detail. Like looking with your eyes at something, say a passing coast line, and then looking at it with 15X binoculars" (*LTRS* 128). As Emily Stipes Watts observes, this description "is simply a statement of simultaneity" (87). She explains:

He was looking at a similar image . . . from different points of view and from several different angles. By arranging the short stories and vignettes in such a way, he was creating a work comparable to the typical cubist guitar which was examined from various perspectives—top, bottom, side, inside, and so on. (87, 90)

Nick's war wound in "Chapter VI," the emotional wounds Nick inflicts on Marge in "The End of Something," the physical wounds Dr. Adams inflicts on the Indian woman in "Indian Camp," and other wounds such as those sustained by the cabinet ministers, the bullfighters and Sam Cardinella can be interpreted as instances of simultaneity. Rather than seeing a "true" view of Nick, of the consummate bullfighter, or of any wounded human being in any one story or vignette, the reader perceives a unity through the several depictions of them that communicates more about their essence than does any individual depiction of them. This technique of presenting several studies of his subjects in *In Our Time* may also have been informed by Hemingway's awareness of Picasso's and other artists' penchants for painting series of studies of the same object under different lighting and in different settings.

Hemingway's tendency to abstract individual characters in *In Our Time* also corresponds to Picasso's tendency to abstract human figures. Nelson explains Picasso's employment of this technique in *Les Demoiselles d'A-vignon* and *Three Musicians*:

Woman and man and child lose their significance as unique and discrete persons, and become interesting in their "folk" or representative roles.... The musicians play their instruments and it does not matter whether they are men or women; the demoiselles are any young ladies of Avignon, attractive in all their naked charm without regard to particular identity. (36)

Similarly, only one character in "Cat in the Rain," George, is referred to by name, and this reference occurs more than halfway through the story. George and his wife are first identified as "two Americans" (91) and later as "the American wife" and "her husband" (91). All other characters in the story are identified generically: "the hotel owner" (92), "a man in a rubber cape" (92), and "the maid" (92). The story is no more a portrait of any particular couple than Picasso's *Demoiselles* is a portrait of five particular individuals. As Nelson says of other, similar Hemingway characters:

The general impression that emerges ... is that uniqueness of person does not matter. What matters is that humankind have had such experiences, thought such thoughts, and done such things. Notably, therefore, Hemingway shares with Expressionist painters the conviction that many things human are ... universal, and can be represented by selected types of persons. (36–37)

Hemingway's abstracted characters demonstrate the extent to which he borrowed not only specific techniques from the Cubists but also broader ways of looking at the world.

Thus, Hemingway's monoplanic style, his resistance to closure, his use of block-shaped interchapters, his repetition of words, phrases, and images to reveal their linguistic essence and to create simultaneity, and his tendency to present characters as abstract types suggest that he learned from Picasso both an ideological approach to realism and representation and several specific techniques of representing. Understanding Cubism helped Hemingway to clarify his cognizance of the linguistic reality of literature, and his observation of the Cubists' revolt against traditional realism contributed to his acknowledgement within the fiction that fiction is a representation of truth rather than truth itself.

2

Le Torero and "The Undefeated": Hemingway's Foray into Analytical Cubism

James Plath

Ernest Hemingway's affinity for Cezanne has been well documented. Yet, when he arrived in Paris in December 1921, Cubist influences were far more prevalent. Cezanne, 14 years deceased, was being hailed as "Cubist in his construction" by Pablo Picasso (Souchere 15), and when Juan Gris returned to Paris the following year, his paintings were on display in three galleries. Gertrude Stein had long since worked through what she termed her "Cezanne phase" and had employed analytical Cubist methods to construct *The Making of Americans*.[1] Although she, like Picasso and Georges Braque, had already moved on to synthetic Cubism, Stein maintained that "in correcting these proofs Hemingway learned a great deal and he admired all that he learned" (Stein, *Selected Writings* 204).

Stein, a financial and spiritual supporter of Picasso and Gris, would later write "that Cubism is a purely Spanish conception and only Spaniards can be cubists and that the only real cubism is that of Picasso and Juan Gris" (Stein, *Selected Writings* 85). To that she added, as if speaking directly to the young man from Oak Park whom she called her "favorite pupil" (202), "Americans can understand Spaniards" because "they are the only two western nations that can realize abstraction" (85).

Although she advised Hemingway to buy paintings from his own generation, he eventually acquired two by Gris: *Guitarist*, painted in 1926 during the artist's synthetic period, and *Le Torero*, painted in 1913 during what was still his analytical period, and later used by Hemingway as the frontispiece illustration for *Death in the Afternoon*. While Emily Stipes Watts, the only scholar to seriously consider "The Undefeated" from a spatial perspective, sees the influence of Goya (116), I would submit that because of the story's multiple perspectives, its emphasis on seeing, its angular language and stylistic echoes of Gris, that "The Undefeated" is instead Hemingway's attempt to apply the techniques of analytical Cubism to fiction—using *Le Torero* as a model.

Stein owned several works by Gris that Hemingway would have seen at her Paris flat. As the second collector to purchase Gris's paintings, she developed a relationship with the artist that included frequent visits, a practice that Hemingway apparently shared. In two letters written in 1921, Hemingway mentions "wanting to go to Juan Gris's" (*LTRS* 121, 126). Though the provenance indicates that Hemingway purchased *Le Torero* when he was living in Key West, when the young writer arrived in Paris in 1921 and took up residence, the painting could be seen at Daniel-Henry Kahnweiler's Galerie Simones, then the legal owner of the work (Cooper 50). That Hemingway was intimately familiar with the gallery—and, by extension, *Le Torero*—seems evident from a letter he wrote to Stein and Alice B. Toklas two months before he finished "The Undefeated" (*LTRS* 133): "There was a fellow here from the states with money, cash, to buy some [André] Massons and Galerie Simones was closed and I didn't have Masson's address" (126).

Given his association with painters and the conscious visual-to-verbal transformations he attempted earlier that same year "trying to do the country like Cezanne" in "Big Two-Hearted River" (*LTRS* 122), it seems probable that Hemingway was trying to create more than simple narrative in "The Undefeated"—especially since he wrote John Dos Passos that the bullfight story "makes a bum out of everything I ever did" (157–158).

In "The Undefeated," the focus is not on the bullfight proper, as it is in the Goya-like miniatures from *In Our Time*, but on the bullfighter himself, as seen from multiple perspectives: through the eyes of a promoter, two waiters, a veteran *picador*, an up-and-coming matador, a gypsy *peon*, a "secondstring" bullfight critic, a single spectator, the collective crowd, the president—even the bull. Hemingway explained to the editor of *The Saturday Evening Post* that with "The Undefeated" he tried "to show it the way it actually is" (*LTRS* 117), and as Kahnweiler, Gris's dealer and biographer, notes, "Cubism was above all a realistic art, since it aimed at as accurate a form of representation as possible" (73). The Cubists, recognizing the limitations a single perspective imposes on "truth," sought to create objects that could be viewed from several points at once, in what Stein and others termed "the simultaneous present." Using fragmentation and recombination of three-dimensional images, Cubists hoped to suggest a fourth dimension: time.

In *Death in the Afternoon* (*DA*), Hemingway even describes the bullfight as a Cubist would, emphasizing the deconstruction of images in order to achieve a simultaneous appreciation of the whole "spectacle built on the planned and ordered death of the bull" (404):

The eye of a person unfamiliar with the bullfight cannot really follow the cape world; there is the shock of seeing the horse struck by the bull and no matter how this affects the spectator he will be liable to continue to watch the horse and miss the quite that the matador has made.... He watches the muleta as something picturesque and the killing may be done so suddenly that unless the spectator has very trained eyes he will not be able to break up the different figures and see what really happens. (193)

The problems with a single perspective are made clear in "The Undefeated," for if each "facet" of the bullfighter is considered separately, widely disparate views occur. Considered as a whole, the bullfighter and a single linear plot become more complete and "true," the bullfight itself protracted in time. Hemingway's bullfighter is even dependent upon simultaneous perspective for his survival because in the bullring

his eyes noted things and his body performed the necessary measures without thought. If he thought about it, he would be gone.

Now, facing the bull, he was conscious of many things at the same time. There were the horns, one splintered, the other smoothly sharp. (26)

Structural similarities also exist between Hemingway's story and Gris's painting. The primary point of visual entry into *Le Torero* are the word fragments from bullfight posters at the top of the canvas, with other dominant areas including an area of high density around the *torero*'s hair or cap—where white half-moons suggest the horns of a bull—and a confusion of triangles overlaid upon the *torero*'s face, rendering it far more complex and less representational than the clearly defined tie and matador's suit.

Likewise, Hemingway's story emphasizes "faces," particularly those of the bullfighter. It begins in a bullfight promoter's office, where "a little man sat behind a desk at the far side of the room. Over his head was a bull's head, stuffed by a Madrid taxidermist; on the walls were framed photographs and bull-fight posters" (1). By emphasizing the man's small size, Hemingway creates an effect where the posters and bull's head dominate the top of the fictional "canvas." His bullfighter also shares a noticeable prop with the Gris counterpart: he smokes a cigarette (2).

The first view of Manuel, by Retana, the promoter, is shaped in part by letters and words—by what he has read in the newspapers about the bullfighter's hospitalization. Almost immediately, Hemingway suggests multiple faces or facets: "Manuel sat down; his cap off, his face was changed" (2). From Retana's perspective, Manuel is a has-been, a risk to put back in the ring—even for a nocturnal. "There aren't any bull-fighters any more," Retana says (2), echoing Hemingway's *Toronto Star* explanation in *By-Line* (*BL*) that it is difficult to find a *torero* who is proficient at "all three acts of the fight"—using the cape to do *veronicas*, planting the *banderillos*, and mastering, then killing the bull (*BL* 85). " 'I'm a bull-fighter,' Manuel said. 'Yes, while you're in there,' Retana said" (3), suggesting the fourth dimension of time that Cubists sought to create.

The second view comes from the cafe waiters on the Puerta del Sol, one of whom sees Manuel and thinks him someone taking part in "the Charlie Chaplin's," a bullfight clown—not the matador.[2] The waiters discuss other bullfighters "in front of his table," adding a comparative perspective that makes Manuel uncomfortable: "They had forgotten about him" (7). In the cafe, the bullfighter becomes a composite figure.

Views of the bullfighter continue to vary. Zurito, his favorite *picador*, sees Manuel in relation to his former self: "You're too old," he tells him (9). The crowd sees him as little more than part of the spectacle: young Hernandez and old Manuel, two facets of matador, preceded by three *peones*, "their capes furled over their left arms in the same fashion" before "the procession broke up into its component parts" (13).

Once the bullfight begins, an ironic note is injected by the "*El Heraldo's* second-string critic" who, watching the bull instead of the matador, writes that "the veteran Manolo designed a series of acceptable veronicas, ending in a very Belmontistic recorte that earned applause from the regulars" (15). Again, the bullfighter is seen not as a single individual, but in comparison with another matador and in relation to the bull. In a story ostensibly about seeing, the critic ironically bases later judgments on crowd response, not on what he has seen of Manuel's performance (19). Zurito, whose perspective is closer, says supportively, "You're going good." But Manuel is not taken in. Given the bullfighter's internal perspective, his sense of potential, "Manuel shook his head" (20). The bull, meanwhile, "had light circles about his eyes. His eyes watched Manuel. He felt he was going to get this little one with the white face" (23). Perhaps not coincidentally, the bull focuses on the matador's white face, just as a small white triangle dominates the nostril area of *Le Torero*. In Gris's painting, an ambiguity of geometric shapes around the head suggests both bull and bullfighter, and eyes are implied by a circle and distinctive half-moon. In Hemingway's version, Manuel notices the "light circles about his eyes" (23), a description that seems more stylized than realistic. In one instance, the point of view even blurs: "The bull looked at him and was no longer fixed. His eyes watched Fuentes, now standing still. Now he leaned back, calling to him" (20).

From another, later perspective, Retana's man exclaims, "Why, that one's a great bull-fighter," whereupon Zurito, considering past performances as well as the present, and the greater perspective that such distance affords him, says, "No, he's not" (25). Eventually, the young matador, Hernandez, sees in Manuel a "damn fool" who should know when to quit, but will not go to the infirmary before he dispatches the bull (30). Finally, a sentence in the last paragraph echoes the bull's perspective, alluding to the dominant white triangle on the face of Gris's *torero*: "The doctor's assistant put the cone over Manuel's face and he inhaled deeply" (32).

Accompanying each shift in perspective are variations of "watching" and "looking" as introductory words, to emphasize that the story is indeed about a way of seeing. Consider these textual fragments:

- The critic looked up to see Zurito, directly below him, leaning far out over his horse. (17)
- Zurito sat patting his horse and looking at the bull charging. (17)
- "Look at him now," Zurito said. (17)
- Zurito watched. (18)
- Now he was facing the bull.... Manuel flopped the cape; there he comes.... Got his eye on me. (18)
- The bull looked at him. Eyes watching, horns straight forward, the bull looked at him, watching. (19)
- Fuentes ... looked at Manuel.... Manuel set down the jug and watched. (19)
- The bull looked at him and was no longer fixed. (20)
- Watch him now. (21)
- They watched. (21)
- The bull, with his tongue out, his barrel heaving, was watching the gypsy. (21)

So Hemingway continues throughout the story, alternating viewpoints in apparently random fashion, but always incorporating different distances and angles, so that the bullfight is seen from the wings of the arena, in the arena itself on foot and on horseback, from box seats, from the higher seats, and, of course, before and after the spectacle—time as distance. At one point, one of the *picadores* says, "He's too damn close" (21), but shortly thereafter Manuel walks "across the arena toward where, up in the dark boxes, the president must be." Immediately thereafter, the reader is drawn from the far background into a middle distance, back again to the front-row seat of the substitute critic (22). Just as quickly, the perspective shifts to Manuel in the arena, then to the bull (23). The Cubists were advocates of what Picasso termed "restrictive or subjective sight," maintaining that a person looking at a face sees only one feature or another, rather than a complete face (Stein, *Picasso on Art* 19). Hemingway's bullfighter experiences similar vision: "Walking forward, watching the bull's feet, he saw successively his eyes, his wet muzzle, and the wide forward-pointing spread of his horns" (23).

During the bullfight, the word "watched" or some such variation occurs

33 times; the word "faced" occurs 11 times; "looked" occurs 19 times; and other variations having to do with sight occur 26 times. Yet, during three moments when the matador is engaged in a life or death struggle with the bull—either being gored or trying to sink his sword between the bull's shoulders—action takes precedent, and not one sight-related word appears. After the bull is killed and the action over, the language of seeing returns: Manuel "looked at the bull going down slowly" and then "looked down for the muleta," and a third time "was sitting down looking" at the dead bull (30). Then the wounded bullfighter is taken to the infirmary, where "he shut his eyes" (31). Until he opens them again, the emphasis shifts to the sense of hearing:

He heard some one coming very heavily up the stairs. Then he did not hear it. Then he heard a noise far off. That was the crowd. Well, somebody would have to kill his other bull.... The doctor smiled at him. There was Retana.... He could not hear his voice.... Manuel could not hear it.... Zurito said something to him. Manuel could not hear it. (31)

Although Manuel must have had his eyes open to notice the doctor's smile and Retana, no mention is made of looking or watching in this section—further evidence of stylistic deliberation. Rather, the emphasis remains on the sense of hearing until, with the final word of the story, Hemingway confirms that "The Undefeated" may indeed have been all about looking: "Zurito stood awkwardly, *watching*" (32, emphasis added). What Hemingway does most successfully in "The Undefeated" is to create striking juxtapositions, the kind of jarring, hard-edged interplay that Picasso first made famous with his collages and that Gris developed even further. In this short story, a paragraph of high energy and tension is often juxtaposed against a paragraph dominated by a lack of intensity, especially during the bullfight proper.

In one instance, the "bull came out in a rush, skidding on his four legs as he came out under the lights, then charging in a gallop, moving softly in a fast gallop, silent except as he woofed through wide nostrils as he charged, glad to be free after the dark pen" (14). Witnessing this in the very next sentence, is a man who takes up the dark pen:

In the first row of seats, slightly bored, leaning forward to write on the cement wall in front of his knees, the substitute bull-fight critic of *El Heraldo* scribbled." (14)

Other times, Hemingway achieves similar planar tensions through the use of implied energy or areas of density, as when Manuel is on his way to the cafe:

He walked down the shady side of the steep street toward the Puerta del Sol. The shade felt solid and cool as running water. The heat came suddenly as he crossed the intersecting streets. (5)

While Hemingway used overlapping planes in "Big Two-Hearted River," which he said was written in the manner of Cezanne, the vocabulary in "The Undefeated" incorporates a language that is harder, more geometrical and angular.

Even more telling is Hemingway's apparent appropriation of another technique the Cubists—and Gris, especially—employed. Kahnweiler explains that one of the painter's essential aesthetic strategies was to use what Gris called "rhymes," where "two forms, generally of different sizes, are repeated" (141). He gives the example of a curved line of guitar "rhymed" in the curve of a bottle or pear, thus producing a stylistic repetition or echo.

In "The Undefeated," such rhymes take shape in the deliberate repetition of words and phrases, but varied slightly each time. The technique, used consistently throughout the story, is established in the first scene. Again, consider these fragments:

- Retana sat, saying nothing and looking at Manuel.
- Retana said nothing but looked at Manuel across the big desk. (4)
- Retana said nothing but looked at Manuel from a long way off. (4)
- Retana was still considering him, leaning back in his chair, considering him from a long way away. (4)

Where Gris varies his objects in size and composition, using shape to draw upon for his "rhyme," Hemingway uses size and distance to create variety, repeating key words to create the rhyme. During the bullfight, such sequences illustrate not only Gris's personal technique of rhyming, but the analytical Cubists' emphasis on geometry:

- Zurito sat there, his feet in the box-stirrups, his great legs in the buckskin-covered armor . . . the reins in his left hand, the long pic held in his right hand, his broad hat well down over his eyes to shade them from the lights. (14)
- Zurito on the white horse . . . the horse facing the bull, its ears forward, its lips nervous, Zurito, his hat over his eyes, leaning forward, the long pole sticking out before and behind in a sharp angle under his right arm, held half-way down, the triangular iron point facing the bull. (15)
- Zurito sat on his horse, measuring the distance between the bull and the end of the pic. (16)
- Zurito sat patting his horse and looking at the bull charging the cape that Hernandez swung for him. (17)
- Zurito, sitting his horse, walking him toward the scene, not missing any detail, scowled. (18)

Such "rhyming" occurs with each participant in the bullfight, at times illustrating the irony of perspective. Manuel thinks, at one point, that the bull is ready to go down: " 'He's all lead,' Manuel thought" (26). But after the sword springs out of the bull's shoulders and into the crowd, young Hernandez comments, "He's all bone" (29).

Le Torero, with its geometric planes and triangular shapes, is typical of analytical Cubist works in that it emphasizes the conceptual and intellectual aspect of the bullfighter, rather than celebrating the imagination and lyricism, as did works in the softer, synthetic mode. In Hemingway's version— emotionally controlled, despite the violence and pathos of Manuel's situation—triangles also dominate, for the story has three settings or "acts," events that take place in the promoter's office, the cafe, and the bullfight arena, with an infirmary postscript. Three *peones* are used in the bullfight, Manuel is thrown to the ground three times by the bull, and, of course, there are three parts to every bullfight, each designated space in the arena: the *tercio de varas*, third of the pic; the *tercio de banderillos*, third of *banderillos*; and the *tercio del muerte*, third of death.

In Gris's portrait, the bull becomes an integral part of the bullfighter, one "fact" by which the latter is defined. In *Le Torero*, this facet is suggested by horn-like shapes and a concentrated area of black around the head. In Hemingway's short story, Manuel's fate also curiously parallels the bull's. Figuratively speaking, in the first act he is "piced" by Retana, getting the "shaft" not only because he is given a nocturnal to fight, but because he is also offered an insulting sum of money to risk his life. In the second act, Manuel endures the *banderillos* or "barbs" of the waiters who further hurt his ego, as well as accusations from Zurito that he is too old to fight. Finally, in the bullfight scene, the third of death, Manuel is beaten—but like Santiago, from *The Old Man and the Sea*, never, ever defeated.

NOTES

1. Stein wrote *The Making of Americans* between 1906 and 1911, but it was not published until 1925.

2. For an interesting discussion of this aspect, see John M. Howell, "Hemingway and Chaplin: Monkey Business in 'The Undefeated'." *Studies in Short Fiction* 27:1 (1990): 89–97.

3

Artists in Their Art: Hemingway and Velásquez—The Shared Worlds of *For Whom the Bell Tolls* and *Las Meninas*

Robin Gajdusek

In the Prado in Madrid one may see, as many of you may have by now seen, a truly remarkable painting by Velásquez entitled *Las Meninas (The Maids of Honor)*.[1] It shows the Spanish Infanta Margarita and her maids-in-waiting dressed in the ceremonial dress of the royal court. It also includes, however, the artist himself, who is engaged in the very act of painting within a painting, perhaps painting the very painting we observe. In a mirror on the far wall, we additionally see the faces of the proud parents, Philip IV and his wife, who while seemingly real subjects being painted by the artist in the painting, are also onlookers almost unseen by us at the scene we witness, a scene in which the Infanta is the one centrally placed and apparently dressed to pose for her portrait. The king and queen are only revealed by their mirrored reflection; they are related to us, the modern spectators, by being, like voyeurs and not participants in the scene we see, outside that scene in history in approximately the same relationship that we are—we seem to stand on the plane where they must have stood—and are only as it were accidentally included within it. This painting, regarded as one of the world's most profound and complex works of art, has inspired many artists to emulate its patterns or to study its composition. It has lead them into making their own creative statements. Although there is no mention of *Las Meninas* in *For Whom the Bell Tolls (FWBT)*, Hemingway was surely well aware of it, and I will try to show that it is almost as though Hemingway were playing with its technique throughout his novel.[2]

There are several overlapping and complex levels of awareness within the scene. There is that of the Infanta, who is looking beyond her time and toward us where we must meet her eyes, and there is that of her maids-in-waiting, who are scattered about the scene but held by the central reason for their existence—the child. There is that of her parents, who observe their daughter together with her friends, and who also observe the artist who paints them and *for* them and *at* their service. They may additionally perceive the illusion of themselves briefly caught in the virtual imagery of a reflecting mirror on a far back wall within the painting. And there is the vision of the artist who can include in his regard all that he chooses to include—one who can alter or distort history at will, by transgressing the boundaries of reality by introducing imagination and fancy in his treatment of it. Staring as he is apparently toward his patrons, who are *in part* there to judge his service and talent, he is also looking directly toward us, for Velásquez has made us seemingly assume approximately the place where these real subjects stand. We are thus the *other* spectators at the scene through whom he undoubtedly acknowledges the posterity for whom he additionally works, concerned as he is for the immortality of his subject and his art. There is another figure, outside the room on its far side on the stairs beyond it, seemingly hesitating momentarily before retreating backward and disappearing into the history from which he briefly emerged. The reflecting interfaces of these several points of view make the canvas an exceptionally thrilling one that connects us to the artist and to his milieu, to his situation and the time he is disappearing into, even as he labors to find a way to transcend them. By the painting we are related to its time, the time and court within which Velásquez painted, where we study his interpretation of himself as well as his environment. We are related also to our own anticipated time, from which we peer into that world of anterior event, trying to interpret images as diverse as those distorted and manipulated within the very painting we contemplate. In the inverted virtual images in the mirror we see images within the painting that intriguingly the artist *within* the work does *not* see, but that are painted and seen by the artist *outside* the work. The artist *within* the work might see us; the artist outside it looks away from us and only engages us, as Perseus did Medusa, by reflection.[3]

I labor details of Velásquez's work that I may better address Hemingway's *For Whom the Bell Tolls*,[4] a work of similar strategy and complexity that presents many of the same overlapping frames of apprehension within it, a work in which its artist and its hero, Hemingway and his Robert Jordan, have taken a stance that is very much that of Velásquez in *Las Meninas*. I am less concerned with the enclosing frames within the novel than I am with the artist's—Hemingway's—portrait of himself that he has, like Velásquez, placed in the center of *his* canvas. But these similar frames are there and I will treat them first.

Robert Jordan is not of the milieu he comes to serve. He is an *out*sider, somewhat like a court painter, who has taken service *in*side the special world where he brings his unique talents. These are talents, as we learn, not only for destruction but for creation. He labors throughout a religiously significant three days to find ways, like an artist, of moving the NOW of dying life to the ALWAYS that the lovers finally do achieve through the techniques of caring love. One of the major questions of the novel, Jordan's concern, is how to achieve eternity and immortality in time, how to expand time and, partly by the powers of love and imagination, master life through ecstacy so that time, which is finite, becomes infinite. The NOW and the ALWAYS become one in *their* passion, and Hemingway suggests that Jordan has managed in three days to live a lifetime. Velásquez as artist similarly challenges time and, in his canvas, unlike the film of a cinematographer, makes it stop, come to a position of seemingly eternal arrest.

Jordan and Hemingway are also concerned, however, with saving Maria from death, and at the end she is sent on by the pen of Hemingway and the planning of Jordan over the hill toward life and also toward posterity. Her salvation, Hemingway pointedly affirms, is also that of her artist/creator, for *as* she survives while Jordan remains behind to die in his duty and craft, she carries with her all that can ever remain of *him*. The last pages of the novel reiterate strongly that in her he lives, that there is no death as long as she, created constant by her fidelity to his memory (that they together through love have fashioned), carries what they have created beyond and into the future, where we the contemporary readers have it to evaluate, to judge, and to experience again. However, she cannot save herself unaided but is carried forward toward the safety that keeps her alive for us by the cherishing attention of her metaphorical adoptive "parents," Pablo and Pilar. Balanced between the two, held there, she is carried over the hill and to that safety that has been identified with immortality. In his painting, Velásquez expressed the concern of the parents for their daughter, whom they are giving to immortality as their patronage yields her to art. It is an obvious parallel. Their cherishing assures the Infanta the later life beyond her aesthetic existence in Velásquez's painting.

The crude outlines of the Spanish court seem also almost parodically drawn in the revolutionary imagery of an anti-aristocratic guerrilla band. Pablo and Pilar are the controlling rulers in that primitive "court" of the cave where the interloping artist/dynamiter comes to grant immortality to them and their "daughter." Spain is the milieu. The Loyalists are those who have given the craftsman/artist Jordan a service to perform for them, a performance that, if successful, will help to perpetuate their order. Pablo and Pilar are the ruling parents who provide Jordan with the dual subject, themselves and Maria, who is to be *his* means to immortality as he brings *her* back to life through the intricately integrated arts of love and bridge destroying. In the foreground is the band of guerrillas that surrounds and guards Maria, who is identified throughout the novel as a parodic, profane manifestation of a raped/virgin Mary; their attention, though scattered, is often fixed upon her. In the background, characters like Agustin, Anselmo and Fernando briefly hesitate on the stairs, if you will—that is, briefly note, observe and judge the Jordan/Maria relationship before they themselves disappear into history—except as they are momentarily captured by the sensibility/craft/memory of Jordan/Hemingway.

I have made too much of a partially arbitrary resemblance, and an expanded metaphor has become a conceit. What matters most are *not* these overlapping congruent frames but rather the figure of the artist in the center of his own canvas, involved and disengaged at once, confronting in one moment the world he is immersed within and is paid to paint and the world beyond it where the spectators and audience wait to appreciate: the man caught in time and the man concerned with its transcendence, aware of death and eternity.

In Velásquez's canvas the girl-Infanta is centrally placed and lit for us and seen therefore to have been a central focus of concern of the artist, while actually the canvas that holds her in her own time reveals that it truly may be her only accidentally seen parents who are the *real if concealed* subject of her artist's craft. It has been suggested by some critics that *For Whom the Bell Tolls* was the novel where Hemingway at last came to terms with his own parents, given as projected surrogates in powerful Pilar, who cows her mate, and cowardly Pablo—who in turn echo *Jordan's* own parents, a bully of a mother who had also intimidated her cowardly suicidal consort—and that this double reflection has its real source in Dr. and Mrs. Hemingway. It has also been suggested that Hemingway's avoidance of explicit profanity, within his elaborate strategy of euphemisms, was one way of making a belated gesture of conciliation toward his morally fastidious parents. Such concern for the mirror-revealed parents who look on at the morally guarded world of the Infanta, and are therefore related to the audience, ourselves, suggests that the artist's real subject was as it was in Velásquez's *Las Meninas*, not the one indicated in the title. The true subject is the dialogue going on between the artist and the audience that observes— among whom are some, the royal parents, who specifically receive the artist's authentic attention—and it is through the reflective strategies of his art that the artist is able to come to terms with them.[5] Certainly Jordan's final reconciliation with Pablo, the cowardly surrogate father, occurs almost simultaneously with Jordan's forgiving-understanding of his real father and, I would affirm, Hemingway's acceptance/forgiveness of *his*.

Like Velásquez, Hemingway paints himself, the artist at work painting the very canvas we witness, in the center of his art. There is enormous daring and effrontery[6] as, on page 444 of a 470-page novel, we have the following exchange:

[*Pilar says violently, raging*] "What passes with that Ingles? What is he obscenitying off under that bridge. . . . Is he building a bridge or blowing one?"

[*Anselmo responds*] "Patience, woman.... He is terminating his work."

[*Pilar*] "But what in the name of the great whore does he take so much time about?"

[*Anselmo*] "Es muy conciuenzudo!... It is a scientific labor."

When Pilar shouts a flood of obscenity suggesting that Jordan's work under the bridge can be regarded as masturbation, Anselmo replies, "Calm yourself, woman.... He is doing an enormous work. He is finishing it now" (444). He who is completing the enormous work is not alone Jordan, but Hemingway, and that the writer's creative endeavor may by the woman be considered masturbation we see well emphasized in *The Garden of Eden* (*GE*) where Catherine describes David's writing as a "spilling of seed" into the waste basket.

There were not many artists when Hemingway wrote who had either the daring or the need to paint themselves at their easel in the midst of and painting the very work the reader is (then) reading. And he does it consistently: this self-reflexive technique determines the shape of *Green Hills of Africa* as well as that of *Death in the Afternoon, Torrents of Spring, The Fifth Column, The Old Man and the Sea*, and *A Moveable Feast*. Hemingway does it in part by making the moral and practical disciplines of a protagonist concomitantly the strategies of the artist. In *For Whom the Bell Tolls* war becomes a mode of art as the artist creator, absolving himself of the subjective personal in his dedication and in his immersion in his subject, annihilates himself that something else, something lasting, can exist: "Once you got rid of your own self, the always ridding of self that you had to do in war. Where there could be no self. Where yourself is only to be lost" (447). Against this sacrificial-redemptive thrust, which describes the writer's self-transcendence as he replaces self with character and situation—"Aloof, indifferent, detached, like a God paring his fingernails"—Pilar, the enemy of absolutes, ridicules the arrogance of the artist: "Thou and thy perfection" (448). She does this as Jordan/Hemingway focuses upon the intricacy of the formal problems he faces in the completion of his great work. The author's delight in his solution of stylistic/narrative problems is one of the delights of reading *For Whom the Bell Tolls*. His sense of what he has solved and the prize he thereby deserves is very real.[7]

As Jordan nears his death at the conclusion of the novel, he thinks, "I hate to leave it, is all. I hate to leave it very much and I hope I have done some good in it. I have tried to with what talent I had. *Have, you mean. All right, have*" (467); and then he reflects, "I wish there were some way to pass on what I've learned, though. Christ, I was learning fast there at the end" (467). It is terribly exciting to witness simultaneously the approaching death of Jordan, the character painted, and Hemingway's exultation at his own aesthetic lessons learned, which have become *his* triumph, *his* way toward life everlasting. Of course, that is what is happening whenever we watch an artist at work, as he translates life-feeling into its death suspension state of abstraction in art, but it is rare that the artist consciously paints the process, or finds an imagery for the revelation of both events. All of this prepares us for the major achievement at the very end of the book as Hemingway/Jordan sends Maria—and we, the readers!—on over the hill toward our own safety. As we exult in our catharsis, we note that it has been purchased at the cost of the victims. As the reader is freed, he should be aware of all that has ceased to be. Jordan and Hemingway recede, retire, and speak further from out of the great silence and darkness into which they now both have gone, while life and feeling are loud within *us*. "If thou goest then I go with thee. It is in that way that I go too.... Thou will go now for us both.... I am thee also now.... You are me now" and "Thou are all there will be of me" (463–464). Crying out against relentless time, Jordan/Hemingway achieves the victory of the artist who lives on through and in the reader/spectator whom he inhabits.[8] The *tour de force* of simultaneous aesthetic, pragmatic and religious levels of victory is obvious as he concludes, "I am with thee" (465). Hemingway has affirmed that the artist only lives in the experience of his reader and that the end of a work of art is in its translation into the sensibility/memory of the one who has possessed it.

Throughout the novel Hemingway has, in the character of Jordan, expressed the problems and dilemmas of the artist who, while thinking and speaking as his life-involved hero, is debating his own aesthetic strategies.

I don't know whether anyone has ever done it before. But there will always be people who will do it from now on, given a similar jam. If we do it and if they hear about it. If they hear about it, yes. If they don't just wonder how it was we did it. (370–371)

His concern is very real that the readers, the recipients of his work, should penetrate its facade—not just wonder about it but study it to learn exactly how it was done to thereby learn truly what it has to pass on, what its real accomplishment was. He knows that what he has to hand on are a set of forms and formulas, the formal solutions that are an artist's ultimate gift to the brotherhood of artists.

The identity of reader and Maria that I have shown is early established as the intensely mentally active Jordan/Hemingway does not wake the sleeping Maria—he goes on planning, plotting, arranging his materials while she remains unconscious of his work. This is, as Jordan says, the "ring" he gives her, the artist's gift to his audience, *unconsciousness* of the details of construction in the midst of aesthetic experience.

Hemingway plays with the alternative identities of his hero who is at once character, Jordan, and Hemingway, artist. The ambiguity creates genuine problems in structure. "Afterwards," Jordan thinks, "I'm going to write a true book. I'll bet, he said. I'll bet that would be easy" (163). Much later he reflects:

All right. He would write a book when he got through with this. But only about the things he knew, truly, and about what he knew. But I will have to be a much better writer than I am now to handle them, he thought. (248)

The reader of such a passage is witnessing the artist *at* work, trying to create readiness, capacity and compassion for the act of identification-understanding that is art. Early Hemingway/Jordan knows, sees, and understands too little to be either in mastery of his situation or of his materials. This is not a critic's observation. It is Hemingway's, the artist's, recognition. Only later, as he warms to his work, does he build to that command over these and find that control of them that leads him to exult at the end of the novel in his powers and his achievement, at the speed with which he has finally worked and the perfection of his execution. During the body of the novel, he again and again girds himself for the task:

No, himself said. You have no right to forget anything. You have no right to shut your eyes to any of it nor any right to forget any of it nor to soften it nor to change it. Shut up, he told himself. You're getting awfully pompous. Nor ever to deceive yourself about it, himself went on. All right, he told himself. Thanks for all the good advice. (304)

This schizophrenic inner dialogue between the involved and the detached, between the character and the author, between the self immersed in and inextricable from the world and the transcendent overseeing spirit, between the passionate and the cold reflective mind is the product of the artist on the canvas, the painter painted standing in the room he paints.

Jordan confronts the catch phrases that possess his mind, to which he, as character and actor, has given absolute assent. They are revolutionary patriotic clichés, and he knows the need to be beyond such immersion, to be disciplined by the detachment of one uninvolved with this war. The problem of being at once immersed in his medium and detached from it, of needing to transcend it while yet being caught in it is the dilemma of God in the flesh, of the author/painter in his medium/time. It is the problem of the Hemingway in Jordan. Hemingway early confronts this problem as he prepares Jordan, caught in history and *his* story, in which he must die, to become Hemingway, the transcendent detached godlike manipulator/overseer and comprehender of that material:

But he noticed, and listened to, and remembered everything. He was serving in a war and he gave absolute loyalty and as complete performance as he could give while he was serving. But nobody owned his mind nor his faculties for seeing and hearing, and if he were going to form judgments he would form them afterwards.

And there would be plenty of material to draw them from. There was plenty already. There was a little too much sometimes. (136)

Hemingway has spelled out this difficulty, this remarkable problem of the author's identification with his creations—God's with his creatures—as he has studied Jordan's dilemma of separation from and concomitant immersion in the world in which he works. Jordan thinks toward the end, "There's no *one* thing that's true. It's all true. The way the planes are beautiful whether they are ours or theirs. The hell they are, he thought" (467).[9] Transcendence and immersion, disengagement and detachment of the transcendent imagination, character caught in the flesh of situation: these alternatives are the author's distance from yet immersion in his protagonist, the painter apart from his subject yet joined to it in the act of painting.

Jordan has recognized that his political feelings have religious analogues—like one's First Communion—but when he elaborates upon them, he finds that politics are inseparable from *aesthetic* response:

It was authentic as the feeling you had when you heard Bach or stood in Chartres Cathedral or the Cathedral at Leon and saw the light coming through the great windows; or when you saw Mantegna and Greco and Breughel in the Prado. It gave you a part in something that you could believe in wholly and completely and in which you felt an absolute brotherhood with the others who were engaged in it. (235)

Reaching for an understanding of his political involvement, Jordan comes upon the brotherhood of artists who share similar aesthetic problems. His split is genuinely between his aesthetic and political-social dedications. This problem is elaborated as Pilar finishes her description of the massacre in Pablo's town.

Pilar had made him see it in that town. If that woman could only write. He would try to write it and if he had luck and could remember it perhaps he could get it down as she told it. God, how she could tell a story. She's better than Quevedo, he thought. He never told the death of any Don Faustino as well as she told it. I wish I could write well enough to write that story, he thought. What we did. Not what the others did to us. He knew enough about that. He knew plenty about that behind the lines. But you had to have known the people before. You had to know what they had been in the village. (134–135)

Here, as author in the midst of his work, whose virtues he attributes to the skill of his character's art, he discusses the basis of the literary technique that has created the very experience we have just had, but it is a basis that we are led to assume neither Hemingway nor Jordan had had. It is perverse: The doubled thinker, who yearns to write the book we are reading, denigrates his own abilities; at the same time, by disassociating himself from them and bestowing them on Pilar, he declares himself superior to Quevedo. It is, again, a magnificent *tour de force* of transcendence of subject in the midst of subject: It is Velásquez standing in the center of *Las Meninas*.

This technique of the artist painted in his art has always been Hemingway's. It accounts in part for the unfortunate tendency to read Hemingway into all of his creations. In Hemingway's work the artist is most frequently inseparable from his subject: Even as Santiago cannot at last extricate himself or keep himself separate from the material he deals with—who is bringing in whom is the ultimate question—so the death-dealing torero must be death exposed, for the medium is the message, and the artist his art.

I am sure that Hemingway enjoyed the deviousness of *Las Meninas*, the exciting and exhilarating sense of being caught in destructive life and simultaneously striking toward immortality that both he and Velásquez gained by placing themselves in the center of the arena of their canvas. Both men were addressing a posterity that might know how to evaluate the suspended brush in the artist's hand[10] and his inextricability from the world he best served by calling its categories in question and breaking its frames.

NOTES

1. *Las Meninas* was completed in 1656, when the Infanta Margarita was about five years old, and when Velásquez was 57. All but one of the figures in the painting were immediately recognizable as a specific member of the court of Philip IV.

2. There is indeed precedent for his so doing, and since his novel was published, the painting has increasingly become the subject or basis of other art. Gustave Courbet's painting. *The Painter's Studio* (1855) was recognized by his contemporaries as playing off parallels with *Las Meninas*. Much more recently Pablo Picasso made the first of his 45 studies based on *Las Meninas* (that are now in the Picasso Museum in Barcelona) on August 17, 1957. Salvador Dali and the Chilean painter Juan Downey have similarly based paintings on the Velásquez work—the latter using a copy of *Las Meninas* as the central theme of an installation and performance event at his New York exhibition in March 1975. It seems apparent that Jean-Luc Godard leaned on Velásquez and his work for his film *Pierrot le Fou* (1965). Antonio Buero-Vallejo's short story "The Only Man" (1933) as well as his controversial play *Las Meninas: A Fantasia in Two Parts* (1960) both indicate the fecundity of Velásquez's conception for the artist.

3. Interpretations of the painting vary widely. The major interpreters see it as a painting of the Infanta Margarita or of the royal family in its courtly setting. Indeed, even after being admitted to the Prado the painting was variously referred to for many years as a portrait of the family, and its name, *Las Meninas* referring as it does to the maids-in-waiting who seem largely incidental to the whole canvas, was either only occasionally used or ignored by critics or official catalogues. Jose Lopez-Rey, who himself uses the title *The Royal Family*, indicates that the title *Las Meninas* was not entered in the Prado catalogue until 1735 (Velásquez: A Catalogue Raisonné of His Oeuvre, London, 1963). One historian, Carl Justi (Diego Velásquez and His Times, Vol. 2, London, 1889), describes it as a portrait of the Infanta

151 964

Margarita at the center of a familial scene in the life of the palace; but he goes on to hypothesize, leaning to some extent on legend, that it is a realistic depiction of a casual event, an instant in time, where the artist, at the suggestion of the king, capitalized upon what the king happened to see as *he* posed with his queen for *their* portrait in the studio—obviously, everything we see is from the standpoint of the king. Justi also says, "It is the picture of the production of a picture" (315), the latter being the portrait for which the royal couple was posing when the king noted the aesthetic possibilities in the scene he, as sitter, looked upon. Bartolome Mestre Fiol (in an article in *Revista Traza y Baza*, 2, 1973, pp. 16f., "El espejo referential en la pintura de Velásquez") speculates that the image in the mirror is that of the full-length portrait Velásquez is painting in *Las Meninas*. Critics like Enrique La Fuente (*Velásquez: Complete Edition*, London, 1943, p. 30), Martin Soria (in a work by George Kubler and himself, *Architecture in Spain and Portugal and the American Dominions 1500 to 1800*, Harmondsworth, 1959, p. 268), and Hugo Kehrer, (in *Die Meninas des Velásquez*, Munich, 1966) conjecture that Velásquez is painting in the picture what the viewer sees and is perhaps even using an unseen mirror behind the king and queen to see what he paints. The author of one study regards the princess as at the center of an allegorical theme that emanates from her. Madelyn Kahr (*Velásquez: The Art of Painting*. New York: Harper and Row, 1976) in a chapter vital for the criticism of this Velásquez painting, "Interpreting *Las Meninas*," writes that the subject of the picture "stated most succinctly, is *The Art of painting*" (171). Luca Giordano, who was a court painter in the 1690s, called it the *Theology of Painting*.

4. Ernest Hemingway, *For Whom the Bell Tolls*. New York: Charles Scribner's, 1968. All page references are to this edition.

5. Madelyn Kahr sees the "intermingling of the reality within the picture and the reality outside, this essentially Baroque breaking of the bounds of the picture space," as "the magic of the mirror" (179). The room in the Prado where *Las Meninas* was solitarily hung, included a mirror, apparently to add yet another dimension to the problem of reality/art.

6. The two major paintings that can be distinguished on the wall in *Las Meninas*, both based on oil sketches by Rubens, are *Minerva Punishing Arachne* and *Apollo's Victory Over Marsyas*. It is noteworthy that both represent a divine chastisement for mortal artistic vanity or human creative acts that arrogantly choose to compete with the Gods. Charles de Tolnay reads the paintings as symbolizing "the victory of divine art over human craftsmanship" (36).

7. The king conferred on Velásquez the title Knight of the Order of Santiago on November 27, 1659; yet in *Las Meninas*, painted in 1656, the cross of the Order of Santiago is plainly visible on Velásquez's breast. Antonio Palomino, in Book III of his *Museo Pictorico* (1724), says this "was painted after his death at the order of His Majesty, and some say His Majesty [Philip IV] painted it, for when Velásquez painted the picture he had not yet been granted this honor by the king" (Kahr 132). Students of Hemingway may well imagine the importance of this order and this title for Hemingway, who had named the protagonist of the novel (for which he himself gained the Nobel Prize) after Santiago, the most important saint, I would hazard to suggest, in Hemingway's pantheon. Santiago is the terminus, the objective of the great pilgrimage route across Europe.

8. Charles de Tolnay ("Velásquez *Las Hilanderas* and *Las Meninas*," *Gazette*

des Beaux-Arts, 35, 1949) states that the self-portrait in *Las Meninas* shows the artist "in a state of dreamy rapture" (36) in order to avoid undignified manual execution in favor of "the subjective spiritual process of creation [that] demonstrates the supremacy of spirit over matter" (37f.). Hemingway's elaborate use of Christian iconography throughout, his creation of a cast of characters having correspondences with a Christian pantheon, and the pattern of the sacrificed-and-to-be-resurrected son that he uses at the end of the novel, as well as Jordan's admonition to Maria at the end, all argue for an intricately laid down message of the supremacy of spirit over matter.

9. Madelyn Kahr writes, "As for Velásquez specifically, he looked upon everything from water jugs to princesses with the same clear-eyed objectivity" (175). This fidelity to "truth" and refusal to be subordinate to subjectivity or bias, one of the major battles being fought in *For Whom the Bell Tolls* by Robert Jordan/Hemingway, surely should explain why Hemingway might well have taken the main idea for his major work from Velásquez.

10. The suspended brush in the artist's hand emphasizes, as Martin Soria says (268), the artist in the act of "considering an idea," thereby emphasizing painting as an act of the mind. Madelyn Kahr sees the arrested moment as implying that Velásquez "did not flinch from the fact that in the end, after thinking, the painter must act" (167). The Hemingway scholar will note that the three days of special life that Robert Jordan is granted—during which he is living apart from the act of writing about his experience that he plans for in the future—is for him, as writer and expatriate, a suspended "moment" in time, and that bridge blower Jordan no less than Hemingway was one to insist upon the integration of thinking and doing, reflection and action.

4

Formal Analogies in the Texts and Paintings of Ernest Hemingway and Paul Cézanne

Thomas Hermann

Hemingway's claim to have learnt how to "do" landscapes from Cézanne has encouraged a number of researchers to take a closer look at Cézanne's landscapes, and the authors of several studies have so far acknowledged that similar impressions are evoked when reading a Hemingway text as when contemplating a picture by Cézanne. The aim of this chapter is to elucidate some underlying formal analogies in their respective works. Since both Hemingway and Cézanne chose to express themselves in a realistic mode, they use no metaphoric devices such as symbols, allegories and so forth. By rigorously subjecting all verbal or visual elements to the overall context, they create a sense of unity, and at the same time of openness, which forces the recipient to construct a meaning. Besides pointing out a few of these context-oriented strategies, it will also be shown that Cézanne—several decades earlier—had theories about art similar to those of Stein and Pound. Thus, although applied to a different medium, Cézanne's theories completed the education Hemingway was receiving from his literary mentors in the Paris of the early 1920s.

Several passages from fictional texts as well as from letters or interviews document the fascination Hemingway had for Cézanne's paintings, especially his landscapes (e.g., "I am trying to do the country like Cézanne" he wrote to Gertrude Stein, *Selected Letters* 122; "He, Nick, wanted to write about country so it would be there like Cézanne had done it in painting," *The Nick Adams Story* 239). Although one is led to assume that the young writer was introduced to Cézanne's art by Gertrude Stein, it seems likely that her influence was limited in that respect. It is true that when Hemingway first visited Gertrude Stein in 1922, the famous *Portrait of Mme Cézanne with a Fan* and a small group of "bathers" still decorated her *salon*. But more than 10 years had passed since Gertrude Stein, together with her brother Leo, had possessed a large collection of Cézanne's works. That was before Leo left his sister and most of the Cézannes were sold. Moreover, 14 years had passed since the publication of Stein's first book, *Three Lives*, a book that she maintains she wrote while under the influence of the *Portrait of Mme Cézanne*. In the meantime, her favorite painters were contemporary artists, above all Matisse and, especially, Picasso, whose Cubist paintings of that period she adored so much that she tried to adapt his style in her fiction and thought of herself as a literary "Cubist." This means that Hemingway, eager to learn, could have tried to imitate artists that were far more "in" at the time than was Cézanne. I therefore argue that his fascination with Cézanne's landscapes was genuine and his desire to "do" landscapes the way Cézanne had done was as self-chosen as was, for example, his disapproval of Dadaism, another movement that was very much "en vogue" during Hemingway's Paris years.

Besides the two pictures at Stein's flat, Hemingway saw at least some 40 to 50 Cézannes in Paris between 1922 and 1924: two in the Musée du Luxembourg, nine in the Louvre and about 30 at different temporary exhibitions. As well as contemplating the paintings as often as possible and discussing them with Stein, Hemingway found another important source of information in Sylvia Beach's bookshop "Shakespeare and Company," from which, according to Michael Reynolds's inventory, *Hemingway's Reading, 1910–1940*, he had borrowed Ambroise Vollard's standard biography of Cézanne. The sharp verbal attacks Cézanne ran against the French academia of his time must have amused the young American, who was about to adopt an equally cynical attitude toward academics. More important, however, were Cézanne's ideas about art: to read them must have sounded like a repetition of what Hemingway was learning about writing from Ezra Pound and Gertrude Stein.

THE CLICHÉS ARE THE PLAGUE OF ART

As of 1850, the impressionists in France started to break with the rigid norms that had been valid for centuries and at the time were still defended by the Académie des Beaux-Arts. Formally, this break manifested itself in the use of different colors (e.g., pastel colors) and especially by breaking up the clear lines. In terms of content, there was a move away from mainly historic and religious themes toward landscapes, a genre that thus far had not been taken very seriously. Cézanne, who for some time moved in impressionist circles, and who was also influenced by some of them, was the one to care least about pleasing the taste of the omnipotent critics and juries. He became more and more radical in his attempt to claim nature as the "supreme court" against which art had to be tested. He was convinced that the painter had to consecrate himself entirely to the study of nature. Consequently, traditional components of art such as allegories or symbols were banned from the canvas. "Clichés," according to Cézanne, are "the plague of art" (Vollard 83). This new perception of nature led to a sober realism and the resulting pictures appear deceptively simple.

A general feeling of breaking away from tradition in the early 1920s, partly due to the horrors of the First World War, led the modernist writers to mistrust literary language and to purge it of its encrusted expressions. It was exactly at this time that Hemingway seriously began to write in Paris, and he subjected his language to the same kind of "diet" as Cézanne had done with his painting a couple of decades earlier. Consciously, he began to use simple English words of Germanic origin wherever possible. He rarely used adjectives or adverbs and hardly ever any symbols. Equipped with these sparse means, the author sought new forms of expression in order to render an experience in a way as unbiased and objective as possible.

I was trying to write then and I found the greatest difficulty, aside from knowing truly what you really felt, rather than what you were supposed to feel, and had been taught to feel, was to put down what really happened in action; what the actual things were which produced the emotion you experienced. (*DA* 7f.)

Later on, in *Death in the Afternoon*, he compares the writer's duty to that of an architect: "Prose is architecture, not interior decoration, and the Baroque is over" (170). The result of this attempt to let the things speak for themselves, without commenting or describing, was a style that, similar to Cézanne's, proved to be deceptively simple and found many imitators.

THE ROLE OF CONTEXT

How did both the artist and the writer succeed in evoking such a feeling of depth by only presenting the surface in their paintings and texts? The answer could be by strictly subjecting all elements to the *motif* or the narrative context, respectively. An individual patch of color (*tache*) does not represent anything real or clearly defined. It becomes significant only in the context of the pictures, and due to its highly abstract nature, it often becomes ambiguous or multi-dimensional. Thus, as Gottfried Boehm has pointed out in his study of the Sainte Victoire pictures, "the same patch of color can evoke the wall of a building, the immateriality of light, a contrast demonstrating depth, the aura of a landscape, etc." (Boehm 59). Cézanne was fully aware of the importance that was given to the exact placing of such meaningless patches in relation to the whole. To Vollard he said: "You know, Monsieur Vollard, if I placed anything accidentally, I would be forced to redo the whole picture from this point" (Vollard 52).

Besides closely interweaving single elements, Cézanne made use of other context-oriented strategies. Sometimes he only hints at things, other things are left out completely and, especially in many watercolors, whole areas of the sheet are left untouched, and it is the contemplator's job to recreate them in his or her imagination. Through such deletions, the things represented gain simplicity and at the same time intensity.

By introducing natural symbols, the context can carry meaning on yet another level. Thus, in order to introduce a religious motif, say of resurrection, into a group of bathers, Cézanne would never use a traditional symbol such as a cross. However, he might arrange trees, which are part of the landscape, in such a way that a horizontal branch of a tree crosses with a cypress, thus providing the symbolic meaning without actually using the Christian symbol but by making use of inherent contextual elements.

If we stay with the cliché of the cross, we can see that Hemingway does exactly the same when he has Santiago walk up to his shack after the unsuccessful fishing expedition with a mast across his shoulder. Although several parallels to the crucifixion could be drawn, neither the word *cross* is used nor are there any overt allusions.

He started to climb again and at the top he fell and lay for some time with the mast across his shoulder. . . . Inside the shack he leaned the mast against the wall. . . . Then he lay down on the bed . . . and he slept face down on the newspapers with his arms out straight and the palms of his hands up. (*The Old Man and the Sea*, 104f.)

In Hemingway's prose the context is further intensified by the use of strictly denotative words which, free of any traditional connotations, share a similarity to Cézanne's color patches and by their relative meaninglessness are made open to new and different interpretations. Taken out of their context, the three nouns in the following sentence of part two of "Big Two-Hearted River": "There was the meadow, the river and the swamp" (220) appear almost accidental. But we all know, of course, that within the story these three nouns function as key words.

Hemingway was convinced that an author can delete the most important things from his story, provided he knows enough about what he is deleting. Thus, his readers are invited to fill in the white spots of a story. They will then come to realize that only on the surface is "Big Two-Hearted River" a story about a young man who goes fishing in a fine landscape. The psychological subtext is about the protagonist's problems of coming to terms with his recent traumatic war experience. Being familiar with the carefully structured stories and the often praised terse style, we can understand the young Hemingway who in fear of editorial changes in his texts wrote the famous lines to Horace Liveright in March 1925: "The stories are written so tight and so hard that the alteration of a word can throw an entire story out of key" (*LTRS* 154). It is possible that when writing these lines Hemingway had the above-quoted sentence by Cézanne in mind—that if anything was accidentally added to the picture, he would have to start again from scratch. In any case, these two quotations show how much weight was given to placing the right word or patch of color at the right place. Only in this way can the appropriate emotions be evoked in the reader or contemplator.

CONSTRUCTION INSTEAD OF DESCRIPTION

Finally, I wish to outline briefly how landscapes are formally realized in their respective media. Traditionally, landscapes are "described" in literature, that is, a place of action is presented to the reader in a (shorter or longer) block description. According to Helmut Bonheim, description is one of the four narrative modes, the others being report, dialogue and comment. Typical for Hemingway's style is the quantitative predominance of report and dialogue. Pure description is relatively rare, comment practically non-existent. His landscapes are comprised mainly of short descriptive sequences, which are mostly embedded in report, like in the sentence: "They walked down the *hill* across the fields and then turned to follow the *river bank*" (176, emphasis added) from "Out of Season." By frequently repeating keywords like *river*, the landscapes are carefully constructed and win a strong presence in the story. The mixing of the narrative modes is part of the strategy to condense the context and helps to present the text as a compact unity.

Cézanne also dreamt of a unity:

Drawing and color are not separate, everything in nature being colored. During the process of painting, one draws; the more the color harmonizes the more the drawing becomes precise. When the color has attained richness, the form has reached its plenitude. (Vollard 81)

As in Hemingway's texts description synthesizes with report, in Cézanne's paintings a unique synthesis of line and color, the basic plastic elements in painting, is attained. The viewer may interpret the concrete motif at first glance, but the single elements require in-depth "reading" and decoding. This becomes especially clear in the late Sainte-Victoire pictures, but it applies also to the earlier works. Where, for example, is the exact border between the river and the opposite river bank, or where exactly does the body of the female bather standing in the river disappear in the water?

Cézanne is often called the father of modern art. The strategies he developed in the second half of the nineteenth century in order to transpose nature into art parallel to a great extent what the modernists tried to realize within literature in the 1920s. The fact that Hemingway realized this parallel enabled him to create literary landscapes that belong to the best in twentieth-century fiction.

II

Our Old Man

5

Repossessing Papa: A Narcissistic Meditation

Mark Spilka

Last summer my friend Edwin Honig, poet and man of many letters, gave me an unusual birthday present—a famous photograph of Ernest Heming-way in boxing trunks and boxing gloves, his manly chest thrust out, gazing at himself in a body-length mirror with a pleased grin on his face. Only it wasn't his own face he now gazed at, it was mine. Honig had imposed a photograph of my head, with a similarly pleased grin on my face, where Hemingway's reflected head should have been. I should add at this point that among his many other books Honig is the author of *The Dark Conceit: The Making of Allegory*. Apparently he had just created another dark conceit, in more than one sense, a pictorial allegory of the critic's conceited identification with, or perhaps repossession of, his authorial subject's sense of his own public image, his publicly visible self, in one of his favorite guises. I have since come to accept this Lacanian effrontery as a legitimate critical act—my usurpation, that is to say, of another man's adult version of infantile self-discovery. This is what we all do as critics if and when we are honest with ourselves, as we attempt to interpret authorial intentions and in that sense begin our own takeover of authorial achievements. By achievements I mean, of course, the books we love or in some sense want to possess by authors whom we also love and want in some sense to possess.

Biographers have for a long time practiced this kind of identification, by which Leon Edel, say, moves at some point from being the James biographer par excellence, the hoarder of all the secrets, all the letters, all the manu-scripts, to being James himself. Great proselytizing critics like F. R. Leavis have long practiced becoming, first T. S. Eliot, then D. H. Lawrence, then in tandem with his wife Queenie, the two, only, and Inimitable Dickens critics of our times. The rest of us have stood back and mocked such pundits for their possessiveness, then gone ahead with our own less flashy takeovers.

I cite these particular usurpations because James, we know, burned all his and everybody else's letters, Eliot tried to depersonalize all poets, Lawrence told us never to trust the artist, only the tale, and Dickens liked to call himself Inimitable; yet all of them have been possessed and indeed repossessed by many a critical and/or biographical admirer. Some of them, Dickens for instance, and maybe Lawrence, and especially Hemingway, have asked for it by becoming public performance artists, creators of their own mythic lives within and without their fictions. Some of them have such a sense of themselves and of their missions that they virtually invite us to accept at face value with our own pleased grins on what used to be their reflected faces.

Consider Hemingway's sense of himself as a great boxer from boyhood days in his mother's music studio to shipboard sparring and mythic matches with Ezra Pound, Morley Callaghan, Wallace Stevens and other Parisian, Cuban and Floridian opponents. Consider too his metaphor of the artist as great boxer taking on all past creators and beating them in story after serious story, meanwhile beating up on discarded contemporary mentors like Sherwood Anderson and Gertrude Stein through stylistic lampoons. If Harold Bloom did not exist, we might well believe that Hemingway had invented him through an exhibited anxiety of influence and rivalry that runs through his life like a loose cannon. Of course, it was his possession by these past and present writers he was trying to throw off or blow off, and in a manner so infectious as to possess us all in his behalf. In these efforts he was more honest, I think, than the depersonalized Eliot sampling all those personal styles of predecessors in his talented extensions of the Great Tradition.

As with writers so with readers. We are all willynilly entrapped within a system of ongoing possessorship and identification. In New Critical times, when Eliot and Hemingway alike were prized for their meaningful forms, the Intentional Fallacy was invented by critics anxious to deny such personal modes of influence. Achieved intention was what mattered, and the only way to determine it was to look at the text. An author's stated intentions were out of bounds, and there was not even a working concept of the personal stylist among these early formalists whereby the similarities between works by the same person might be described. Later reformers like Wayne Booth invented such terms as the author's second self or the implied author to overcome this odd exclusion, this appropriation of anonymous works by oddly possessive readers, who often wound up writing their own stories into other peoples stories. Then came poststructuralism and deconstruction, semiotics and the new historicism, postcolonialism and multiculturalism, neo-Marxism and neo-Freudianism, feminism and gay and lesbian regenderings, and reader response in all its infinite varieties.

We are all familiar with the anarchic marginalizations and decenterings of our profession in recent times, the heightened cynicism as to language and reality, the undermining of authority and authorship and of literature itself, the devastating discoveries of gaps and antisocial codings in works reduced to texts and read in terms of cultural viability and political correctness, and with an infinite plurality of meanings. As aging members of one of the 42 author societies still extant in the Modern Language Association in America—and of similar throwback societies elsewhere—we are all puzzled about what to do in the wake of these devastating new theories. In an essay in the Sunday *New York Times Book Review* (January 12, 1992) Frederic Busch offered what many of us would like to see, a formula for "Reading Hemingway Without Guilt." The idea was that we live in a violent age, as Hemingway among others has shown us, that Hemingway himself saw writing as a life and death affair, and that this combination absolves him and us from the new academic payload of cultural guilt. One problem with that approach is that even dying is a value-laden and relational experience; it can be abusive or non-abusive to female partners, for instance, and is therefore bound like so much else by those gender considerations that Busch wants us to discard as reasons for not reading Hemingway. Well, we can't discard them, can't stick our heads in the sand and pretend that Hemingway and other writers we have loved still stand essentially untarnished. The problem is to confront such rejections with the same awareness that Hemingway himself showed for moral mixes, and to make our own cases for reading him in that problematic light.

Problematics is a buzz word these days, but let's embrace it and see where it takes us. The problem of dying in Hemingway's fiction is related, for instance, to the problem of killing, and not just of killing oneself, which is what Busch seizes on to prove Hemingway's lifelong sense of urgency and despair about widespread violence: There is also the problem of killing others. Hemingway liked to kill people. First in "Soldier's Home," then in *For Whom the Bell Tolls*, he described a taste for killing people in his fiction. He invested himself so often in war, moreover, as a medium for hard-boiled heroics, as to be sometimes called a war lover. It was partly true: He loved wars and considered himself the best writer about them in his times; hence his outraged vanity when Scribner's published a young rival's work, *From Here To Eternity*, after World War II, after his own book on that war had proved to be unsuccessful. Probably this not-so-secret attitude made him a great writer of anti-war novels, made him struggle, that is to say, with his own pro-war propensities, the better to seize on the fashionable anti-war movements of his time and write about war against the grain, using his wound in World War I, his two weeks experience of life at the front, and his longer experience of life behind it, to write better than anyone else what needed to be written, as in that great anti-war novel, *A Farewell to Arms*. Maybe that also explains his reluctance to take on the Spanish Civil War, to which Martha Gellhorn dragged him as her lover, after which he wrote about it with epic power, or to take on World War II, until she shamed him into following her example, with less happy results.

But my subject here is not merely his long-known propensity for killing men, but more importantly his newly noted propensity for killing women. I am concerned with Judith Fetterley's devastating reading of *A Farewell to Arms* in her powerful feminist study of American fiction, *The Resisting Reader* (1978) and especially with her resonant conclusion that for Hemingway the only good woman is a dead woman. I come to that problematic with a longstanding belief that Hemingway made a mistake in selecting senseless death in pregnancy as the equivalent for women of the male fate of senseless death in battle—hence the need to say farewell to arms erotic as well as martial. By 1918, however, there was no longer any great statistical danger of death in childbirth. The real danger for women, then and now, is from men; they are more likely to be killed, maimed, or physically and emotionally damaged by their male partners than by childbirth. Hemingway did not know this when he wrote *A Farewell to Arms*; he would not begin to slap, revile, and frighten his wives with violent behavior until his third and fourth marriages, but his hostilities where mounting, and I think he early began to sense his own propensities for marital violence with Pauline, whom he abused in more evasive and verbal ways throughout their 23 years together. I want to use my narcissistic license, my own white male stake in coping with such powerserving propensities, to speculate on those possibilities. Meanwhile, as should now be apparent, I am recommending that we read Hemingway *with* guilt, not without it if we want to persuade others to read him, or want simply to be honest with ourselves.

This brings me back for a moment to contemporary criticism and its cultural and semiotic gambits. Among them is the repeated announcement of the death not only of God but of the author, and particularly the white male author, subsumed by the very language he employs, or by its codes, unable to create works afresh like God, condemned only to repeat and reflect the governing social codes and language forms that control him— the biases, that is to say, of race, gender, class, and style that determine the texts and intertexts (not works) that issue forth under his name. I want to concentrate here on the contemporary theorist whose work I know best, my friend and colleague Robert Scholes, whose position in *Semiotics and Interpretation* I have elsewhere examined with regard to Lawrence, and whom I would now like to approach in Hemingway's behalf. I have no quarrel at all with Scholes's formidable case against Hemingway's gender-bashing in that mean-spirited tale, "A Very Short Story." But I do want to question Scholes's semiotic system. At the end of "Decoding Papa," for instance, Scholes tells us why he prefers his own approach to such fictions to New Critical exegesis:

A semiotic approach...allows critic, teacher, student, and reader more scope for thought, more freedom and more responsibility, than merely exgetical one. This Hemingway text is neither the greatest story every told nor a horrible example. It is, in miniature, a model of all fictions—better than the man who made it, because he worked hard to make it that way, but still flawed, still a communication to be tested and weighed, not an icon to be worshipped. For all forms of idolatry, whether of gods, men, or literary works, teach us finally the worst of all lessons: to bend the knee and bow the head, when what we must do instead is examine everything before us freely and fearlessly, so as to produce with our own critical labor things better than ourselves.

One problem with this oddly Joycean response to academic idolatries is that it grants aesthetic efficiency to the author but denies him or her the same moral braveries and freedoms that it assigns to the critic, teacher, student or reader. Granted, it allows the author to be morally flawed, as we too may be flawed; but we are in a better position, apparently, to be free and fearless, perhaps because we are still alive and writing, and therefore not bound by the same generic and cultural restraints and codes as idolized authors are, and thus more likely to unlock those codes.

Another problem with this approach is that it takes as its "model of all fictions" a well-made text with moral flaws, which suggests that it refuses any valid moral dimension to all fictions, or perhaps more to the point, any mix of valid and flawed assumptions. In most of his better and more complicated fictions, Hemingway, like any other author, presents such a mixture of which "A Very Short Story" is scarcely a helpful model. One reason for this difference, in Hemingway's better works, is that he is usually critical of characters like himself. Another and perhaps more generic reason is that, like every writer worth any salt, he is a creative semiotician himself, a critic of cultural codes who offers some sense of alternative possibilities and directions. It is from the past performances of these writer/pioneers, then, that Scholes and others draw their powers and braveries, assign them to critics, teachers, students—all those text-producing academic animals to whom Scholes allows humanity—and deny them to code-bound and/or idolized writers of the past. The point of his system is that we are all as good as or better than they are and need not kneel or worship.

I want to posit a different tack: As text-producing animals these writer/pioneers are at least as good as and often better than we are, and accordingly we may be able to learn from, and admire and even profit from, their struggles with their own mixture of flaws and virtues. In particular I want to look at Hemingway's struggles with himself in writing *A Farewell to Arms*. The easiest place to begin here is with his love of war and killing. One of the obvious self-critical functions of the text is to show Lieutenant Henry's milder struggle with himself and his modest military authority— milder, that is, than Ernest's early delight in being at the front and even at being wounded, and his postwar pride in such matters, which he first tried to catch through a younger version of Frederic named Emmett Hancock, then wisely modified with a hero closer to his presently chastened outlook.

In the novel's famous opening chapter, for instance, the narrator, Frederic Henry, presents a muted argument from nature against war. Noting first the troop movements that dust the trees, causing the leaves to fall early, he then contrasts the rich crops of summer with the pregnant appearance of soldiers, wearing heavy cartridge belts and the leafy branches used to camouflage the long barrels of big guns mounted on moving tractors. Then come ironic comments on the fast mud-splashing cars bearing officers and the inquisitive little king on inspection tours of the front, and on the rain bearing cholera, which kills only 7,000 soldiers that year.

In the second chapter, Henry similarly presents the futile argument from religion against war in the person of the baited priest in the officers' mess hall. Thus the priest is mocked for the secret sexual and economic basis of the spiritual life: "Priest every night five against one," the major says, with appropriate onanistic gestures; and "The Pope wants the Austrians to win the war.... That's where the money comes from" (7). When the priest then asks Frederic to spend his coming leave with his family in Abruzzi, where there is good hunting and the cold air is clear and dry, his messmates tempt him with urban centers of culture and civilization, where beautiful girls abound, then call him away to the officers' whorehouse.

In the third chapter, when Henry returns from his phantasmagoric leave, it becomes clear that Abruzzi is a pastoral alternative to, and a religious retreat from, the drunken debaucheries of those urban centers and their front-line equivalents. Thus, when the embarrassed Henry tries to explain to his respected friend the priest why he did not go to Abruzzi, he ends by granting him an oracular wisdom about love and war in those famous lines: "He had always known what I did not know and what, when I learned it, I was always able to forget." These lines are frequently applied to Frederic's selfishness in love, which calls rather for sacrifice and service to another person, as the priest tells him after he has been wounded (72). But even earlier in the same chapter (XI), the priest argues that the war is what Frederic is always able to forget: "You do not mind it," he tells him. "You do not see it ... even wounded you do not see it" (70); then he pointedly adds that Frederic is "nearer to the officers than to the men," that he identifies with the officers who make the war, rather than with the rank and file who oppose it (71).

What Frederic does not see, or sees imperfectly for himself, is the extent of that identification. Thus, early in the novel, as he records such anomalies as "two bawdy houses, one for troops, one for officers" (5), he begins also a series of meetings with enlisted men who oppose the war and officers who do not. In Chapter VII he feels sorry for and unsuccessfully tries to help a limping straggler near the front who curses the war and admits that he has deliberately thrown away his truss to get out of it. In Chapter IX, just before being wounded, he listens to the mechanics who hate the war, tries at one point to persuade them that defeat is worse than war, but lets them go on talking when they dismiss his arguments. As one of them pointedly observes, Henry likes to hear their rebellious talk and will soon be converted by it (51). Later, in a Milan hospital, he becomes alarmed when a patriotic barber mistakes him for an Austrian officer and almost cuts his throat while shaving him. During the Milan sequence he also meets some American Italians in a bar, including a thrice-wounded fellow officer named Ettore whose friends call him a militarist but whom Frederic sees as a "legitimate hero" who bores everyone. "I don't mind him," he pointedly tells Catherine, who cannot stand his conceited pride in rank and medals, and who shortly afterwards confesses to her fear that either she or Frederic will die in the rain. On his way back to the front, moreover, Frederic buys a used officer's pistol but is soon forced to yield his saved seat on the train to an outraged captain, who outranks him. Still later, as the wild retreat from Caporetto begins, Frederic forgets such warning signs, takes out his used officer's pistol, and shoots with it a fleeing sergeant who defies his orders. His confidence is shaken, however, when rearguard Italian patriots similarly shoot one of his men. Another deserts to the enemy, and the groundswell of retreating troops he joins near the Tagliamento begin calling themselves the Peace Brigade. Soon after, when he becomes himself the target of crazed officers and rearguard patriots, who take away his pistol and threaten his life, he says farewell to the absurdities and abominations of war and to his own participation in them.

I dwell on this conversion process because Scholes has no place for it in his semiotic scheme as a valid moral and social anti-war coding with known historic impact; and because Judith Fetterley similarly forgets its anti-patriarchal direction in her zealous feminist case against this white male author whose protagonist survives the death in childbirth of his beloved partner. Apparently Frederic Henry is in good company in his ability to forget important truths. But then so are we all.

One truth I would now like to recall from the historic context of literary and social codings surrounding this novel is the phenomenon of mass promiscuity that began in our century with World War I and the pressures it created for a step-up in random sexual activity as an apparent response to wholesale random slaughter. Hemingway's awareness of this phenomenon seems to me self-evident, but we tend to forget how closely interwoven it was with what might be called his novel's anti-seduction plot. His sympathetic treatment of Catherine Barkley's war-induced madness seems to me in this respect to be one of his finest and least acknowledged achievements. Judith Fetterley ignores it, but then so does everybody else. I want to speak to it now as what might be called a pre-feminist argument.

As I have elsewhere noted, Catherine Barkley's madness is related to

Catherine Linton's madness in Emily Bronte's *Wuthering Heights*. We have no problem noting the pre-feminist nature of Bronte's argument: The original Catherine is pulled apart by the selfishness of her bourgeois husband and her rebellious adolescent lover, each of whom claims her for his own. She is trapped by limited and conflicting choices in a patriarchal world, by social and emotional pressures that shake her sanity. Catherine Barkley is similarly but perhaps more subtly maddened by the social and emotional pressures of modern warfare. Her fiancé, the boy she was engaged to for eight years before the war, has been killed during the horrendous random slaughter of trench warfare in the battle of the Somme in France in 1916. She had imagined herself nursing him at the hospital where she worked. He would come there with a sabre cut and a bandage round his head, or a shot through his shoulder: "Something picturesque" (20). Instead he is blown to bits. She tells this story to Frederic Henry in Chapter IV, when she first meets him. She is carrying "a thin rattan stick like a toy riding crop, bound in leather" (181), which had been returned with his things and sent to her by his mother. The sequence, I need not remind you, is a characteristically ironic undercutting of shattered romantic illusions, rather like Hemingway's account of the explosion of the young soldier's marital expectations in "A Very Short Story." In "Decoding Papa" Scholes shows interestingly that it is impossible for Luz, rather than the soldier, to narrate that stacked story. Henry narrates this one by having Catherine tell it during their first conversation. It is not a stacked story but a newly encoded one like those which Paul Fussell records in *The Great War and Modern Memory*. Compare Hemingway's play with things picturesque in *The Sun Also Rises* (*SAR*), and elsewhere, where male narrators like Jake Barnes respond: "Isn't it pretty to think so?" Catherine Barkley knows that it is not; Frederic Henry is learning why, but keeps forgetting what he learns. Is not Catherine's position here privileged by the author in an extraordinarily significant way? She *knows* what Frederic and the reader have to learn. The woman knows. She uses the word "silly" quite a lot, and she has often been considered silly by critical detractors. But in Hemingway's world she has just been given a privileged position of considerable import.

Her friend Fergie seems to know it, too, in the hospital chapters in this novel. When Frederic Henry asks if she will come to his wedding with Catherine Barkley, she responds that they will never get married, that they will either fight before they marry or they will die: "Fight or die. That's what people do. They don't marry" (109). When Frederic, seeing that she is about to cry, tries to take her hand, she brushes him off, saying angrily, "Watch out you don't get her into trouble. You get her in trouble and I'll kill you.... I don't want her with any of these war babies" (109–110). Her prescient and well-taken anger is prefigured briefly back in Chapter V when Frederic calls again on Catherine, tries to kiss her, and gets slapped for his courting plans: "I'm dreadfully sorry," she then apologizes. "I just couldn't stand the nurse's evening-off aspect of it" (26). Both nurses are reacting at such moments against wartime pressures—newly coded expectations to make themselves sexually available to men who are about to die—or in World War II parlance, to put out for the troops. In the first war especially, for the first time anywhere, men literally died by the thousands—60,000, for instance, on the first day of the battle of the Somme, 370,000 in three months at Passchendaele, 8 million in the four years of war. The pressure to put out, in the face of such slaughter, was horrendous, and it makes our current concerns with on-the-job sexual coercions seem paltry by comparison: It was patriotic to put out, it was male entitlement with flags waving and drums pounding, and quite enough to make any woman feel unsexed and demeaned and angry and a little crazy when faced with her own newly coded failure to perform to expectations.

It is in that pressured context that Catherine's mad and sometimes silly-seeming behavior becomes extraordinarily meaningful. Though like Frederic Henry, Robert Scholes, and Judith Fetterley, we have all forgotten the context, it is resonantly there in the text and lends poignancy to such early lines as "I could have given him that anyway" and "You see I didn't care about the other thing and he could have had it all. He could have had anything he wanted if I would have known" (19) and to such later lines as "I want what you want. There isn't any me any more. Just what you want" (106) and to those frequent allusions to being his "good wife" and his "good girl." Even Catherine's fevered rivalry with the prostitutes whom Frederic has known becomes an understandable measure of the degree of her need to seize the wartime day, to ease the pressure of loss and guilt by becoming what she knows she must become to make up for her supposed feminine failure. Hemingway's recognition of this new type of madness, his obvious ability to listen to what someone like Agnes von Kurowsky or one of her Fergie-like friends must have told him, strikes me as admirable, as is his use of Catherine's madness to check his hero's greater folly, his cynicism and selfishness, and to sharply expose his sense of male entitlement.

Consider what Frederic now says to himself when Catherine asks him, in effect, to replace her lover by saying, "I've come back to Catherine in the night":

I thought she was probably a little crazy. It's all right if she was. I did not care what I was getting into. This was better than going every evening to the house for officers where the girls climbed all over you and put your cap on backward as a sign of affection between their trips upstairs with other officers. I knew I did not love Catherine Barkley nor had any idea of loving her. This was a game, like bridge, in which you said things instead of playing cards. (30)

What Frederic likes here is actually quite similar to the artificial affection shown by the prostitutes. The difference is that the previous lover is dead and that his own exploitive job is to resurrect that once and future lover. But even Catherine knows that they are both playing rotten games, and she soon pulls him up short by saying so. It is her reactive game, moreover, not his, that he now agrees to play; and the problem for both of them is to get beyond such substitions, to break through into loving each other directly.

Presumably this is what happens when he arrives wounded at the Milan hospital to which she has been transferred and immediately falls in love with her, and she with him. Apparently they both arrive at love by acting out the terms of her original romantic illusion, her dream of nursing her slightly wounded fiancé back to health, and of giving him the love she failed to give him before he died. They are "cured," supposedly, by testing that dream against the inroads of reality; but it is a shared androgynous dream they test, in which they both enjoy a measure of passive androgynous control and work together to create provisional homes in hospitals or hotels—defensive inner spaces, as Judith Fetterley nicely puts it, against the outside world. The right to name reality is always Catherine's, however, as when she feels like a prostitute in the hotel scene on Frederic's return to the front and so undercuts his untested early dream of a hotel rendezvous with his crazy sweetheart.

Her aggressive subservience in these chapters has been called a form of male wish-fulfillment by many feminist critics. It seems to me, however, to be more nearly a possible type of female response to mass wartime male coercion, which Hemingway now consciously records. Frederic's continuing boozy struggle with his own selfishness and forgetfulness is its male complement. *Thus*, if we take as our paradigm their favorite sexual game with Catherine's undone hair, which falls over the supine Frederick's face like a sheltering tent, then we are forced to conclude that Catherine in her passive aggressiveness and greater and more sober knowledge of the realities of love and war is always protectively on top—always doing what Frederic wants and what she wants to do for Frederic, and with an edge of playful madness that never leaves the text.

In *The Resisting Reader*, Judith Fetterley crosses these ideas with a number of similar assumptions. She believes the text is governed by an underlying hostility to women for which Catherine is the primary scapegoat. She believes that Catherine defines herself by men, that "her self-image is a result of internalizing male attitudes" and is "consistently negative" (67). She believes that Frederic is selfish, egocentric, paranoid, and fundamentally hostile to Catherine, whose "ritual death" allows him to survive his supposedly unwitting betrayer. Though I have no quarrel with most of these assumptions, it seems to be equally true that the text is also governed by an essential sympathy for Catherine's plight as a victim of wartime sexual coercion, that Hemingway is on both sides of that problematic pressure and is struggling through Frederic with his own ambivalence. There is little or no allowance for that struggle in Fetterley's relentless chapter. She never says that Hemingway sides with Catherine in important ways, and she frequently fails to say that Hemingway opposes most of the rude male misogyny she cites, and that Frederic struggles with *his* subtler failings. Nor does it ever occur to her that Frederic, along *with* Ernest, is attracted *to* Catherine as a possible solution for unresolved ambivalence.

The problem for me, in my own divided reading, is how and where to define the workings of that ambivalence. There are signs of it, as Fetterley well observes, in Frederic's treatment of older nurses in the hospital who oppose his will and perhaps also in those alcoholic hazes that Hemingway endorses as his own manly form of wartime madness. For me the main takeover begins with the escape to Switzerland. It also has something to do with the problem of Frederic's identity as well as Catherine's, and with the implications of their androgynous union, their frequent assertion of being and/or wanting to be the same person. If Frederic's male identity has been defined by his work as an ambulance driver on the Italian front, and if Catherine's female identity may be defined as a form of martial coercion, then their rebellious break with wartime society, their flight to Switzerland, severs their connection with the defining source of their separate identities. Their essentially passive androgynous union, which served so well as a defense against wartime intrusions, is now open to its own shortcomings. They do not fight much in this novel, as Fergie predicts in her fight or die formulation; but in one way or another, a wartime romance is bound to end when the war is no longer there to sustain it. Hemingway's way is to submit his lovers to the priest's religious world at Abruzzi, or rather to its secular Swiss equivalent, the mountain resort at Montreux where the cold air is clear and dry and the peasants respect you and where selfishness may be overcome for a time through an androgynous fusion of two unselfish persons. It is here, I think, that Hemingway's attempt to convert mutual wartime madness into idyllic mutual unselfishness goes astray.

Thus the beard that Frederic grows to pass the time becomes an unspoken biological trap, which the novel leaves undefined: It reminds us, as Hemingway almost seems to know, that Frederic no longer has any supporting form of male identity to keep the idyllic androgynous union going. Nor does Catherine have her own supporting form of female identity. Hemingway's solution to this fluid imbalance is to kill Catherine through outmoded death in childbirth and to leave Frederic to mourn her in the implicative rain. This seems to me, as to Fetterley, a sentimental form of male self-aggrandizement and disguised hostility. The only good woman is a dead woman after all.

But there are two Catherines in Hemingway's as in Bronte's world. In *The Garden of Eden* the girl-child whom Catherine and Frederic were going to name Catherine is androgynously reborn as a writer's wife named Catherine Bourne. The good woman is alive and well in the south of post-war France! Only she is no longer good, and not too well, since her new form of madness is androgyny itself, reinvigorated by a creative form of penis envy that leads toward hospitalization and suicide. I have no time or space to delineate this new kind of madness, which in any case I have already developed at some length in my book on *Hemingway's Quarrel with Androgyny* (1990). But I do want to point out how it meets the present understandable objections to Catherine's aggressive subservience by matching her with a demonic double, an aggressively self-serving heroine who makes her husband do what she wants, then demonstrates that he wants it too. This kind of deliberate reversal, cast as a different form of madness, argues for Hemingway's conscious awareness of that ongoing struggle with himself that is my primary theme, and for which such heroines function as externalized aspects. Thus Catherine Barkley herself recurs in this novel in the form of the lesbian pickup, Marita, who becomes the aggressively subservient mistress of the mystique of writing through whom the male protagonist, David Bourne, is able to regroup his creative energies and to re-write the African tales of men and boys without women, which his mad wife Catherine has burned. David's androgynous subservience to both heroines becomes an obvious key, moreover, to this parable of the male artist's struggle with his own demonic and subservient feminine muses; and David argues often and openly in this context with his self-serving wife. Thus all the unresolved elements of a *A Farewell to Arms*—fighting and dying, male and female identities, androgynous fusions, selfish and unselfish loves—are recreated and marshalled for another and more ambitious failure in self-knowledge and creative change and growth. It seems to me a more instructive failure, moreover, because it involves what E. L. Doctorow rightly calls "the most informed and delicate reading Hemingway has given to any woman" (44–45).

Hemingway's return to such problems, at the end of his life, is my closing argument for attending to a writer's struggle with himself and his world. His portrait of this "brilliant woman trapped into a vicarious participation in another person's creativity" (Doctorow 44–45) seems to me as historically prescient, in this regard, as his sympathetic coding of Catherine Barkley's victimization by wartime sexual coercion. Thus, as with Zelda Fitzgerald and to some extent any of Hemingway's four wives, Catherine is destructively jealous of her writer husband's creativity. When she sets him the task of writing about their life together and then seeks out Picasso to illustrate that private book, she buys his time and work with her money. When she finally burns his rival African stories of men and boys without women, she tries to punish him for denying her existence as his true demonic muse. Above all, she tries to assert some comparable form of creativity for herself, chiefly through artful conversations that speak to her own humanity as a text-producing animal, but also through tanning, haircut, and dressing styles through which she not only imposes her own androgynous demands upon her husband, but also advertises their private sex-life to the world. Like

Brett Ashley in *The Sun Also Rises*, she functions as a fashion-setter in the new androgynous life-styles of the postwar age, and, perhaps more importantly, as a forerunner of our own regendered times.

Once more, then, Hemingway functions, or tries to function, as a writer/ pioneer. Working from his personal knowledge of Parisian postwar mores, and from his own postwar propensities along the Riviera, he predicts and prefigures in the 1950s the new social codings of the 1990s. Indeed, his attempt to portray what it means to be spectrally "possessed" by androgyny as a kind of private obsession, which in the Riviera atmosphere of changing fashions and amoral upheaval becomes implosively corrupt, comes remarkably close to our own end-of-the-century ferment over gender liberations and politically correct salvation. He seems in all these respects braver than you and I, and Robert Scholes and Judith Fetterley, and more worthy of critical study—though I want to add, in all fairness, that it is the brave work of Scholes and Fetterley that enables me to say this.

I have been moved also by their arguments to place possessorship and identification somewhere between the false extremes of idolatry and author-bashing, and to define them as endemic to the literary trade. Further, I have been moved to define Hemingway as a creative semiotician and to defend his humanity as a producer of textual codings that speak to our own cultural predicaments, and to our own humanity in confronting them. I am most reminded of that humanity, moreover, by two passages in *The Garden of Eden* manuscript in which the writer David Bourne speaks of his desire to make his characters Nick and Barbara Sheldon come alive for his readers, and he singles out Catherine Bourne especially as someone whom he cannot personally help, but whom he can make as alive in the story of their life together as she was in life itself. However fictive, and however much it runs against that old shibboleth about characters as mere words upon a page, that kind of self-reflexive male authorial responsibility for doing justice to the humanity of a female character whom he obviously resents is my model for our own responsibility to the humanity of problematic authors and their problematic characters. Perhaps it explains also why this discussion has moved from a narcissistic meditation on repossessing Papa to a narcissistic meditation on the madness of two Catherines and their hostile husbands— and with a reading that insists on the common humanity of all such victims and victimizers who struggle to be better than themselves. But then to read Papa with that kind of struggling guilt is to repossess his own text-producing humanity, along with ours.

6

Hemingway's Influence on Sportswriting

Larry Merchant

We all know of the influence that the seminal American sportswriter Ring Lardner had on the young Ernest Hemingway. I am writing to repay that debt on behalf of all the sportswriters, myself included, whom Hemingway influenced.

Directly and/or indirectly he influenced us in a number of ways.

He influenced us first by giving a certain dignity to the world we covered, a fun-and-games world that before Hemingway seemed too frivolous to be treated seriously or even not seriously by serious people.

He influenced us by cleaning up the language of its rhetorical excess, forcing us to observe and report and write better.

He influenced us by baring the human behavior and the human heart of the athlete, and by the strong and sometimes contradictory code of ethics by which he judged athletes. He showed us that losers could be at least as interesting as winners.

And finally he influenced us by the sheer force of his personality and presence.

In the few pages I have here, I will elaborate on these themes, examine some of the sports references in the Hemingway library, and tell a few stories. As one who has devoted his life to this sporting life, I feel a bit intimidated among scholars, a mere parishioner at the College of Cardinals. But onward. Grace under pressure.

Some background. A noted sportswriter, Paul Gallico, said that sportswriters were "one peg up from the office cat" on the ladder of letters. Gallico, like Ring Lardner and Damon Runyon, turned to what I think of as light fiction. Others, like Heywood Broun and Westbrook Pegler, graduated to political punditry. They were fleeing a craft dominated by mythmakers and hero worshipers and cheerleaders. The best of the breed moved on.

That is the tradition my generation teethed on. At the high end of the mythmaking was Grantland Rice, our Kipling. After the Black Sox Scandal of 1919, when the rainbow bubble of America's innocence was punctured by the fixing of the World Series, Rice led a movement to restore that lost innocence. In poetry and prose he bathed sport in epic grandeur. He "godded up" athletes, as Red Smith put it. The most famous lead, probably the most famous words, or music, ever written by a sportswriter were Rice's:

Outlined against a blue-grey October sky, the Four Horsemen rode again. In dramatic lore they were known as Famine, Pestilence, Destruction and Death. These are only aliases. Their real names are Stuhldreher, Miller, Crowley and Larden.

That was about a football game.

Sportswriting rose a few pegs after World War II with the perspective and humor of Red Smith and Jimmy Cannon, who were daily columnists, and A. J. Liebling and John Lardner (Ring's son), wonderful writers who occasionally wrote about sports in magazines. Cannon, Liebling and Lardner, like Hemingway, had been war correspondents. Smith and Cannon, and Rice and Runyon, were friendly with Hemingway in New York and/or Cuba. Cannon's style often resembled Hemingway's and itself was widely copied.

How Hemingway's revolutionary impact on writing influenced all of these writers is impossible to know. But it absolutely influenced the mass of mythmakers and hero worshipers and cheerleaders, the fans who wrote sports. More accurately, it influenced the journalists who replaced them.

Death in the Afternoon, for example, was so crammed with acute observation, with detail, and ultimately with passion, told directly, that it had to kill the bull in sportswriting. Pretty or careful or oblique writing, filled with jargon, elegant variation, clichés and overblown metaphors, would in time be dragged out of the ring. Hemingway's less-is-more style required us to pay attention, to get it right, which, I believe, contributed to the demystification of athletes, from Giants with a capital G to giants with a small g. He often complained that too much was made of his style because after all it was just a means to an end. An editor once said to me, "If you have the story, tell it! If you don't, write it."

At that newspaper, the *New York Post*, where I succeeded Jimmy Cannon, I frequently wrote about the losers because the columnist who had seniority chose to cover the winners because that's what most readers wanted to read about. I couldn't have been happier, having discovered that there are only a few ways to win and a hundred ways to lose. I liked them all, noble losers and ignoble losers, especially if you got them to truly tell their stories in the straightforward dialogue Hemingway taught us.

Point: I assume you are all familiar with Manuel Garcia, the journeyman bullfighter who does not conquer but endures. Hemingway called him "The Undefeated."

That human touch—unsentimental and true—was our ambition. So too was the Hemingway magic of building, one word and sentence and paragraph and page at a time, toward what actors call "being in the moment," whether catching a fish or a punch or an emotion. Good luck if you can get it.

In common with all sportswriters, I became one because it seemed like a pleasant and exciting dodge. Reading Hemingway in college, along with Smith and Cannon and others, broadened the possibilities. Sports could be used as metaphor and prism as well as fun and games. In his journalism, his short stories, his books on bullfighting and in some of his novels, Hemingway recognized sport for the significant part of the culture we knew it to be. Maybe we weren't always relevant, thank heaven, but surely we weren't always irrelevant.

Lillian Ross's "Profile of Ernest Hemingway" in *The New Yorker* (May 13, 1950) was further inspiration for my ilk. While literary types cringed at her revelations of his odd ways—his drinking, his pseudo-Indian talk— I was amused with the great man's damn-them-all silliness and regular-guy act. Here are some of the things he said in that piece and others.

On critics: "It is like being a third baseman and protesting because they hit line drives to you. Line drives are regrettable, but to be expected."

On his betters: "It's like a miler running against the clock rather than simply trying to beat whoever is in the race with him. Unless he runs against time he will never know what he is capable of attaining."

On his plane crashes in Africa: "There is nothing you can do anyway about broken ribs except to hope that you receive them in the ninth round of a ten-round fight instead of the first."

On his wife: "Miss Mary can do with a few words what Maureen Connolly can do with her forehand."

It is amazing that Hemingway had the sports field to himself among serious writers for three decades. The only exception was Irwin Shaw's short story, "The Eighty-Yard Run." My guess is that the baseball passages in *The Old Man and the Sea* followed by "The Dangerous Summer" in the 1950s gave permission to Bernard Malamud, Mark Harris, Norman Mailer, John Updike, Philip Roth, Robert Coover and others to get into the game. This further reinforced sport as one of the glues that bind us.

Earlier I mentioned that Hemingway and Grantland Rice were friendly. An odd couple, you might imagine. While Rice was creating myths and heroes, Hemingway wrote "Fifty Grand" about a fixed fight and "My Old Man" about a father who breaks his son's heart by saying, "It sure took a great jock to keep that Kzar horse from winning." That was Hemingway's response to the Black Sox scandal that involved one of the Chicago teams of his boyhood.

But there was a strong philosophical or moral connection between Hemingway and Rice. It was Rice who also said "When the one great scorer comes to write your name, it isn't whether you won or lost but how you played the game." Hemingway of course also felt that how you played the game—how you shot the lion, how you caught the fish, how you fought the fight—was crucial.

How Joe DiMaggio played the game was no doubt why Hemingway used him in *The Old Man and the Sea* as Santiago's hero. There was an aspect of the bravest bullfighter in "the great DiMaggio." When a pitcher tried intimidation by throwing a baseball that could kill at him, DiMaggio would scarcely flinch, moving only enough for the ball to miss him by a millimeter. He was the essence of less-is-more: understated, elegant, classic, yet dramatic.

I once saw Hemingway and DiMaggio at a prize fight in New York. I can't remember whether they sat next to each other or a few seats apart. It was a Sugar Ray Robinson fight. Robinson was the DiMaggio of boxing.

How Jack Dempsey played the game probably was why he was the only name athlete Hemingway trashed. The fact that Dempsey was considered a draft dodger in World War I could not have endeared him to Hemingway either. One of the trove of Hemingway articles uncovered recently by the *Toronto Star* is entitled "The Superman Myth," a systematic, logical explanation of why Dempsey wasn't the fighter he appeared to be, how he had been manufactured into a star attraction because of his whirlwind style, why he might fall to Georges Carpentier, the challenger, who happened to be a French war hero. Dempsey, Hemingway revealed, had been training on Broadway, which "has stopped more fighters than all the left hooks and right crosses in the world."

Having been logically wrong a few times myself—Dempsey knocked out Carpentier in the fourth round—my sympathy is with Hemingway. What is interesting to me is that he missed what in hindsight were the essential truths of the Dempsey phenomenon. One, after the war America was flexing its muscle and dancing its feet, and Dempsey, like another swing-from-the-heels superstar, Babe Ruth, captured the spirit of the times. Hemingway could not make the leap into their revolution against conventional order. Two, who said, "Never risk anything unless you are prepared to lose it completely"? Hemingway. And that was exactly what Dempsey was doing. But let us remember: Hemingway was 22 then.

Two major league pitchers were mentioned by Hemingway, in a preface to the paperback edition of Lillian Ross's profile. They were Joe Page and Hugh Casey, both tough, hard-drinking relief pitchers. Relief pitchers fascinated Hemingway because they are the purest gunslingers in sport, expected to enter games in pressure situations and perform with no-mistake skill and poise—like hunting lion.

Which brings me to a story, or two.

The year after Hemingway committed suicide a former ballplayer named Billy Herman told me that in 1947, when the Brooklyn Dodgers trained in Havana, Hemingway befriended some of them and took them shooting at his club. He invited four of them, including Casey and Herman, to dinner at his home one night. They all drank. After sizing up Casey during dinner, Hemingway challenged him to a fight. Casey wasn't interested but when his host put on boxing gloves and continued to insist, Casey agreed and started to pull on gloves too. Hemingway, who felt that how you played the game was crucial, sucker-punched Casey on the jaw. A brawl ensued, Casey pummeling Hemingway until they were separated. Then, according to Herman, Hemingway went to another room and came back with two pistols and said they would have to settle the matter outside. The ballplayers, having more common sense and better social graces, fled.

There's a postscript. Four years later Casey killed himself with a gun. I've learned that Hemingway was deeply affected.

There's a second postscript. Showing how foolish and how swinish he could be with guests, Hemingway also challenged the ex-heavyweight champion, Gene Tunney, who incidentally had done to Dempsey what Hemingway thought Carpentier would—outboxed him. Apparently Hemingway hit Tunney in the stomach without warning. Tunney countered with a body shot of his own and then flashed a lightning hook and stopped it at Hemingway's whiskers, saying, "Don't you ever try anything like that again."

Allow me to comment on the Stanley and Steve Ketchel question in "The Light of the World," which I understand has brought forth scholarly debates. Why did the fat blonde hooker insist that she had gone to bed with Steve and not Stanley—his real name—Ketchel, the middleweight champion? My first thought, based on my experiences with athletes, is that Stanley didn't want anyone to know that he went to bed with a fat hooker, so he told her his name was Steve. My second thought is that it doesn't matter whether they did or not because this is a story about how some ordinary people deal with mortality, by trying to connect with immortality.

Also, a friend of mine, Stan Isaacs, of the newspaper *Newsday* in New York, once sent a letter to Scribner's advising them to correct the misspelling of Frankie Frisch, a famous ballplayer, in *The Sun Also Rises*. Twice he is spelled "Fritsch." Stan received a letter from an editor advising him that Hemingway might have spelled it that way to indicate that Jake Barnes was drunk at the time. It seems unlikely. It seems more likely that Hemingway or Scribner's blew it. It remains "Fritsch."

In *The Sun Also Rises* there is a passage about a fight someone saw. A black fighter was hit by a white fighter, got angry and knocked the white fighter out. The promoter refused to pay the black fighter on the grounds that he had agreed not to do that to the white fighter. That may have been Hemingway's spin on two well-known fights. Jack Johnson, the first black heavyweight champion, knocked the horny Stanley Ketchel out after Ketchel had knocked him down. In Paris, when Hemingway was there, George Carpentier defended his light-heavyweight title against a fighter who had been discovered as a boy in Africa by a French actress on location and raised in France. He was known as Battling Siki. Siki agreed to lose the fight for a substantial amount of money, but when Carpentier hit him harder than he expected, he lost his head and knocked Carpentier out. I don't know how much he was paid, but it was enough to buy the leopard that he walked around with at the end of a leash.

If Hemingway could composite a fight, he could composite a character. Harold Loeb, a friend of Hemingway's, complained that he was a model for Robert Cohn. Hemingway indicated that only Cohn's whineyness might have been borrowed from Loeb. How then did Cohn become a Princeton boxing champion? Well, let me introduce you to Moe Berg, the first and perhaps the only Jewish star athlete at Princeton. He was a baseball player and when he was in the major leagues it was said of him that he spoke 10 languages and couldn't hit in any of them. He was also a linguist, a lawyer, and a spy. More importantly, he attended the Sorbonne in the 1920s, and he was a fabled womanizer who specialized in wealthy beauties, like Brett Ashley. Loeb and Berg. It's a theory.

Some closing thoughts.

In word and deed, Hemingway showed us that active, rugged individualism and writing were not mutually exclusive. That, however, does not mean that we swallowed whole his obsession with physical courage and his manic competitiveness. "The hardest thing in the world," he said, "is to write straight honest prose about human beings." His commitment to that good fight was his real courage.

His achievements and his stature as an icon insinuated themselves into us. I never even considered his influence until a critic took me to task for writing a column about a fight between two fighters who weren't quite championship caliber. For loving what they did, I was labeled "the spoor of Hemingway."

I was flattered.

Mythmaking, Androgyny, and the Creative Process, Answering Mark Spilka

Donald Junkins

No writer in the twentieth century has been lampooned, caricatured, parodied, ankle-nipped, imitated, despised, adored, and appropriated by his heirs for market advertising as much as Big Bad Ernest Hemingway. Hemingway the sadist, Hemingway the macho American, Hemingway the daring romantic sportsman, Hemingway the international gun-toting war correspondent, big game hunter, wounded war hero, airplane crash survivor twice in one day, double daiquiri record-setting drinker in the Floridita bar in Havana, German submarine chaser in a fishing boat, palsy-walsy friend of Cary Cooper, Ingrid Bergman, Marlene Dietrich and 15 Spanish bullfighters—and winner of the Nobel Prize for Literature when he was 52 years old. How many Ernest Hemingways are there?

The biographers tell us that Ernest is Legion, not unlike the Devil, that he wears a coat of many colors, that he is a psychically wounded, compensating boy in a man's body, a compulsive friend-destroyer, penny-pinching woman exploiter, braggadocio, contract-breaker, ingrate, soul-torn parent despiser who wrote his literal life into his fiction where that life can be explained for the asking and where those explanations can be simplified, morally evaluated and labeled. Philip Young's fascination with Jake Barnes's half penis gave birth to half-truths about Hemingway's psychological turmoil. Kenneth Lynn's fascination with Freudian simplicities led him into an imagined Gothic sanctorum of Grace Hemingway's sexual disturbings of young Ernest, and now Mark Spilka's fascination with Hemingway's psychologically undifferentiated maleness focuses a Hemingway crippled by his quarrel with androgyny. In *Hemingway's Quarrel With Androgyny*, Mark

Spilka out-Eastmans Max, out-Meyers Jeffrey, and out-Bells Millicent, and the mythicizing of Ernest Hemingway deepens.[1]

BIOGRAPHICAL TERRAIN AND THE CREATIVE PROCESS

The legitimate terrain of the literary biography, psychographic or cultural, obviously, is the writer's life, and the legitimate intent is a clarifying aesthetic inspiration. There may be strange threads weaving through a personal and racial past, co-mingling with private remembrances, obsessions, passions, sublimations, regressions, fantasies, suppressions, projections, compensations, horrors, dreams, dreads, wish fulfillments—the whole laundry basket of contemporary psychoanalytic terminology that aspires to and fails to describe the artistic process of making new things out of age-old human warpings and woofings—but there must be no jargonizing, and no didacticism. Moral speculation breeds sensationalizing and fosters caricature. The history of Hemingway as a mythological figure bulges with popular romantic fascinations engendered by cult passions and moral judgments in the service of fetishes political, cultural, and social, exploiting generalizations and simplifications. The literary biographer must evaluate, but the evaluation must be inherent in the writer's clarified life and art, both against the historical screen of culture and society, and within the timeless framework of aesthetics.

Historically, the biographical critics have played into the hands of the Hemingway pop-culturalists and their academy allies, the new political left: the anti-textualists, the radical feminists, and the multi-cultural extremists. Photos of the lean Hemingway (recently recovered from dysentery) in Africa, big game rifle in hand, raised leg planted on a dead kudu, handsome in the manner of Clark Gable and Errol Flynn, simplify Hemingway at the same level that the academic pop-Freudians do when they sensationalize Hemingway's inner life. By sensationalize, I mean that the biographical critics have almost totally neglected the study of the creative process in favor of psychologizing in the most surface ways. The abandonment of the study of Hemingway's art as process has caused by default the obsessive focus on popular mythic generalizations, dramatized as eccentricities in Hemingway the artist. His biographical critics have Gothicized Hemingway's art by Freudianizing it. It is what Spilka does when he refers to Hemingway's "hard-boiled prose"[2] and illustrates this critical evaluation with moralisms about Hemingway and his fictional characters. Professor Spilka and the biographical critics have turned the creative process into rational equations and have thrown open the field to the new-left Hemingway-haters.

They have done this in three ways: (1) consciously crossing over between Hemingway's life and his prose; (2) shunning the creative process as the soul of aesthetic significance; (3) caricaturing psychology itself as naive Freudian jargon. The crossings-over have pinpointed and literalized the origins in Hemingway's art in such a way that the ego of Hemingway replaces the multi-faceted egos of his characters, at the same time that the fictional characters make linear and one-dimensional the complexity of Hemingway's psyche. The shunning of the creative process has moralized the context of Hemingway's life rather than clarifying it. The Freudianizing both obscures the central truth that origin does not determine validity, and it monopolizes, in the form of jargonizing, psychological truth itself. The final irony of moralistic criticism is that it wishes that the writer had lived a different life. Unlike Jake who says, "You paid some way for everything that was any good....Either you paid by learning about them or by experience, or by taking chances." (*SAR* 148). Also unlike Hemingway itself, who said, "There are some things which cannot be learned quickly, and time, which is all we have, must be paid heavily for their acquiring. They are the very simplest things and because it takes a man's life to know them the little new that each man gets from life is very costly and the only heritage he has to leave" (*DA* 191, 192).

ANDROGYNY, SPILKA'S QUARREL AND SOURCES

In the dim light of Mark Spilka's statement 20 years ago that Ernest Hemingway's hard-boiled prose could never accommodate the deepest human emotions, the book *Hemingway's Quarrel With Androgyny* recalls attention to Spilka's ongoing fascination with Hemingway's life. Centering on androgyny, Spilka rightly focuses on the subject crucial to the polarization of male/female difference and male/female differentiation in current American literary studies. Unfortunately, much contemporary mythicizing of Hemingway's life, and consequent diversion once again from the study of Hemingway's art, has emanated from popular separatist views of so-called male versus female creativity. These views are political, social, and sexual, and they have reinforced popular genderizing fads, which, in addition to distorting Hemingway's true androgynous vision in his art by focusing on his failures to reconcile masculine/feminine polarities in his nonartistic life, have destructively genderized a whole body of contemporary literary criticism.

Professor Spilka has written a brilliant book in which he calls himself a neo-feminist critic; yet he seems narrowly, even prudishly, separatist: feminist. He often genderizes, and he subjects Hemingway's life to an ongoing litmus test of various versions of what he calls "tenderness," "softening feminine influences" and "hardened male attitudes." I can find no definition of "androgyny" in his book and can only conclude that Professor Spilka seems to think of it in general terms as merely an exchange of sexual roles in dress, lovemaking, and personal attitudes. He uses the term almost always as an adjectival weapon in such phrases as "androgynous remarks" (208), "androgynous emulation" (263) and "androgynous complicities" (309) and appropriates the word to mean gender reversals that not only establish the incompletenesses in Hemingway's life, but also in both Hemingway's art and in the historical circumstances and cultural milieu that shaped his childhood upbringing. Unfortunately, Spilka appropriates the concept of androgyny in the service of, not gender clarification, but gender stereotyping.[3]

The lack of precision in Spilka's use of the term *androgyny* begs the question of authorial intent and calls into question such a source-centered critical methodology. ("Source-centered" meaning not only (1) the actual literary sources of plots and characters, but also (2) psycho-source speculation with Freudian weaponry that makes no distinction between the writer's personal life and the lives of his fictional characters.) For argument, I would ask Professor Spilka: (1) if we could trace the actual genesis of all artistic ideas and syntheses, what would we have in the end? An aesthetic or psychological enrichment of the work of art? If the answer is yes, I would ask how it furthers our pleasure before a painter's canvas if we discover the secret trauma associated with that artist-child's blue bedroom wallpaper that has become a green bird, or the yellow ribbon in his second lover's braid that has become a wheatfield on a rain-drenched day? I would ask of the amateur Freudian critic (2) what is the nature of a created art that is exclusively experienced as being psychologically derivative? Professor Spilka tells us that Hemingway's characters in *The Sun Also Rises* "are not only puppets and caricatures, unable to stand by themselves, they are also products of sentimental failure founded in impotence" (198–199). He assures us that Hemingway's objection to Allen Tate's review that stated this is, furthermore, a "disclosure of [Hemingway's] personal impotence" (200). Professor Spilka speculates on Hemingway's employment of the honorable tradition of impotent heroes. Why did Hemingway create an impotent Jake? For the answer, Professor Spilka probes the original manuscript of *Garden of Eden* where

the hero engages in androgynous forms of love making with his adventurous young wife in the south of postwar France, and at one point in the original manuscript imagines himself as one of the lesbian lovers in a mysterious statue by Rodin, called variously Ovid's Metamorphoses, Daphnis and Chloe, and Volupte, and deriving from a group called The Damned Women from the Gates of Hell. Since the hero also changes sex roles with his beloved, we have one interesting explanation for Hemingway's postwar choice of a symbol for his own unmanning by war wounds and the American nurses who tend them: for if Jake remains "capable of all normal feelings as a 'man,' but incapable of consummating them," as Hemingway told George Plimpton in a famous interview, his physical wound suggests also the female genitals as men erroneously imagine them, at least according to Freud . . . which again makes us wonder if Jake is not in some sense an aspect of his beloved—not really her chivalric admirer, like Robert Cohn, but rather her masculine girlfriend, her admiring Catherine from the novel years ahead who similarly stops her car on the return from Nice to kiss her lesbian lover, then tells her androgynous husband about it and makes him kiss her too—or, in Jake's more abject moments, her selfless Catherine from the novel next in line. (203)

I find the above paragraph ingenious; yet I confess to a personal preference, not for a discussion of Hemingway's possible motivation for using Jake's wound as a metaphor of the traditional impotent hero (although Jake is not impotent), but for a discussion of Jake's wound as a metaphor for the psychological wounds in all the major characters in *The Sun Also Rises*. My own critical preferences notwithstanding, however, it seems clear that Spilka's real test is not only his quarrel with Hemingway but with the alchemical nature of the creative process and with the classical psychological androgyne mythically described by Plato, psychologically focused by Carl Jung, and further focused and clarified by June Singer in her book, *Androgyny: Towards a New Theory of Sexuality*.[4]

To illustrate Professor Spilka's method, early in his own book, *Hemingway's Quarrel with Androgyny*, in discussing Hemingway's early boyhood, Spilka notes that Ernest's sister "Marcelline's hair was cut short to resemble Ernest's. Her suffering from that tonsorial reversal must have deeply impressed her brother, who would later imagine a heroine raped and cropped by Spanish fascists." (47). Later, in his discussion of *For Whom the Bell Tolls*, Professor Spilka says,

Since the novel is dedicated to Hemingway's third wife, Martha Gellhorn, it suggests that Hemingway felt that Martha—a St. Louis girl like his first two wives—was in some sense an extension of Pauline's beneficence (an idea that he would develop, over the next two decades, through the menage à trois in *The Garden of Eden*). But the ambitious Martha contributes only physical features to Maria; that "little rabbit" in her selfless caring for the novel's hero, Robert Jordan, is more like Hadley or the younger Pauline in Spanish guise. Having been raped and cropped by Spanish fascists, she is also more like Hemingway's twin sister Marcelline, whose hair was cropped by his mother to resemble his, one childhood summer, and who suffered for it, as we have seen, for sometime after. So Maria is Grace's gift as well as Pauline's in the novel's psychogenesis, and that strong woman Pilar may owe as much to Grace as she does to Pauline. She is the tough, outspoken gypsy mother Ernest would have preferred, apparently, to the one he got, whom in many ways she nonetheless resembles. (246)

Six pages later, Professor Spilka adds, about Maria and Robert Jordan, "As a heterosexual pair, at any rate, this fictional couple wouldn't last six months back in the academic circles at the University of Montana" (252).

Professor Spilka on *The Garden of Eden*:

As his frequent chapter notations—'Hair,' 'Hair Cutting,' 'Hair Symbol'—attest, hair was for Hemingway the public expression of his own private obsession with androgyny, his easy, imaginative access to a woman's breasts and womb; his unconfessed desire to rest confident in her supine passivity; and his honest awareness of her oppression of men much like himself. (291)

Professor Spilka on *A Farewell To Arms*:

It may be too that Catherine's small hips—that androgynous feature—have determined her fate in more ways than one. The love she offers so absorbs male identity that she is as threatening to it, finally, as any bitch heroine; and though she dies bravely, like a true Hemingway hero, it may be that she is sacrificed to male survival—so this time the Indian in the upper bunk lives on! (215)

Professor Spilka on Catherine and Brett:

To be a woman like Brett is finally more attractive, for men as well as women, than to be a woman like Catherine Barkley. But that may be precisely because with Catherine something in Frederic, and by the same token something in his creator Ernest, is lapsing or dying—namely his capacity for nurturing tenderness, his sympathetic sameness, his identification with women in their selfless suffering rather than in their bitchy independence. . . . The androgynous secret behind this kind of fusion, the androgynous threat to male identity, is finally more threatening and absorbing than abject service to the bitch goddess Brett Ashley, which at least drives men back upon themselves. So the extremely female Catherine dies that Frederic/Ernest may regain his maleness. (219)

Two final notations of Professor Spilka's detective work: the sources of (1) the charging lion in "The Short Happy Life of Francis Macomber," and (2) Frederic Henry's preference for the names of towns and dates where battles were fought, rather than the words "honor" and "sacrifice."

In [Marryat's] *Percival Keene*, which is on the Oak Park Public Library list for 1904, variations on the lines [from Shakespeare's "A man can die but once; we owe God a death and let it go which way it will he that dies this year is quit for the next"] appear three times. In the same novel, moreover, a cowardly clerk runs screaming before a charging cow in one comic chapter, even as Hemingway's hero runs wildly before a charging lion in the Macomber tale; and in the next chapter, Marryat's hero is shot in the back of the head in a hunting "accident" which later proves intentional, even as Hemingway's hero is shot there "accidentally" in the Macomber story. (90)

A charging cow, a charging lion. A shot in the head and a shot in the head. Oak Park Library reading list when Hemingway was five years old.

In Kipling's *Stalky & Co.* [also on the Oak Park Library reading list] where

"a fatuous M. P. addresses the college on the glories of service to the Empire [and] they are appalled by his sacrilege: 'In a raucous voice, he cried aloud little matters, like the hope of Honor and the dream of Glory, that boys do not discuss even with their most intimate equals, cheerfully assuming that, till he spoke, they had never considered these possibilities. He pointed them to shining goals, with fingers which smudged out all radiance on all horizons. He profaned the most secret places of their souls with outcries and gesticulations. He bade them consider the deeds of their ancestors in such a fashion that they were flushed to their tingling ears. Some of them—the rending voice cut a frozen stillness—might have had relatives who perished in defence of their country. They thought, not a few of them, of an old sword in a passage, or above a breakfast-room table, seen and fingered by stealth since they could walk. He adjured them to emulate those illustrious examples; and looked all ways in their extreme discomfort. The years forbade them even to shape their thoughts clearly to themselves. They felt savagely that they were being outraged by a fat man who considered marbles a game.' (256–257) [Spilka comments] The genesis of Hemingway's famous dismissal of patriotic rhetoric in World War I in *A Farewell to Arms*, seem evident in this imperial lament. (100)

ALCHEMY: HEMINGWAY AS ANDROGYNE

Although Professor Spilka does not define androgyny, it is clear that he thinks of it merely as "an exchange of sexual identities," (9) thus diverting from the real meaning of androgyny as defined in contemporary psychological scholarship. Compare Professor Spilka's narrow definition of androgyny with two sentences from June Singer:

1. Androgyny is the rhythmic interplay of Masculine and Feminine within the psyche of one individual. (266)
2. The conscious aspect (as Jung understood the term) corresponds to the ego-image which in men is masculine, and in women, feminine . . . plus the inward unconscious extension of our being which we call "soul," (and which Jung called "anima" in men and "aniumus" in women). (164)

The androgyne, then, is a whole human being, psychologically differentiated, inter-sexually correspondent, gender friendly in inter-sexual rhythms, at peace with both masculine/feminine selves. The androgyne is the fulfilled person, creative in the self-interactions of conscious and unconscious sexuality. The androgyne is the individual psyche managing creatively its double gender. The androgyne mirrors the cosmic unity of all things and personalizes the truth of the psychological doctrine of opposites: health achieved and contained in the resolution of contradictory forces. The androgyne has achieved "an innate sense of a primordial cosmic unity, having existed in oneness or wholeness before any separation was made. The human psyche is witness to the primordial unity; therefore the psyche is the vehicle through which we can attain awareness of the awe-inspiring totality" (Singer 20).

Obviously, we are not talking in the previous passage about Big Bad Ernest Hemingway whom Dos Passos called "The Monster,"[5] who chewed up and spit out three St. Louis wives and tried to drive out a fourth from

Walker, Minnesota, whose personal foolishnesses, anti-literary prejudices, domestic mismanagements, parental lapses, exaggerated heroisms, public embarrassments, private blackass sufferings, cyclical venomous lacerations, human unfairnesses despising of academics, in short, his humanity, became reconciled in his creative unconscious. When Professor Spilka fails to come to terms with the meaning of the word *androgyny*, he fails to come to terms with the alchemical resolutions that the creative process engenders. Hemingway's conscious night journeys in the darkness of the whale's belly, notwithstanding Professor Spilka's distractedness, are alchemized in the unconscious deliverances of his artistic self. Crucial to any understanding of Hemingway's art are the failures in his personal life. What Meyers, Lynn, and Spilka, to name only three, have done is to magnify the grotesqueries in Hemingway's life and to overlay those grotesqueries onto his art as one might overlay a cartoon transparency over an oil painting, thus disparaging not only Hemingway's life and art but also Art itself.

Contrast this with the historical alchemists who understood the necessity of destruction and despair in the transforming of matter, the *prima materia*, from darkness into light, and how that transformation parallels the healing process in the human psyche by reconciling masculine/feminine opposites. The psychologist Ralph Metzger describes such a working out of opposites within a person's psyche as an alchemical conjunction: "The first fusion of male and female energies, known as the 'conjunction,' is the central process of alchemy" (quoted in Singer 142). My answer to Professor Spilka is that the artist in Hemingway, the androgynous Hemingway, negotiated the male Hemingway and the female Hemingway together, despite the obvious fact that the person Hemingway failed to do this in his non-artistic life. As a writer, Hemingway was to writing what Mercurius was to the alchemical process, "the agent of creation" (143).

Alchemically, Hemingway's turbulence fueling his conscious self-destruction was the forge in which he purified the irreconcilable polarities in his domestic and personal relationships. Singer explains clearly how this is a process requiring tremendous work on the part of the androgyne, that destruction and despair are necessary, that the task of healing requires purification, that the process requires a facing of the personal shadow ("the realities of our nature instead of pathologies") and that in the long and complicated process of discovering the contrasexual other within ourselves, the miracle and the mystery of the work produces the *filius philosophorum*, the son of the philosopher. "It does not simply happen, it is not a gift of grace, but it is the result of hard work and devotion and the application of man and woman to the process in the right spirit" (144–149). This is a perfect description of Hemingway separating himself in the mysterious conjunctions of his art from the darkness and often despair in his non-creating life. In his creative unconscious, the transforming agent, Mercurius in Hemingway, transformed the prosaic iron into gold.

My intention is not to document Hemingway's masculine/feminine resolutions in the characters of his prose—others have done that and will
continue to do so—but rather to signify the deeper resolutions in Hemingway's aesthetic consciousness, that is, his darker unconscious self where the
alchemy of creation took place.

MYTH BECOMES ART: HOW MANY HEMINGWAYS ARE THERE?

My answer, also, is "Legion": the female Hemingway, the male Hemingway, all the versions of Hemingway finding themselves in the characters
of his art, and all the versions of Hemingway contradicting themselves in
his life. He failed time and time again in his life, and he succeeded time and
time again in his art where he did not represent anyone else's view, and
where he did not moralize. Hemingway presented a world to us, incomplete,
personal, flawed, multi-layered, punitive, price exacting, and devastating,
and he presented it truly. Unfortunately, he did not inspire humility in his
biographical critics, and none has been restrained by Carl Jung's warning
that "a human being is only half understood when we know how everything
in him or her came into being."[6] They have been too quick to psychologize
after the insights of Freud, have been neglectful of Jung's studies of the
shadow side of the human personality, have dramatized a view of the creative
process that is not only naively rational, but is too often morally pragmatic.
Everything we know about the wellsprings of human creativity leads us to
a context of amoral energies combining into resolutions greater than the
sum of life experiences. Jung said it: "The highest and lowest, the best and
the vilest, the truest and most deceptive things are often blended together
in the inner voice in the most baffling way."[7]

In *Green Hills of Africa*, Hemingway writes:

We have been there in the books and out of the books—and where we go, if we
are any good, there you can go as we have been. A country, finally, erodes and the
dust blows away, the people all die and none of them were of any importance
permanently, except those who practiced the arts, and those now wish to cease their
work because it is too lonely, too hard to do, and is not fashionable. A thousand
years makes economics silly and a work of art endures forever.... If you serve time
for society, democracy, and the other things quite young, and declining any further
enlistment make yourself responsible only to yourself, you exchange the pleasant
comforting stench of comrades for something you can never feel in any other way
than by yourself. That something I cannot yet define completely but the feeling
comes when you write well and truly of something and know impersonally you have
written in that way and those who are paid to read it and report on it do not like
the subject so they say it is all a fake, yet you know its value absolutely; or when
you do something which people do not consider a serious occupation and yet you
know, truly that it is as important and has always been as important as all the things

that are in fashion, and when, on the sea, you are alone with it and know that this Gulf Stream you are living with, knowing, learning about and loving, has moved, as it moves, since before man, and that it has gone by the shoreline of that long, beautiful, unhappy island since before Columbus sighted it and that the things you find out about it, and those that have always lived in it are permanent and of value because that stream will flow, as it has flowed, after the Indians, after the Spaniards, after the British, after the Americans and after all the Cubans and all the systems of governments, the richness, the poverty, the martyrdom, the sacrifice and the venality and the cruelty are all gone. (109, 148–149)

The true gold of Ernest Hemingway's life is his art. The style of his clear, simple, wonderfully compound and complex sentences and the freshness of his uncompromising vision bring us to the edge of that vision and perhaps even if we are lucky, bring us to ourselves. Each one must choose who to read for nourishment. I read Hemingway because he gives me courage—not to live, but of beauty and the courage of utter and total honesty. For me his prose is transformative and redemptive. I would wish on his biographical critics, and on all of you, that experience.

NOTES

1. Mark Spilka, *Hemingway's Quarrel with Androgyny*. (London: University of Nebraska Press, 1990).

2. Mark Spilka, "The Necessary Stylist: A New Critical Revision," *Modern Fiction Studies* 6, no. 4 (Winter 1960–1961): 283–297.

3. Other Spilka usages: "oddly androgynous sexual roles" (18), "raising the children androgynously" (22), "androgynous household" (42), "androgynous extension" (140), "androgynous ironies" (145), "androgynous actions" (156), "androgynous forms of lovemaking" (201), "androgynous remarks" (208), "androgynous husband" (204), "a lesson in androgyny" (211), "androgynous nature of their fusion" (214), "androgynous bliss" (215), "small hips—that androgynous feature" (215), "androgynous secret" (219), "androgynous threat" (219), "androgynous fact" (250), "androgynous infancy" (250), "motherly-sisterly androgynous love" (251), "androgynous yearnings" (252), "androgynous fantasy" (252), "androgynous lovemaking" (260), "androgynous emulation" (263), "androgynous mergings" (274), "dangerously androgynous" (274), "androgynous couples" (277), "androgynous relations" (274), "the wilds of androgyny" (278), "androgynous sexual practice" (281), "androgynous direction" (282), "barbershop androgyny" (283), "biographical scramble androgyny" (284), "androgynous experiments" (287), "androgynous love" (287), "more androgynous love" (288), "androgynous changes" (288), " 'possession' by androgyny" (288), "androgynous coiffures" (289), "conversion to androgyny" (289), "he considered his mother androgynous" (297), "androgynous swimming" (300), "androgynous propensities" (298), "androgynous weakness" (299), "threatening androgyny" (306), "androgynous complicities" (309), "androgynous option" (309), "androgynous wife" (310), "androgynous parents" (331), "androgynous son" (332), "androgynous leanings" (334), "androgyn-

ous propensities" (335), "androgynous wounding" (335), "quarrel with androgyny" (335).

4. June Singer, *Androgyny: Towards a New Theory of Sexuality* (New York: Anchor/Doubleday, 1976).

5. John Dos Passos, in a letter to Sara Murphy, 8 September 1948, as quoted in *Letters from the Lost Generation*, Gerald and Sara Murphy and Friends, ed. Linda Miller (New Brunswick, N.J.: Rutgers, 1991) p. 307.

6. Carl Jung, *On The Psychology Of The Unconscious.* "Two Essays," as quoted in *The Essential Jung*, ed. Anthony Storr, (Princeton: Princeton University Press, 1983) p. 152.

7. Jung, as quoted in Storr, p. 209.

III

On Spanish Earth

8

"The Undefeated" and *Sangre y Arena*: Hemingway's *Mano a Mano* with Blasco Ibánez

Susan F. Beegel

For a comparatively simple short story that Ernest Hemingway insisted he had "invent[ed] completely," "The Undefeated" has a surprising number of sources.[1] Richard B. Hovey and Robert O. Stephens have both recorded its indisputable basis in a July 1923 bullfight where Manuel Garcia, Maera, sprained his wrist during repeated unsuccessful attempts to kill a "cement bull," yet remained in the arena to complete his estocada despite considerable pain.[2] Scott MacDonald has observed that the protagonist of "The Undefeated" has "much in common" with matadors Manolo Martinez and Manolo Bienvenida, while I have noted Hemingway's probable indebtedness to Spanish newspaper accounts of Manuel Garcia, El Espartero, killed in the Madrid ring in 1894.[3] John M. Howell has even located a basis for Garcia's grotesque pratfalls in the popular film antics of Charlie Chaplin.[4] However, "The Undefeated" is most indebted to a literary source, Vicente Blasco Ibánez's 1908 novel of the bullfight, *Sangre y Arena—Blood and Sand*. In his useful survey, *Hemingway and the Hispanic World*, Angel Capellán mentions the Spanish novel's influence on the American short story:

There is little doubt that *Sangre y Arena* counted as a source in Hemingway's early writings on bullfighting, even though the American far surpassed Blasco's fictionalization of bullfighting. Hemingway's picture of a raging public—the real beast of the bullring—in "The Undefeated" and in the unpublished "A Lack of Passion" has very strong precedents in Blasco's novel.[5]

Yet "The Undefeated" owes far more than its portrayal of a bloodthirsty bullfight audience to *Sangre y Arena*, and the indebtedness noted briefly by Capellán merits more extended consideration. Indeed, when read side by side with the novel, "The Undefeated" emerges as a kind of literary *mano a mano*, a combat for ascendance between two matadors. The unknown American challenger, Ernest Hemingway, imitates the renowned Spanish master of bullfighting fiction, Blasco Ibánez, in pass after pass, striving to outdo him in technique, the creation of emotion, and a daring and significant kill.

Hemingway wrote "The Undefeated" in the autumn of 1924, and he was certainly familiar with Blasco Ibánez's fiction in general, and *Sangre y Arena* in particular, before composing the short story.[6] According to Capellán, Blasco Ibánez was "by far, the most popular Spanish novelist in the first third of this century," with "twenty-six of his books brought out in English translations and widely reviewed in the United States."[7] In 1919 and 1920, Blasco Ibánez made a "widely publicized trip to the United States," coincident with the English translation of *Sangre y Arena*, which Hemingway may have seen reviewed in *The Dial* or *The Bookman*.[8] Published by E. P. Dutton of New York, the 1919 translation was sufficiently popular to go through ten printings in its first year. The manuscript of Hemingway's 1921 *Toronto Star Weekly* article "Why Not Trade Other Public Entertainers Among the Nations as the Big Leagues Do Baseball Players?" contains a vignette on Blasco Ibánez, satirized as author of "The Sands and the Tortilla."[9] By 1924, Hemingway was probably also aware that John Dos Passos had published a scathing commentary on *Sangre y Arena* in the 1922 collection, *Rosinante to the Road Again*.[10]

Michael Reynolds's inventory of Hemingway's library shows that he owned a pocket-sized, heavily abridged, and bilingual edition of *Sangre y Arena*, titled *La Corrida*, or *The Bullfight*, and published in London by G. G. Harrap in 1919.[11] Offering an English translation by C. D. Campbell, this now rare, little book features Spanish and English versions of the text on facing pages, and it may have been the direct inspiration for "The Undefeated."[12] The unabridged *Sangre y Arena* opens with the matador Juan Gallardo, at the height of his career, nervously awaiting the afternoon's corrida. The novel's first chapter follows Gallardo as he copes with hangers-on, dresses for the fight, and proceeds in a state of superstitious dread to Madrid's Plaza de Toros. There he triumphs through a combination of suicidal abandon and extreme good luck, and he is carried from the arena on the shoulders of the crowd. Chapter two of *Sangre y Arena* turns back the clock to Gallardo's beginnings as the half-starved son of a shoemaker's widow, tramping the dusty roads of Spain in search of amateur capeas where he may spread a scrap of home-dyed linen before a bull. The rest of the novel chronicles Gallardo's rise to wealth and fame, and his fall from popularity after a goring that costs him his courage. *Sangre y Arena* concludes with Gallardo's death in the bullright, jeered into recklessness by a contemptuous crowd.

La Corrida condenses the 354 page novel into a 64 page short story. The abridged version begins with the opening pages of chapter one—Gallardo at a bullfighter's pension, dressing for the fight, proceeding to the Plaza—and then, omitting the entire center of the novel, concludes with Gallardo's death in the ring. Because Blasco Ibáñez's first chapter is heavy with foreshadowing and information about the matador's background and character, the *La Corrida* abridgement is surprisingly effective, implying much about the omitted life that ends on the horns of a bull. The result is a short story remarkably like "The Undefeated"—a moving chronicle of a broken-down bullfighter's final hours. Hemingway may have found inspiration for his celebrated theory of omission in C. D. Campbell's ability to compress an entire novel into the restricted space alloted a long short story.

La Corrida has not hitherto been recognized as a source for "The Undefeated," but I by no means wish to imply that Blasco Ibáñez's obvious influence on the short story was derived from *La Corrida* alone. Hemingway also owned two full-length versions of *Sangre y Arena*, the 1908 Spanish edition, and the 1919 English translation by Mrs. W. A. Gillespie published by Dutton.[13] Of the three texts, Hemingway probably relied most heavily on the Gillespie translation during the composition of "The Undefeated." In 1924, he had visited Spain just twice, and as his possession of the bilingual *La Corrida* suggests, his mastery of Spanish was far from perfect. Although Hemingway was studying tauromachic Spanish at this time with a self-prescribed reading list including bullfight newspapers like *El Toreo*, *Toreros y Toros*, *Tauro*, *La Lidia*, and *Sol y Sombra*, his command of the language was probably insufficient for reading Blasco Ibáñez's novel without an English trot.[14]

The affinities between Blasco Ibáñez's Juan Gallardo and Hemingway's Manuel Garcia are manifold. Both men are aging matadors. Although Gallardo is not yet 30 when he goes to his last fight in the Madrid arena, his oft-injured body has grown old for so physically demanding a profession as bullfighting. As he is dressed by a servant for the corrida, Gallardo bemoans to his surgeon the necessity of having cotton stuffed between his toes and his feet tightly bandaged:

"Age, doctor!...We are all getting older. When I fought both bulls and hunger at the same time I did not want all this. I had feet of iron in the capeas."[15]

Manuel Garcia too is aging, but unlike Juan Gallardo, he refuses to admit it, despite such reminders from the picador Zurito as:

"You're too old," the picador said.
"No," said Manuel, "You're ten years older than I am."

"With me it's different."
"I'm not too old," Manuel said.[16]

Not only are the matadors aging, but each goes to his final corrida barely recovered from a near-fatal goring. Gallardo's cogida, in the words of his banderillero, El Nacional, has involved "one leg broken to bits: a gore underneath one arm, and besides what, I know not!" (*BAS* 237). The matador's condition was so grave that, when he was carried unconscious from the arena, his patron pronounced that only "a miracle" could save him (*BAS* 238). Gallardo has survived, but the imperfectly healed break pains him greatly, and he is "obliged to recognize" that his legs, a matador's most valuable physical equipment, are "neither as light nor as steady as formerly" (*BAS* 326). Manuel Garcia too has been the victim of a cogida so serious that Retana, the bullfight promoter, greets him with "I thought they killed you" (*SS* 237). His goring has also involved a grave leg injury. Just out of the hospital, still pale and not looking well, Hemingway's matador again differs from Blasco Ibáñez's in his refusal to admit weakness. Garcia curtly denies any problem with his leg:

"I heard they'd cut your leg off." Retana said.
"No," said Manuel. "It got all right." (*SS* 236)

In *Death in the Afternoon*, Hemingway observes that bullfighting is governed by certain rules "formulated by years of experience, which, if known and followed, permit a man to perform certain actions with a bull without being caught by the bull's horns.[17] A matador, according to Hemingway, may increase his danger "at will in the measure in which he works close to the bull's horns" (*DIA* 16). It is to a bullfighter's credit "if he does something that he knows how to do in a highly dangerous but still geometrically possible manner," to his discredit "if he runs danger through ignorance, through disregard of the rules, through physical or mental slowness, or through blind folly" (*DIA* 21). Because "it is the business of a matador not to be killed or gored but to kill the bull," in Hemingway's view, "the greatest bullfighters die in bed between sheets."[18]

By this definition, Juan Gallardo, who openly expresses his contempt for the rules of bullfighting, cannot be considered a great or even a skillful matador:

Gallardo laughed at the ancient aficionados, grave Doctors of Tauromachia, who judged it impossible that an accident should happen if a torero conformed to the rules of his art. Rules forsooth!...He ignored them and took no trouble to learn them. Bravery and audacity only were necessary to insure victory. (*BAS* 43)

Gallardo works very close to the bull, feeling its "breath moist with slaver" fall on his face and right hand, and performs reckless circus tricks, placing his hat on the bull's head or lying down and rolling beneath the animal's nose (*BAS* 47, 345). He kills by throwing himself on bulls he has not fixed and that are waiting to charge. When Gallardo is luckiest, he emerges from these encounters with only his clothes torn and disordered by the bull's horns (*BAS* 48). In the jargon of the arena, he is *carne de toros*—meat for the bulls—and pays a high price for his inept but daring actions. Even before the penultimate cogida that costs him his fitness and courage, Gallardo's body is covered with "the scars of ancient wounds" (*BAS* 24). His critics shake their heads and mutter: " 'very brave,' 'very daring,' 'suicidal,' but that was not art" (*BAS* 49–50).

While Manuel Garcia is able to design "a series of acceptable veronicas" and can sometimes dominate the bull with the cape, as an artist he is no more skillful or worthy of the epithet "great" than Juan Gallardo (*SS* 249, 253). Hemingway's matador works dangerously close to the bull, but in violation of the rules as the animal is not fully under his control: "He shook his cape at the bull; there he comes; he sidestepped. Awful close that time. I don't want to work that close to him" (*SS* 252). Like Gallardo, Garcia feels "the hot, black bull body" touch him as it passes "too damn close" (*SS* 358–359). And again like Blasco Ibánez's matador, Garcia performs at least one reckless trick, kneeling in the center of the ring and provoking a charge from the bull (*SS* 259). His manner of killing is more scientific than Gallardo's; he thinks about "the need to profile himself toward the left horn, lance himself short and straight, lower the muleta so the bull would follow it, and going in over the horns, put the sword all the way into a little spot about as big as a five peseta piece," but will still charge at a bull that is unfixed and "waiting" for him (*SS* 260, 262).[19] Garcia has paid for his audacity on "plenty of operating tables"—the preparations for surgery in the Plaza infirmary are "all familiar" (*SS* 265–266). The ignorant mistake his suicidal bravery for greatness, but the wise old picador Zurito, like the "Doctors of Tauromachia" who shake their heads over Gallardo, knows better:

"Why that's one great bull-fighter," Retana's man said.
"No, he's not," said Zurito. (*SS* 259)

Blasco Ibánez and Hemingway emphasize the recklessness of their respective matadors by contrasting them with skillful and prudent members of their cuadrillas. For Gallardo's friend and banderillero, El Nacional, the question of approaching a fighting bull on foot and sticking darts in its rage-swollen crest is one of business, not art, of "earning his bread" (*BAS* 44). Keenly aware that "down in Seville he had four little ones, who, if he died would find no other father," El Nacional displays neither grace nor daring, but simply does his duty, placing the banderillas "like a journeyman of Tauromachia," not seeking applause, but only trying to avoid hissing (*BAS* 44–

45). El Nacional is not a coward; when Gallardo is gored, the banderillero deliberately risks his life to draw the bull from the fallen matador. He simply places a higher value on the uses of courage. El Nacional will risk his life to save a friend, but not to please a crowd (*BAS* 235). He urges Gallardo to adopt a similar perspective, but with a tragic lack of success.

In "The Undefeated," Zurito is the exemplar of skill and prudence (*SS* 250). "The best picador living," Zurito is able to punish the bull properly while preserving himself and his horse from harm (*SS* 244). The old picador's skill resides in his ability to control danger, rather than be controlled by it, while simultaneously creating a graceful picture of consummate horsemanship. He takes risks—in a bravura performance that has the crowd roaring "olés," he learns far out over his horse and pushes on the pic with all his weight—but they are carefully measured risks justified by his skill. Because he lacks Zurito's control, Garcia's pride, like Gallardo's, only increases the likelihood of his meeting a bloody end in the ring.

Both faltering matadors are being urged to retire by family or friends. Gallardo's manager, Don Jose, wants to get a medical certificate that will allow his protégé to cancel his contracts and rest. Gallardo's wife, Carmen, writes that "he ought to retire at once, 'cut off his pigtail,' as they said in his profession, and spend his life quietly at La Rinconada or in his house in Seville with his family, she could bear it no longer" (*BAS* 303). Zurito admonishes Manuel Garcia—" '*You* got to quit,' he said. 'No monkey business. You've got to cut the coleta.' " (*SS* 244).

The concern expressed for the matadors is well-founded. Gallardo has begun to draw crowds who attend his fights in hopes of seeing him killed:

Everyone thought he was destined to die, gored to death in the Plaza, and for this very reason they applauded him with homicidal enthusiasm, with a barbarous interest, like that of the misanthrope, who followed a tamer everywhere, awaiting the moment when he would be devoured by his wild beasts. (*BAS* 43)

Manuel Garcia lacks even this dubious distinction. His skill will not suffice to draw a crowd, and he is too obscure for his possible death to arouse any public interest:

"Why don't you put me on next week?" Manuel suggested.

"*You* wouldn't draw," Retana said. "All they want is Litri and Rubito and La Torre. Those kids are good."

"They'd come to see me get it," Manuel said, hopefully.

"No, they wouldn't. They don't know who you are any more." (*SS* 237)

Economic necessity drives both men to remain in the arena when their careers are over. Wealthy and famous, Gallardo has nevertheless "played high" and led "an expensive and ostentatious life," purchasing a beautiful but unprofitable farm, La Rinconada. For him, retirement would mean "curtail[ing] his expenses, pay[ing] his debts ... [and] bring[ing] into ways of order and economy all these people who had hitherto lived at his expense with happy carelessness and openhandedness" (*BAS* 304–305). He wants to be a "torero of the old-fashioned style, lavish, arrogant, astonishing every one with scandalous extravagances, but always ready to help misfortune with princely generosity" (*BAS* 304). Impoverished and forgotten, limping through Madrid with his suitcase, unable to command contracts or hire his own cuadrilla, Manuel Garcia is already living from hand to mouth. Yet like Gallardo, who rejects the idea of farming, he does not want to "get a job and go to work," as Retana suggests. "I don't want to work," Garcia insists. "I am a bullfighter" (*SS* 236).

As Garcia's emphatic pronouncement suggests, professional pride is as much a part of his decision to remain in the arena as economic necessity. He insists that he has "a lot of stuff" to show the crowds, that, despite his recent goring, he is "going good" (*SS* 244). Gallardo too has his share of professional pride—he cannot bear the thought of his enemies saying he had retired through fear (*BAS* 304). In an unpublished portion of the *Death in the Afternoon* manuscript, Hemingway comments on the "blind pride" that killed the historic matador Manuel Garcia, El Espartero, who knowingly risked a "horn wound rather than let a difficult bull humiliate him."[20] "I have no right," Hemingway continues, "to deny his greatness purely on results obtained since greatness in bull-fighting demands a quality of heart which carried to excess proves fatal."[21] Both Gallardo and Garcia share this fatal "quality of heart."

"Ignorant m[e]n who live in continual danger," they also share, as Blasco Ibánez puts it, a belief "in every sort of adverse influence and supernatural protection" (*BAS* 37). Gallardo is badly shaken when his servant puts out a crimson suit of lights like that El Espartero wore on the day of his death:

"Curse you! Don't you know anything about the profession? ... Corrida in Madrid,—bulls from Muira,—and you put me out red clothes like those poor Manuel, El Espartero, wore! You are so idiotic one would think you were my enemy! It would seem you wished for my death, you villain!" (*BAS* 18)

The crone-like mother of a boyhood friend killed by a bull also unnerves the matador with her begging, and he is further distressed when on the way to the bullring his carriage must halt for a funeral procession, and El Nacional refuses to remove his hat in respect for the passing cross. Manuel Garcia, not coincidentally the namesake of the unfortunate El Espartero, is also superstitious.[22] He knocks on wood when Retana says "I thought they'd killed you" (*SS* 235) and knocks again when they discuss the unlucky business of substituting for a gored matador (*SS* 237). Zurito is superstitious on his friend's behalf, forcing Retana's man to knock on wood three times when he suggests that Garcia's reckless behavior in the ring will send him to the hospital "damn quick" (SS 259).

Both Hemingway and Blasco Ibánez play as well upon the superstitious dread of their readers. In both *Sangre y Arena* and "The Undefeated," the matadors' deaths are foreshadowed by disturbing encounters with stuffed bulls' heads. Returning home drunk after a disastrous performance in the arena, Juan Gallardo feels "his anger rise" as he looks at "the shaggy head with its threatening horns" hanging on his wall (*BAS* 280). The matador recalls how this particular bull humiliated him until the crowd whistled, threw bottles, and insulted his mother, and sees "the brightly varnished muzzle twitch, and the glass eyes flash with peals of concentrated laughter" (*BAS* 280). Transferring his rage against the matador's destiny to the head, Gallardo is overwhelmed with hatred toward "those bulls with perverse minds, so cunning and reflective . . . the evil causes of a worthy man being insulted and turned into ridicule" (*BAS* 280). "Impelled by ungovernable rage," he takes a revolver from his desk drawer and fires twice at the mocking head, shattering one of the bull's glass eyes and leaving "a round black hole . . . surrounded by singed hair" in the center of its forehead (*BAS* 281).[23]

In "The Undefeated," Manual Garcia too has a confrontation with a stuffed bull's head—this one mounted on the wall of Retana's office.

Manuel looked up at the stuffed bull. He had seen it often before. He felt a certain family interest in it. It had killed his brother, the promising one, about nine years ago. Manuel remembered the day. There was a brass plate on the oak shield the bull's head was mounted on. Manuel could not read it, but he imagined it was in memory of his brother. Well, he had been a good kid. (SS 236)

Unlike the drunken and hysterical Gallardo, Manuel Garcia responds soberly and calmly to the bull's head.[24] Yet his failure to be equally outraged is both tragic and ironic, for this bull too mocks the matador—albeit more subtly. Unable to read or write, Garcia believes that the brass plate commemorates his dead brother, a young matador of promise. In fact, the plate commemorates the bull and his aristocratic breeder, listing the death of Garcia's brother (and seven horses) as among the well-bred animal's accomplishments:

The plate said: "The Bull 'Mariposa' of the Duke of Veragua, which accepted 9 varas for 7 caballos, and caused the death of Antonio Garcia, Novillero, April 27, 1909."

Garcia's illiteracy allows him to conserve intact his ill-founded belief that the discipline of tauromaquia prizes the courage and skill of men above those of animals, and it blinds him to his exploitation by Retana, a bullfight promoter who buys and sells men's lives for public entertainment and keeps mementos of their deaths as office souvenirs.

Neither the dictates of common sense nor of superstitious dread prevent Juan Gallardo and Manuel Garcia from going to their final bullfights. In both *Blood and Sand* and "The Undefeated," the matadors' deaths result from the action of the crowds' derision upon the toreros' fatal "quality of heart." Gallardo, badly gored on so many previous occasions, has difficulty with the estocada, reflexively turn[ing] away his face and shorten[ing] his arm at the moment of killing" (*BAS* 350). When this happens at an important Madrid bullfight he hopes will restore his tarnished reputation, Gallardo is as sorely goaded by the "whistling and protests" of the crowd as his reluctant bull has been by fire sticks:[25]

Curse it!...Was this same thing always going to happen to him? Could he not put his arm between the horns as formerly and drive the rapier in up to the hilt? Was he going to spend the rest of his life as a laughing-stock for the public? An ox whom they had been obliged to fire! (*BAS* 350–351)

Determined to redeem himself, Gallardo stands opposite the waiting bull and places himself "in profile," with his muleta hanging to the ground, and his sword held at eye level. The audience rises to its feet as he "throw[s] himself in to kill as on his best day" (*BAS* 351). Man and bull form one single mass, moving together for a few steps, and the connoisseurs prepare to applaud—it seems a " 'true' estocade" (*BAS* 351). But somehow, mysteriously, Gallardo has failed to kill the bull:

Suddenly the man was thrown out from between the horns by a crushing blow, and rolled on the sand. The bull lowered his head, picking up the inert body, lifting it for an instant on his horns to let it fall again, then rushing on his mad career with the rapier plunged up to the hilt in his neck. (*BAS* 351)

Gallardo stands and the Plaza bursts into "uproarious, deafening applause," but the matador is able to stagger only a few feet before falling flat on the sand, and he is dead on arrival in the bullfight infirmary, where the doctors undress him and reveal that the bull has disemboweled him like a picador's decrepit horse (*BAS* 351–353).

Manuel Garcia's problem with the estocada is anything but an instinct for self-preservation. Again and again he profiles for the kill and launches himself on the bull, but the animal seems to be "all bone," without any vulnerable spot for sinking the sword (*SS* 263). Twice Garcia is tossed by the bull, and twice his sword buckles as he endeavors to plunge it into the bull's neck. These failed attempts, at least according to Hemingway in *Death in the Afternoon*, are not dishonorable—"If...the sword strikes bone and refuses to penetrate...the merit of the attempt at killing is as great as though the sword had gone all the way in and killed, since the man has taken the risk and the result has only been falsified by chance" (*DIA* 247). Garcia, then, is "going good," but the crowd does not see it that way. Finally, as in *Blood and Sand*, their unappreciative derision goads the matador into recklessness:

The first cushions thrown down out of the dark missed him. Then one hit him in the face, his bloody face looking toward the crowd. They were coming down fast. Spotting the sand. Someone threw an empty champagne bottle from close range. . . . Oh, the dirty bastards!
Dirty bastards! Oh, the dirty lousy bastards! (*SS* 263)

Without profiling himself for the kill, Garcia steps close and jabs the reluctant animal in the muzzle to provoke a charge—"The bull was on him as he jumped back and as he tripped on a cushion he felt the horn go into him, into his side" (*SS* 263). The crowd's "homicidal enthusiasm" and "barbarous interest" (*BAS* 43) has proven to be Garcia's undoing both emotionally, by impelling his incautious assault on the bull, and physically, by mining the arena with cushions—dangerous obstacles for a matador, whose life depends on his unencumbered agility.[26]

Garcia arises from this goring "coughing and feeling broken and gone," but he nevertheless manages, in his sixth attempt, to kill his bull (*SS* 264). There follows an epiphanic moment when Garcia, apparently dying from a cornada in the chest,[27] experiences a profound identification with the dead bull:

All right, you bastards! He wanted to say something, but he started to cough. It was hot and choking. He looked down for the muleta. He must go over and salute the president. President hell! He was sitting down looking at something. It was the bull. His four feet up. Thick tongue out. Things crawling around on his belly and under his legs. Crawling where the hair was thin. Dead bull. To hell with the bull! To hell with them all! (*SS* 264)

The moment derives from the conclusion of *Blood and Sand*, where the banderillero El Nacional, grieving for Gallardo, draws a similar parallel between the fate of matador and bull:

He thought of the bull who was now being dragged out of the arena, with his neck burnt and bloody, his legs stiff, and his glassy eyes gazing up at the sky. Then he thought of the friend lying dead a few paces from him, only the other side of a brick wall. His limbs also rigid, his stomach ripped open, and a mysterious dull light shining through his half open eyelids. Poor bull! Poor espada! (*BAS* 354)

In both *Blood and Sand* and "The Undefeated," the bullfights continue after the mortally injured matadors have been carried from the arena, emphasizing the mob's indifference to the fates of men who risk their lives to entertain them. Blasco Ibáñez makes this point in the famous final sentences of his novel, as the banderillero El Nacional, driven from the infirmary by the heart-wringing sight of his dead friend, hears the noise of the crowd and the sound of music emanating from the Plaza:

And suddenly, as noisy cries of delight burst out in the circus applauding the continuation of the spectacle, El Nacional closed his eyes and clenched his fists. It was
the roaring of the wild beast, the true and only one. (*BAS* 354)

For Hemingway, the point is more subsidiary than climactic, but he makes it nonetheless, perhaps in a nod to *Sangre y Arena*. Lying on the operating table, stripped for surgery, Garcia can hear the sounds of the crowd re-sponding to "the continuation of the spectacle":

He heard some one coming very heavily up the stairs. Then he did not hear it. Then
he heard a noise far off. That was the crowd. Well, somebody would have to kill
his other bull. They had cut away all his shirt. The doctor smiled at him. There was
Retana. (*SS* 265)

It is not coincidental that the noise of the crowd commingles with the arrival of Retana, the promoter who profits from their savagery.

How differently do Blasco Ibánez and Hemingway handle their very sim-ilar stories? An antimonarchist who advocated a republican Spain, Blasco Ibánez was twice exiled and once imprisoned for his leftist political views before his election in 1898 to the Spanish parliament, where he would serve for seven terms.[28] His major works of fiction, written during the years in parliament, reflect his concern for the poor and socially disadvantaged. In *Sangre y Arena*, Blasco Ibánez uses literary naturalism to create a profound indictment of the Spanish national spectacle, and by extension, of the deep-ening socioeconomic problems experienced by Spain at the turn of this century, dangerous political currents carrying the nation inexorably toward civil war. His Old World vision acknowledges that the fates of the individual and society are inseparable—Gallardo, the poor son of a shoemaker's widow manipulated by wealthy aficionados, is both the representative of his class and the victim of its lust for spectacles.

Sangre y Arena, then, aligns the bullfight with the gladiatorial circuses of imperial Rome. Spain, in Blasco Ibánez's view, has been neither softened nor civilized by Christianity. It is still driven by a pagan appetite for cru-cifixions that supports such ironic institutions as the chapel—"a dark place terrified by . . . cries of pain"—at Madrid's Plaza de Toros (*BAS* 339). In *Sangre y Arena*, the corrida is neither art nor tragic ritual, but a barbaric spectacle that lacks an aesthetic or spiritual component and is provided to appease an oppressed population's lust for violence. The novel's protagonist, Juan Gallardo, is never an artist, only an illiterate athlete, fighting with a recklessness born of ignorance. He dies the pawn of a socioeconomic system that has exploited his stupidity and egotism to control with "bread and circuses" masses of equally poor and ignorant men.[29]

Despite borrowing many plot elements of "The Undefeated" from *Blood and Sand*, Hemingway, like all strong artists, transforms his borrowings to serve his own agenda. Paul Smith, reviewing the short story's critical heritage, notes "unusual critical unanimity" about that agenda. He ascribes scholarly consensus about "The Undefeated" to "the ancient and archetypal aura of the corrida," "the romantic associations with the torero," and Hemingway's apparent use of "the familiar design of tragedy," accruing to the story "not only the prestige but also the classic interpretations of that venerable tradition."[30] According to such interpretations, the corrida for Hemingway is a tragedy, and, like a Roman soldier devoted to the exclusively masculine cult of the bull-slaying god, Mithras, he perceives the bullfight as fraught with aesthetic and spiritual significance.

The bullfight, when perceived as tragedy, constitutes a ritualized enactment of man's confrontation with and triumph over death. The matador is the artist-hero of that tragedy, giving his audience, if he possesses sufficient artistry and genius, a feeling of immortality "profound as any religious ecstasy" (*DIA* 206). Manuel Garcia, protagonist of "The Undefeated," is brave, honorable, and even skillful, but he nevertheless has no artistry. He is one of those bullfighters who, in the language of *Death in the Afternoon*, "will always be one of the day laborers of bullfighting and paid accordingly" (207). Unable to create with cape and sword a satisfying metaphor for man's triumph over death, Garcia instead gives his unappreciative audience the reality of a different kind of victory—a literal fulfillment of his *brindis*, the matador's pledge to kill his bull or die in the attempt. Despite exploitation by greedy promoters, sadistic crowds, and unfeeling critics, despite the fierce commercialism that has overwhelmed the modern bullfight, Garcia is truly "undefeated," more tragic hero than hapless victim. He has earned the right to keep his coleta, the matador's badge of honor, by sacrificing his life to the spiritual requirements of his ancient art. Death be not proud, such readings seem to say; the matador is prouder.

This type of interpretation suggests that in "The Undefeated" Hemingway's naturalism thinly disguises a point of view more romantic—and American—than that of the Spanish novel it imitates. Manuel Garcia seems like a Western hero, the individual leaving "snivelization" behind to confront the beast in the wilderness; the lone gunfighter despising the craven violence of society who steps into the sun-drenched street to fulfill the higher law of the code duello. Hemingway, with his American nostalgia for individual affirmation through confrontation with nature's dark forces, seems to possess an affinity for the ancient uses of the bullfight inimicable to Blasco Ibáñez, who viewed the corrupt contemporary state of this uniquely Spanish cultural institution as a mirror of his nation's deteriorating civic health.

Yet study of the indebtedness of "The Undefeated" to *Sangre y Arena* suggests the need to review the short story's critical heritage. Its borrowed elements of social criticism—Garcia's exploitation by Retana, his illiterate misunderstanding of the plaque honoring the Duke of Veragua's bull, the drunken bullfight critic who departs before the fight's conclusion, the homicidal mob, the fatal transference of Garcia's rage from the murderous crowd ("Oh, the lousy, dirty bastards!") to the doomed and guiltless bull ("All right, you dirty, lousy bastard!"), the priest absent when needed most, and finally, the matador's death capping the artless slaughter of the bull—all hint that "The Undefeated" may bear a profoundly ironic title (*SS* 263). The many parallels between Hemingway's short story and Blasco Ibánez's novel lend new credence to the dissenting critical voices of Scott MacDonald, who asserts that Zurito allows Garcia to keep his coleta solely to prevent his sitting up on the operating table, and John Howell, who emphasizes the black comedy of Garcia's grotesque performance.[31]

Comparison of "The Undefeated" with *Blood and Sand* at the very least teaches us that it is past time to add Vicente Blasco Ibánez to the ever-lengthening roll of Hemingway's literary mentors. A long, dense novel rich with anecdotes about bullfighting, *Blood and Sand* has influenced not only "The Undefeated," but also the entire range of Hemingway's tauromachic fiction. The bullfighting interchapter of *In Our Time* commencing "They whack-whacked the white horse" is indebted to Carmen Gallardo's nightmarish encounter with disembowelled picadors' horses (*BAS* 340–342). "A Lack of Passion" echoes the career of "El Manitas," a teenaged mama's boy pressured into the bullring by an ambitious father (*BAS* 288–292). Brett Ashley's affair with matador Pedro Romero in *The Sun Also Rises* has origins in that of the aristocratic and promiscuous Dona Sol with Juan Gallardo, while the broken-down matadors and homemade mechanical bull of "The Capital of the World" have antecedents in the tavern torero and bullfighting school portrayed in *Blood and Sand* (*BAS* 317–320).

In *For Whom the Bell Tolls*, Hemingway rewrites Gallardo's encounter with the stuffed bull's head in Pilar's tale of the tubercular matador Finito, and, like Blasco Ibánez before him (as well as Spanish artists from Goya to Picasso) uses bullfighting archetypes to emphasize the human capacity for atrocity.[32] When Robert Jordan leaves the Montana of the High West to become a Spanish "rider of the mountain" like *Blood and Sand*'s radical brigand, El Plumitas, the courage of the once fiercely individualistic American hero, as well as the literary naturalism of Ernest Hemingway, make common cause with barbarous but beleaguered humanity (*BAS* 188–217). To Blasco Ibánez, then, Hemingway owed an early introduction not only to the rich subject matter of tauromaquia, but also to its host of thematic possibilities.

NOTES

1. Ernest Hemingway to Maxwell Perkins, 16 Nov. 1933, in *Ernest Hemingway: Selected Letters 1917–1961*, ed. Carlos Baker (New York: Charles Scribner's Sons, 1981), 400.

2. Richard B. Hovey, *Hemingway: The Inward Terrain* (Seattle: University of Washington Press, 1968), 26–27 and Robert O. Stephens, *Hemingway's Nonfiction: The Public Voice* (Chapel Hill: University of North Carolina Press, 1968), 367–369.

3. Scott MacDonald, "Implications of Narrative Perspective in Hemingway's 'The Undefeated'," *Journal of Narrative Technique* 2 (Jan. 1972), 15 and Susan F. Beegel, "The Death of El Espartero: An Historic Matador Links 'The Undefeated' and *Death in the Afternoon*," *The Hemingway Review* 5.2 (Spring 1986): 12–23.

4. John M. Howell, "Hemingway and Chaplin: Monkey Business in 'The Undefeated'," *Studies in Short Fiction* 27.1 (1990): 89–97.

5. Angel Capellán, *Hemingway and the Hispanic World* (Ann Arbor, UMI Research Press, 1985), 203.

6. Hemingway to Robert McAlmon, 15 Nov. 1924, *Selected Letters*, 133.

7. Capellán, 201.

8. Ibid.

9. Hemingway, Files 833, 833a, John F. Kennedy Library, Boston, in Capellán, 202.

10. John Dos Passos, *Rosinante to the Road Again* (New York: George H. Doran, 1922), 120–132.

11. Michael S. Reynolds, *Hemingway's Reading: 1910–1940: An Inventory* (Princeton: Princeton University Press, 1981), 100.

12. I am indebted to Pamela Roper Wagner of the Library of Congress and Barbara Andrews of the Nantucket Athenaeum for helping me to obtain a copy of this rare edition. The book is listed in the *National Union Catalog* under its English title, *The Bullfight*.

13. Reynolds, 100.

14. For this reason, the Gillespie translation of *Sangre y Arena* will be cited henceforward as the text most likely to have been the principal influence on "The Undefeated."

15. Vicente Blasco Ibáñez, *Blood and Sand*, trans. Mrs. W. A. Gillespie (New York: E. P. Dutton, 1919), 25. All citations in parentheses commencing *BAS* refer to this edition.

16. Hemingway, "The Undefeated," in *The Short Stories of Ernest Hemingway* (New York: Charles Scribner's Sons, 1954), 243. All citations in parentheses commencing *SS* refer to this edition.

17. Ernest Hemingway, *Death in the Afternoon* (New York: Charles Scribner's Sons, 1932), 16. All citations in parentheses commencing *DIA* refer to this edition.

18. Hemingway, File 58, *Death in the Afternoon* mss., John F. Kennedy Library, Boston.

19. Hemingway, ever obsessed with craftsmanship, analyzes in detail every aspect of Garcia's technique in a manner that would never occur to Blasco Ibáñez, intent on not valorizing the corrida, and writing for a Spanish audience literate in tauromaquia.

20. Hemingway, File 58, *Death in the Afternoon* mss., John F. Kennedy Library, Boston.

21. Ibid.

22. Beegel, 12.

23. A footnote to the W. A. Gillespie translation of *Blood and Sand* confides that

a similar anecdote was told about the matador Frascuelo (Salvador Sanchez, 1842–1898).

24. Garcia's sobriety in this scene is temporary—like Gallardo, he sometimes drinks too much when overcome by his professional difficulties. After leaving Retana's office, Garcia drinks himself to sleep in a cafe near the Puerta del Sol (*SS* 239–241).

25. Special banderillas used on bulls determined to be cowardly, the fire sticks are fitted with explosive charges that terrify, burn, and galvanize a reluctant animal when jabbed into its withers. In *Blood and Sand*, the savage mob demands their use on Gallardo's last bull (*BAS* 346–348).

26. Bullfight crowds have not changed. The English edition of a *Programa de Toros* distributed at the Madrid bullring in 1984 bears this warning—"Caution: cushion throwing at the arena strictly prohibited against a severe fine."

27. Although "The Undefeated" concludes with Manuel on the operating table, inhaling anesthetic, there is critical consensus that he is dying. Only John Howell, exploring the short story's comic aspects in his essay "Hemingway and Chaplin: Monkey Business in 'The Undefeated'," has argued that Manuel will survive.

28. The fervent republicanism of Vicente Blasco Ibáñez (1867–1928) forced his removal to Paris in 1889, and to Italy in 1895. During 1896–1897, he was imprisoned for his political activities. His parliamentary terms spanned the years 1898 to 1923, and he also served as an active propagandist for the Allies during World War I.

29. The phrase "bread and circuses," "*panem et circenses*," comes from the *Satires* of Juvenal, critic of vice in imperial Rome.

30. Paul Smith, *A Reader's Guide to the Short Stories of Ernest Hemingway* (Boston: G. K. Hall, 1989), 106–108.

31. MacDonald, 10; Howell, 89–97.

32. Ernest Hemingway, *For Whom the Bell Tolls* (New York: Charles Scribner's Sons, 1940), 184–189. One thinks of the strong affinities between Goya's two series of etchings, *Desastres de la Guerra* and *La Tauromaquia*, drawn during and immediately after the Peninsular War in Spain (1808–1814), and of course Picasso's famous black-and-white oil painting of the Spanish Civil War, *Guernica* (1937), depicting the horror of the first aerial bombardment of a civilian population.

9

Reality and Invention in *For Whom the Bell Tolls*, or Reflections on the Nature of the Historical Novel

Allen Josephs

"The truth is that what really interests me is telling a story."
—Gabriel García Márquez

In a recent interview Gabriel García Márquez talks about his novel, *Love in the Time of Cholera*, but his remarks are equally valid regarding *For Whom the Bell Tolls*, and, I believe, for any "period" or historical novel. "Have you ever noticed," he queries, "what Flaubert did with the distances between places in Paris? You find that the French writers have their characters take walks that are impossible.[1] It's a poetization of space" (137).

In the novel García Márquez placed the Cafe de la Parroquia—which is actually located in Veracruz, Mexico—in Cartagena, Colombia. Why? Because, as he explains,

"The Cafe de la Parroquia *could* be in Cartagena perfectly well. The fact that it isn't is purely incidental.... [It] *would* be in Cartagena if the Spaniard who built it had immigrated to Cartagena instead of to Veracruz.... How marvelous to have the freedom to be a writer who says, 'Well I'm going to put the Cafe de la Parroquia where I want it to be.' Every day I'm writing I say to myself how marvelous it is to *invent* life." (136–137)

There are more germane thoughts in this splendid interview, such as: "I am also quite disrespectful of real time and space," and "I don't write with historical rigor," but here is the most important for our purposes: "This novel isn't a historical reconstruction. Rather it contains historical elements used poetically. All writers do this" (136).

I do not know if all writers do this. I doubt it, and in any case, perhaps I am putting the cafe in the wrong place by starting with García Márquez. But criticism is sometimes as much an invention as fiction is, only starting with a different base. At any rate, we can safely say, I think, that certainly Hemingway and García Márquez do *this*, that is, they invent, and when necessary they move cafes—or bridges—to suit their own purposes.

There are, I believe, three ways to look at this particular novel called *For Whom the Bell Tolls*: (1) We can look at it as a documentary novel—a literal picture—of the Spanish Civil War. (2) We can see it as a historical novel. (3) We can consider it a novel—without the almost pejorative, hybrid restriction, "historical"—that is, as a work of the imagination, as an invention. The way we choose to focus on the work may well determine what our eventual critical opinion will be.

As a documentary, as a picture of the real war, *For Whom the Bell Tolls* is a failure because the picture is at least partially false. That falseness is one reason Spanish writers such as Arturo Barea, Francisco Ayala, Julio Alvarez del Vayo, and Juan Benet have taken such fierce umbrage with *For Whom the Bell Tolls*. From this critical vantage, Barea's well-known criticisms are mostly correct.

Less familiar (because it has not been translated into English) is a short piece by Spanish novelist and sociologist Francisco Ayala, called "Spanish Eccentricity." Ayala laments that Hemingway's overly sentimental, overly dramatized novel takes place against the backdrop of a universally critical moment in history; in the precise moment that Spain needed to be understood by the outside world, here was Hemingway reverting to the bullring and the *leyenda negra*, the black legend, giving us a construction covered with false local color. It is similar to Barea's essay but without quite the same sense of wounded pride.

An admittedly indignant Julio Alvarez del Vayo claimed to know from personal experience that "the Spanish Civil War was fundamentally alien to [Hemingway]," that his "was the Spain of the running of the bulls" (188), and so forth. And the preeminent Spanish Civil War novelist Juan Benet remarked to Martha Gellhorn and me at lunch at a Michigan State conference on the literature of the Spanish Civil War several years back (Nov. 19–21, 1987) that, in his opinion, *For Whom the Bell Tolls* was more unbearable (*insoportable*) than the movie made from it, that its error was that it was written to be a success, that it was just cardboard figures and stereotypes, that there was no enigma in it, nothing of the human heart, that it was old-fashioned as all historical novels are. Traditional, I wondered; yes, he said, probably the most traditional of all his books.

From the point of view of the documentary novel, all these criticisms, even the exaggerations, have merit, including the criticism (some of it my own; "Poor Spanish") that realistically speaking the novel, especially linguistically, does not work. For her part, Martha Gellhorn, whose antipathy to her ex-husband is well known (Kert), added that she thought the "literally translated Spanish was awful" and that she told him so at the time.

But the real question is, is this critical point of view valid for understanding the book? Is it not—my own article included—excessively literal-minded?

As a historical novel—and I am not altogether sure precisely what a historical novel is—For Whom the Bell Tolls seems unsatisfactory in that some of the same doubts from the first category creep into our thinking. Robert A. Martin, for one, observes quite sensibly that the book is a "masterful blend of fact and fiction" and that that is what gives it the "status of a classic war novel" (219). Jeffery Meyers writes that "Hemingway's insight about the complexity of the Spanish tragedy, written immediately after the events it records, makes For Whom the Bell Tolls the greatest political novel in American literature" (16–17). But he must assert that strong opinion, I am afraid, in the face of Senores Barea, Alvarez del Vayo, Ayala and Benet who collectively and not unconvincingly contend that Hemingway was, in fact, naive to the point of being absurd, ridiculous at times, wrong at times, confused, and self-serving. This middle-of-the-road point of view probably involves us in a critical box canyon. At the very least it leads nowhere, except to shouting matches.

More balanced, or at least less literal, is the point of view of Michael J. B. Allen, who sees the war as symbolic, allegorical, and parabolic, concluding that Hemingway is a "myth maker, and it is the manifest quality of the myth rather than the accuracy of the reporting which accounts for the novel's enduring fascination" (212).

I admit that the question of fact and fiction in For Whom the Bell Tolls is a vexing one, a question that has troubled me for years. Omniscience is part of the problem. In The Sun Also Rises and A Farewell to Arms we look through Jake Barnes's or Frederic Henry's eyes, but in For Whom the Bell Tolls, Hemingway-God is our guide. The manuscript shows us that it began as a first-person narrative but that Hemingway quickly abandoned the forgiving limitations of single-mindedness for the difficult world of all-knowing (John F. Kennedy Library [JFK] 83). Hemingway was clearly aware of this problem. During final editing (August 26, 1940), he wrote to Max Perkins, remarking: "I don't like to write like God" (LTRS 515).

I do not think the problem of fact and fiction especially as they are seen as accuracy and inaccuracy will ever be resolved with regard to this novel. The atheists will never be able to accept Hemingway-God's flaws and the Hemingway fundamentalists will continue to insist on the infallibility of his-His word.

In the long run the rawness of the so-called factual errors will probably fade and the mythic qualities will likely assume a larger critical profile. Perhaps it is appropriate to ask at this juncture whether Russian-language critics continue to look at *War and Peace* as a historical novel.

Also, Hemingway's self-professed method of writing—inventing from experience, or as he put it literally, "out of what you know" (*LTRS* 407), which is a kind of oxymoronic negation of any absolute categories of fact and fiction—becomes more difficult in the third person. How do you invent from experience omnisciently? It is one thing in a tightly controlled short story but altogether another in a long novel about a "foreign" civil war. Rather than fact and fiction, perhaps we should speak of the real war and the invented or imaginary war, especially since much recent critical theory has blurred or even erased the difference between fact and fiction.

The writing about the real war, by which I mean the Spanish Civil War as Hemingway actually saw it, includes his political articles and war dispatches; the play, *The Fifth Column*; and the Civil War short stories, "The Denunciation," "The Butterfly and the Tank," "Night Before Battle," "Under the Ridge," and the recently published "Landscape with Figures" in *The Complete Short Stories of Ernest Hemingway* (CSS). In the play and in these stories, Hemingway was writing from actual experience, and, although he was to some extent inventing from that experience, these pieces were largely crafted from events in which Hemingway took part. He even made his own hotel room the scenario for the play and, in part, for the story "Night Before Battle," and his favorite bar, Chicote, the locale for "The Denunciation," "The Butterfly and the Tank," and for the beginning of "Night Before Battle."

These stories of the Spanish Civil War have two characteristics in common. The first-person narrator is clearly Ernest Hemingway himself—correspondent, film maker, writer, raconteur, personage. There is no making himself up as in the Nick Adams stories and the occasional use of a fictional name—Mr. Emmunds in "The Denunciation" and Edwin Henry (A relative of Frederic Henry?) in "Night Before Battle" and "Landscape with Figures"—only makes his real identity more obvious.

The second characteristic is that the real subject of all these stories, sometimes overtly, sometimes subtlety, is the political nature of the conflict at hand—or perhaps I should say Hemingway's increasing distaste for politics and the political nature of the conflict as the Spanish Civil War came to a close.

These stories, Hemingway realized at the time, were not his best work. In February 1939 he wrote a letter to Max Perkins about his dreams, remarking: "Last night I was caught in this retreat again in the goddamndest detail. I really must have a hell of an imagination. That's why I should *always* make up stories—not try to remember what happened" (*LTRS* 479, emphasis his). On March 25, 1939, he wrote to Perkins about the first 15,000 words of *For Whom the Bell Tolls*: "It is 20 times better than that

Night Before Battle which was flat where this is rounded and recalled where this is invented" (*LTRS* 482). The real war, in other words, was not as good as the imaginary war, a sentiment that echoed something Gertrude Stein had told him years before in Paris: "The parts that fail are where [you] remember visually rather than make up" (*LTRS* 310).

Regardless of their literary merit, the Civil War stories as a group do have a function. For better or worse, the stories and the play present the real war as Hemingway experienced it, an experience that included being on the losing side. As he would express it to Max Perkins in a Key West letter: "Well we've lost another war" (*LTRS* 478).

In two important earlier letters, written while he was still in Europe, he refers to these stories and to his general sense of malaise. As he wrote to Arnold Gingrich on October 22, 1938, "Things here are so foul, now, that if you think about it you go nuts" (*LTRS* 473). Less than a week later he would write to Perkins about the "carnival of treachery and rotten-ness" (*LTRS* 474). Although Hemingway is alluding here to the general state of affairs in Europe, especially the Munich agreement, there is little doubt the defeat in Spain was central to his sense of disillusionment.

What these stories did, I believe, precisely because they were autobiographical and political, and accurate, was to purge the real war and the real loss of the Spanish Republic from Hemingway's fiction. Perhaps nothing could really purge such a loss personally, but literarily at least he got the dreadful reality of the war as he had experienced it out of his system. The stories and play as a group became a kind of cathartic fictional memoir.

That catharsis led straight into the writing of *For Whom the Bell Tolls*, which was rounded rather than flat, invented rather than recalled, and exciting, and 20 times better than "Night Before Battle." Whether the inventing was altogether a good idea is another question, but had Hemingway not written the stories, it might have taken him as long to get to *For Whom the Bell Tolls* as it did to write *A Farewell to Arms* after the First World War. In a letter to Perkins he mentions that after writing "Under the Ridge," the last and most cathartic story in the group, finished just before he began the novel, that he had "started on another [he'd] had no intention of writing for a long time" (*LTRS* 482).

Martin Light[2] has written that these stories "can be seen as part of Hemingway's search for a true way to recreate the Spanish experience" (77). I think they are that and more—they also readied him to write the great romantic war novel he so badly wanted to do. As he wrote to Tommy Shevlin on April 4, 1939: "It is the most important thing I've ever done and it is the place in my career as a writer I have to write a real one" (*LTRS* 484).

Years later, looking back, he would write to Charles Poore: "Dr. Tolstoi was at Sevastopol. But not at Borodino. He wasn't in business in those days. But he could invent from knowledge we all were at some damned Sevastopol" (*LTRS* 800). Hemingway was not at the Guadarrama offensive (he was in Bimini at the time; Baker, *Life* 313), just as he had not been in the retreat from Caporetto. But he knew the territory, and, as the Civil War stories show so well, he was in the Casa de Campo and in the heights at Pingarron and at the Arganda Bridge over the Jarama.

These stories about the Spanish Civil War—the real war—were Hemingway's Sevastopol. They show very clearly that he could write accurately and well about the war. "Under the Ridge" is a wonderful and undervalued story, one that Hemingway revealingly referred to in a letter to Charles Scribner as "warming up" for *For Whom the Bell Tolls* (*LTRS* 486; my remarks about the Civil War stories are adapted from "Hemingway's Spanish Civil War Stories"). And *For Whom the Bell Tolls* was his Borodino. That is to say, it was an attempt to create his own twentieth-century equivalent to *War and Peace* from the Spanish Civil War.

If I am right about any of this (and if I am not, I will add parenthetically), *For Whom the Bell Tolls* may be a failure. I am trying to get us to a critical juncture, or point of departure, that affirms that *For Whom the Bell Tolls*, the totality of *For Whom the Bell Tolls*, was invented. It was invented for two reasons: (1) because Hemingway was disgusted with, had dealt with and was through with the real war; and (2) because invention, as he often said, could be realer than reality. He was no longer interested in the *ethos* of the Spanish Civil War; he wanted its *mythos*. Juan Benet said there was nothing of the human heart in it, but it was precisely the human heart that Hemingway was after, not the realism but the romance, through word, through story, through legend, in a brave attempt to arrive at the universal particular.

Here is a modern analogy: I have never known anyone who was in the war in Viet Nam who likes the film *Apocalypse Now*; but there are those of us who, not having been in the southeast Asian conflict, think it is a brilliant film. *Film*; not documentary film—art film. I have finally come to believe that understanding how Hemingway's inventive process worked, how he played out on the visualized, mental stage of his imagination the war that he created in his mind, is a higher critical question than the accuracy of his details of the actual conflict.

That brings us to the fascinating question of just how much of *For Whom the Bell Tolls* is completely invented, not invented from reality but entirely imagined, or at least so changed in the smithy of his imagination that it is not recognizable. The answer is, of course, a great deal. For our purposes here, I have identified four areas for the briefest consideration: the war, the geography, the characters, and the language. These areas, as we shall see, are not always separable. My most important sources have been unpublished materials in the Kennedy library and first hand investigation in the terrain.

The War. Aside from the real versus invented war I have already mentioned, there are two interesting pieces of information to discuss. The first is that from the Spanish military maps of the front at the time of the Guadarrama offensive, or more specifically, the La Granja offensive in late May and early June of 1937—the precise time of the novel—it is clear that the *guerrilleros* in the novel were not behind the lines at all, but rather in the Republic's, which is to say their own, territory. In other words, the whole plot of the novel based on *guerrilleros* working behind the lines is invented. Second, all local authorities in that area that I could consult, including people who were living there at the time, maintain flatly that no *guerrilleros* ever, at any time during the war, operated in the area, which is to say that they too are an invention—or at least a transposition—of Hemingway's. There were *guerrilleros* in the war, including one or two Americans such as Irving Goff, but they operated mostly in the south and not in the Guadarrama area (Wyden 316–317). So the plot is invented and so are the characters, or at least the characters' function.

The Geography. The river, the Eresma, is real enough; the description of the countryside is quite accurate. You can drive through much of it and walk the river and the *caminos* forestalls—the logging roads under the supervision of ICONA, the Instituto de Conservacion de la Naturaleza, the Institute for the Conservation of Nature—and see how exact Hemingway's descriptions are. As he told Charles Poore, "The country you know, also the weather. Then you have a map 1/50,000 for the whole front or sector; 1/5,000 if you can get one for close. Then you invent from other people's experience and knowledge and what you know yourself" (*LTRS* 800). Hemingway is referring to *A Farewell to Arms*, but the procedure for *For Whom the Bell Tolls*—or for any of his books—was close enough. The terrain and the weather were exact, except for two small details, the bridge and the cave.

There is a bridge, but it is a stone bridge. It is not metal and it is not a suspension bridge; in fact, it is a rebuilt Roman style arched bridge. The best guess is that Hemingway (as García Márquez had done with the Cafe de la Parroquia) took the metal suspension bridge over the Jarama at Arganda and put it, for effect, high in the mountains over a stream far below. Hemingway had been at the Jarama and knew all about that bridge—the story "Under the Ridge" takes place exactly there near the bridge at the battle of the Jarama. But for the novel, he transposed it—a poetization of space, in García Márquez's words—to the Eresma (Wyden 303).

And the cave—if you get a detailed map of the area, you will find something on it called "La cueva del monje," the Monk's Cave, but you will be disappointed if you walk into it. It is only a dolmen-like rock overhang. It turns out that the entire area is granite and that a real *cueva*, a cavern large enough to house people and cook in, is a geological impossibility, another poetization of space.

The Characters. All but the historical characters are, of course, invented. Much has been written about this, but much unfounded supposition is among what has been said, such as that Pilar is based on Grace Hemingway or Gertrude Stein. All you have to do to know whom Hemingway had in mind for Pilar is to read his *Selected Letters*. On page 508 in a letter to Max Perkins about how the bridge had to be steel and not stone on the book's cover, and about the smell of death passage, he wrote, "I didn't put in Pilar's husband (really Rafael el Gallo)." That identifies her concretely not as Gertrude or Grace but as the flamenco dancer and singer Pastora Imperio, who also appears in the book under her own name, mentioned by Pilar—a little inside joke by the *maestro* (187).

There is an unpublished letter to an incensed Catalan reader that bears this out explicitly: "Anyway I respect your viewpoint, understand your attitudes, do not agree with your facts always, and I wish you luck. The dig about Carmen is all right with me. I know it is not like Carmen anymore than Pastora Imperio (Pilar) is like Kate Smith" (from Sun Valley to Jose Alemany, Nov. 8, 1940; *JFK*). Suffice it to say Pilar/Pastora had absolutely nothing to do with Gertrude or Grace and that Pastora was Spanish essence personified and a brilliant choice for the model of a real person in such a fictional situation.

Then there is Maria. I will limit myself to saying that there are two unpublished fragments (*JFK* 522a, 824) that link Martha Gellhorn and Maria, shall we say, intimately. The most interesting is one in which the "girl" in the Hotel Florida tells the narrator that he must not call her rabbit—something he continues to do despite her objections—since they have just eaten rabbit for dinner (522a). There is no doubt material for an entire paper here, but I will just leave this tip of the iceberg exposed for you to imagine.

The Language. Mutatis mutandi we see the way language—Hemingway's nickname (whether fictional or real is unimportant) for Martha Gellhorn—becomes Maria's and creates a, shall we say, congested problem. This problem has been so much discussed that I will not dig us deeper into that critical pit. Again suffice it to say that the whole problem of language as invention—especially inventing from what you know when what you know is not enough—is still one of the novel's spiniest problems. And it is not remotely solved.

I do not have any earth-moving conclusions. But here is a beginning: As Hemingway got older he invented more and more. In some ways that tendency was more ambitious than his early work, but it was also more dangerous the farther he got from actual experience. It entailed more risk but also involved more mythic reverberations. For better or for worse, what seems to have interested him most in *For Whom the Bell Tolls*—all literal and factual considerations aside—was what interested García Márquez and what seems to interest all great writers of fiction. As García Márquez put it in the epigraph with which I began: "The truth is that what really interests me is telling a story" (138). For Hemingway, too, telling a story was always the highest form of truth, and in *For Whom the Bell Tolls* he has told his most extended, his most ambitious, his most moving and for many readers his best story.

Probably those of us who worry too much about where the real lines were, about the real cave, about the actual politics of the war or about the specific linguistics of the Spanish language in *For Whom the Bell Tolls*—perhaps we should consider something Hemingway wrote about *War and Peace* for *Esquire* in December 1934:

Then when you have more time read another book called *War and Peace* by Tolstoi and see how you will have to skip the big Political Thought passages, that he undoubtedly thought were the best things in the book when he wrote it, because they are no longer either true or important, if they ever were more than topical, and see how true and lasting and important the people and the action are.

NOTES

1. The Colombian novelist could as well have been describing the long, intentionally altered Paris walk in *The Sun Also Rises*, a walk that becomes part of what H. R. Stoneback has aptly called a *paysage moralisé* (136, 143).

2. "Of Wasteful Deaths: Hemingway's Stories about the Spanish War," *Western Humanities Review* 23 (1969).

10

Nostalgia, Its Stylistics and Politics in Hemingway's *For Whom the Bell Tolls*

Erik Nakjavani

"Tu ne me chercherais Das, si tu me n'avais pas trouvé."
—Blaise Pascal

"So we beat on, boats against the current, borne back ceaselessly into the past."
—F. Scott Fitzgerald

The nature and the considerable role that nostalgia plays in *For Whom the Bell Tolls* have not yet been adequately explored in Hemingway scholarship. One may attribute this inadequacy to the lack of a precise definition of nostalgia. Such a definition requires a double act of theorization and formulation. Accordingly, first, I develop a theory of nostalgia in distinction to memory. Subsequently, I test the validity of this new theory by applying it to the passages from which, I contend, it emerges. Finally, I formulate the triadic relationship of this new theory of nostalgia to the stylistics and politics that it generates in the novel.

The title of this chapter proposes a triangular conceptual relation that a certain reading of *For Whom the Bell Tolls* makes manifest: nostalgia and its consequent stylistics and politics. To grant primacy to the text of the novel in any theoretical reading of it is to affirm that it is the text itself that suggests such a reading. The theoretics of any literary text falls within the text's general significations. Since textual significations are inherent and inexhaustible, by extension, the theoretical horizon of the text is also unlimited. From time to time, a specific mode of reading discovers and explores a theoretical dimension of the literary text, which is by definition non-exhaustive. However, it is always the text itself that offers the possibility of such theoretical reading in its inevitable, unique, reciprocal relation to a reader. The movement from textual reading to theoretical articulation represents a trajectory of moments of critical reflection upon the text. These moments of reflection produce more or less extensive texts that are extensions of the original texts and dependent upon it. What such theoretical texts produce is no more than an attempt to transform what is perceptual in the novel to what one may regard as conceptual.

A theoretical formulation of the triangular relationship between nostalgia and its stylistics and politics in *For Whom the Bell Tolls* demands a clear definition of each of these three terms. Since I hold the concept of nostalgia to be the foundational psychical principle of the passages in the novel that I intend to treat, I find it useful to begin by providing a definition of nostalgia. I will then delineate the consequent stylistics and politics of it.

DEFINING NOSTALGIA, STYLISTICS, AND POLITICS

By nostalgia I mean a maximally intense "longing" for a reality that always characterizes itself in the present by its very absence.[1] From a combined experiential and ontological viewpoint, nostalgia presents us with a double dictum: *absence as presence and presence as absence*. Nostalgia as a hypertensive *absent presence* confronts us with a *paradox*. This is as it should be because the definition that I have just provided goes beyond the *doxa* of nostalgia, that is, the pathological and politically regressive connotations commonly associated with it today. In these distinctions lie the significance and the contribution of the new definition. This definition somewhat coincides with the Greek origin of the word *nostos* (to return), and *algos* (pain). Therefore, nostalgia is experienced as a rather painful yearning to return home or "homesickness." *Homesickness* is the synonym the dictionary offers for *nostalgia*. The German word *Heimweh* too, expresses this meaning.

Nostalgia is then a painful desire for "homecoming." It acquires its widest and deepest possible meaning as the primeval and ever-present dream of a known but not specifically geographic homeland. All human aspirations find their fulfillment in this motherland of hope. Nostalgia permeates one's life as incessant quasi-conscious hope. Nostalgic hope should not be equated with optimism. It persists as a belief in the eventual realization of the infinite potentialities of the human spirit when no reason for optimism exists. Nostalgia begins where despair ends.

The psychic homeland called nostalgia is a place both lived in and anticipated. Past, present and the world to come harmoniously dwell in it. Nostalgia is a memory of the perfect future realizing itself at the crossroads where the immemorial past meets the future in the eternal present. Nostalgia defines the "pastness" of the past and the "futurity" of the future in the actuality of the present.

Nostalgia is a yearning for perfection. That is why there is always and inevitably an intimation of the Platonic in nostalgia. One may add that nostalgia as dream of perfection manifests itself in human experience as the transient hyper-reality of paradise lost. This paradise stands for the ground of the possibility, of the possible in human self-fulfillment. An immense promise of salvation resides in it. It appears as the horizon of human life with which human beings can coincide only momentarily in our time. This coincidence takes place in existential circumstances that Karl Jaspers defines as "limit-situations."

In this sense, the immutable rigid boundaries of an ideal and, therefore, *valorized* or *privileged* past, no longer hold nostalgia in confinement. Nostalgia negates the arbitrary and mechanical temporal divisions of past, present and future. Time flows through nostalgia forward and backward simultaneously. This simultaneity of forward-backward movements of temporal maneuvers in nostalgia makes for its plasticity as a psychic phenomenon. In other words, nostalgia as the consciousness of an absent presence provides a spider web of connective temporal tissues. Wherever one touches this web, its expansion and contractions are felt everywhere. Nostalgia constantly offers us the *future perfect* of the recollective discourse of ancient human longings whose fulfillment remains forever deferred, forever in flux. Nostalgia takes root and grows in the realm of transcendence. The transcendental obviously defies a thoroughly theoretical approach; it incorporates theory and goes beyond it. Perhaps the best way to deal with nostalgia would be through transcendental meditation or contemplation, as Ralph Harper has done in his book *Nostalgia*. In any case, it is useful to have certain passages in *For Whom the Bell Tolls* as a guide for our own brief meditative forays into the notion of nostalgia.

I define politics simultaneously in its most cogent and widest possible sense: the stringent dialectical progression from the ideological, defined as "lived-experience," to the political defined as "scientific discourse" or political theory—that is to say, political science. This progression is primarily grounded and initiated in the semi-conscious, the sensual, the perceptual and then gradually makes its way toward the conscious, the conceptual and the theoretical. In short, it moves from the buzzing, booming confusion and indeterminacy of experience to the rigorously clear and scientific.

Finally, I refer to stylistics as the ensemble of phonological, lexical, grammatical, and syntactic features that transform the denotative language of communication to the connotative language of literature. Stylistics "foreground" and set apart the literary discourse or "poetic language," from the norm of the "standard language," which constitutes its "background" (Mukarovsky 997).

I would reiterate that these definitional formulations derive from a specific reading of the narrative discourse of *For Whom the Bell Tolls* itself. My task is now to locate the various sites of nostalgia in passages that best approximate a mode of prose-poetry in the novel and search briefly for nostalgic traces in the development of the novel's political and stylistics dimensions. First, I must demarcate the borderlines of memory that surround nostalgia on every side. Subsequently, I need to differentiate between nostalgia and memory. This differentiation, in turn, should lead me to discover and explore passages in the novel where nostalgia resides in the fold of prose-poetry.

EIDETIC MEMORY IN DISTINCTION TO NOSTALGIA

The knowledge that informs Hemingway's fiction in its entirety is an aggregation of various modes of remembering. As Martin Heidegger tells us, "Memory, Mother of the Muses—the thinking back to what is to be thought is the source and ground of poesy" (11). This remembering is a type of "recollective knowing," to borrow another term from Heidegger. *For Whom the Bell Tolls* is no exception to this recollective and, therefore, "subjective" epistemology; in fact, it presents a striking example of it.

Robert Jordan declares, "He fought now in this war because it had started in a country that he loved and he believed in the Republic and that if it were destroyed life would be unbearable for all those people who believed in it" (163). Clearly, he firmly situates his declaration in recollective knowledge. Jordan's love for Republican Spain is a disclosure that draws its authenticity from memories of the country and its threatened political system. The memories burst forth from his having lived "parts of ten years in Spain before the war" (135).

Jordan's love of Spain does not only involve a *remembrance of things past* à la Proust but also a pronounced *remembrance of things future* as well. As a militant intellectual, Jordan projects his memories into Spain's political future. On the personal level, his love of Maria carries the kernel of his own possible future survival. After his horse falls upon him in retreat, crushes his right leg and he is left behind, Robert Jordan tells Maria, "Now you are going fast and far and we both go in thee" (464). So, there exists an implied notion of personal survival in Robert Jordan's love for Maria, either spiritual or reproductive.

The various modes of "thinking-back" (*An-denken*) or commemoration in *For Whom the Bell Tolls* stimulate regressive-progressive movements that approximate significant features of nostalgia as I have defined it. However, thinking-back does not wholly coincide with recollection. There is a difference between the two. This proximity and difference between recollection and nostalgia in *For Whom the Bell Tolls* is a subtle and crucial point to keep in mind.

Recollective passages abound in *For Whom the Bell Tolls*. Robert Jordan is not the only character who provides such passages in the novel. Pilar, Maria, Anselmo, Andres and, to a lesser extent, other characters do so as well. Pilar, much like Robert Jordan himself, is capable of producing alternately recollective passages of great joy, power and beauty or of numbing sorrow, futility and ugliness. Her long strands of reminiscences of Valencia produce something akin to a sensual fugue in prose. Or one may consider it as a tableau in which eidetic visual images create from memory a lyrical, an occult (hidden) visibility that brings to mind Andrew Wyeth's poetic hyper-realism, say, in the Helga pictures. Pilar draws the following word-sketch of Valencia:

We went to the beach and lay in the water and boats with sails were hauled up out of the sea by oxen. The oxen driven to the water until they must swim; then harnessed to the boats, and, when they found their feet, staggering up the sand. Ten yokes of oxen dragging a boat with sails out of the sea in the morning with the line of the small waves breaking on the beach. That is Valencia. (85–86)

Yes, that is Valencia, or an artistic rendering of it that is truer than true: Valencia recollected and commemorated in words that are at once magically transformative and supremely precise. The visual images then metonymically shift to gustatory images:

We ate in pavilions on the sand. Pastries made of cooked and shredded fish and red and green peppers and small nuts like grains of rice. Pastries delicate and flaky and the fish of a richness that was incredible. Prawns fresh from the sea sprinkled with lime juice. They were pink and sweet and there were four bites to a prawn. Of those we ate many.... All the time drinking a white wine, cold, light and good at thirty centimos the bottle. And for an end; melon. That is the home of the melon. (85)

These gustatory images in turn give way to memories of Pilar's lovemaking with the bullfighter Finito in a room

with the strip wood-blinds hanging over the balcony and a breeze through the opening of the top of the door which turned on hinges. We made love there, the room dark in the day time from hanging blinds, and from the streets there was the scent of the flower market and the smell of burned powder from the firecrackers of the *traca* that ran through the streets exploding each noon during the Feria. (85)

Would it be inaccurate to call Pilar's reminiscences contemplation on the theme of Valencia, or more precisely, a recollective meditation on the *absence* of Valencia? I think not. There is something of the immediacy and cohesion of masturbative or Onanistic, to extend Robert Jordan's reference to Onan (342), in Pilar's descriptive images. I make this comparison not to emphasize the erotics of her descriptions but rather their extraordinary eidetic acuity. Pilar provides images that are naturally and powerfully *appropriative* as well. This is not surprising because recollection is a selective appropriation of the self in relation to the world. Pilar's Valencia is a desperate but successful effort to capture a double absence: Valencia as experienced reality and Valencia as a tangle of memory traces.

The question now is: What specifically characterizes these passages as *memorial* rather than nostalgic? First, I would say that the time of the syntax of memory is primarily the perfect (simple) past ("We went to the beach and lay in the water" or "We ate in pavilions on the sand" or "We made love in the room"). Since memory is always unaware of its multiple transformative functions of selecting, repressing and, eventually, preserving and foregrounding, it immobilizes the past experience and freezes it forever in a temporal frame—the absolute past. Memory unconsciously suppresses its alterations of past experience to take it up again as a finished product beyond change or even the possibility of change. Through the unconscious processes of selective recollection, the objects of past experiences emerge sharper than sharp and clearer than clear, as they do in dreams.

Recollection is truly a *fictive* operation. To recollect is to spin the narrative yarn of a *created*, pristine, ontological state. Recollective discourse emerges from the "once upon a time" quality of all narrative fiction. The eidetic images of a keen memory are photographic only if one considers photography as at once a highly sensitive recording device and transmutive art. What a photographic memory such as Pilar's produces merely pretends to be an exact reproduction of particular experiences. The work of her photographic memory is in reality more akin to a composition of certain aspects of the remembered experience rather than an accurate reporting of it. It is a work that the quasi-conscious but indelible marks of memory has made on her mind. The reality of Pilar's remembered Valencia to Valencia is comparable to El Greco's Toledo to Toledo. Thus the transformative and fictional nature of memory constitutes its first characteristic.

The result of all these alterations of memory is the appearance of a specific temporal dimension in the psyche and, by extension, in the narrative: *the discourse of the absolute past*. The borders of memory are linguistic to the extent that recollection takes place in language and images that can only fully realize themselves in spoken or written words. Consequently, the linguistic features of recollection constitute the second essential characteristic of memory.

The most revealing and dominant trait of recollective passages given to Pilar is their direct and highly stressed *referentiality*. The intent of Pilar's sensuous remembrances of Valencia or the macabre violence in her city at the beginning of the Spanish Civil War is above all *communication as informative discourse* in and through language. Pilar's remembrances demonstrate a lyrical quality of lexicon and unusual syntactic dilatation. These stylistic qualities bring the narrative discourse of her memories close to the status of poetic-prose; nevertheless, they remain essentially within the category of communicative prose. They lack the self-referential and polysemic dimensions of poetry and prose-poetry on the semantic level. In that respect, they fall short of attaining the status of poetic language. The aim of recollective communication is a one-on-one coincidence of the eidetic images as signifiers and their extra-linguistic signifieds. Robert Jordan is not thinking metaphorically when he finds that drinking the "liquid alchemy," absinthe, helps him to bring back memories of

the evening papers, of all the old evenings in the cafes, of all the chestnut trees that would be in bloom now in this month, of the great slow horses of the outer boulevards, of book shops, of kiosques, and of galleries, of the Parc Montsouris, of the Stade Buffalo, and of the Butte Chaumont, of the Guaranty Trust Company, of Ile de la Cité, of Foyot's old hotel, and of being able to read and relax in the evening." (51)

The length of the sentence that comprises this passage is mainly a matter of economics of style. As every attentive reader of Hemingway's work knows, what constitutes the Hemingway style is not the predominance of short, choppy, declarative sentences everywhere in his work. His style often includes an arabesque of long, complex sentences, both in his fictions and nonfictions. In the sentence that I have just quoted, the chain of signifiers pushes itself forward *associatively* in memory. The whole sentence progresses metonymically and continually signifies what lies beyond it in the remembered past. There is no specific lexical, grammatical, or syntactic violation of the norm of the standard language in this sentence, only certain slight modifications of it. As a result, there is nothing that would allow this sentence to acquire the semantics of what one may call "surplus meaning." Poetry draws incessantly from the inexhaustible resources of "surplus meaning." As we shall see in due course, one encounters that "surplus meaning" or semantic multiplicity in *For Whom the Bell Tolls* only in passages marked by a specific mode of consciousness. Fred Davis calls it "nostalgic consciousness" (81).

The binary opposition between "good" and "bad" memories is the third essential feature of the act of recollection. Memories are consistently either good or bad. Indifferent memories do not exist; they are forgotten memories. Indifference precludes memory. Forgetfulness and indifference are the same psychic phenomenon in temporal terms. The selective operations of recollection excise from our mind memories of indifference. As a rule, one only remembers the *memorable*. Memory discards what the psyche perceives as trivial. Memory is the repository of the consequential.

Pilar's hymnal tribute to Valencia finds its reverse side in her reminiscences in Chapter Nine. She describes in this chapter a brutal massacre at the beginning of the war in her unnamed town. Consider in the following passage the treatment of the Fascist Don Guillermo before his murder, as he passes through two lines formed by a mob that Pilar describes as "drunkards and worthless ones" (119):

Then some drunkard yelled, "Guillermo!" from the lines, imitating the high cracked voice of his [Guillermo's] wife and Don Guillermo rushed toward the man, blindly, now with tears running down his cheeks and the man hit him hard across the face with his flail and Don Guillermo sat down from the force of the blow and sat there crying, but not from fear, while the drunkards beat him and one drunkard jumped on top of him, astride his shoulders, and beat him with a bottle. (118)

Such a passage possesses nothing of what Anselmo, the admirable old guerillero, refers to as *"pride* of remembrance [my emphasis]" (40). The passage overflows by an inescapable horror associated ordinarily with nightmares. It is a diurnal nightmare. And it is so much more frightful because it is real, all too real. Perhaps one may think of it as a meditation on the real intrusion of the chthonian on everyday human existence. It is a frightful struggle between the Devil and the Good Lord, as it were, that tends to demolish any vestige of optimism about the essential goodness of the human race. This remembrance of things demonic is only heightened by Maria's description of her savage humiliation in a barber's chair and her gang-rape by Fascists on a couch in her father's office. I believe the binary opposition between good and bad memories establishes the psychical borders of recollection in general and in *For Whom the Bell Tolls* in particular.

NOSTALGIA AND ITS TEMPORAL DIMENSION

What are the constituents of the *difference* between nostalgia and memory in *For Whom the Bell Tolls*, as I have defined these terms? It is helpful to refer immediately to one of the narrative passages in the novel that appears in Chapter 37 and that, for me, makes manifest the specificity of nostalgia. One reads:

Then they were together so that as the hand on the watch moved, unseen now, they knew that nothing could ever happen to the one that did not happen to the other, that no other thing could happen more than this; that this was all and always; this was what had been and now whatever was to come. (379)

At the outset, it is the temporal aspect of the passage that is immediately discernible. Robert Jordan and Maria were in time and aware of it before "being together." This time is clock-time, *chronos*, arbitrary and mechanical time, artificially superimposed on the temporal dimension of all that lives and *endures*. *Chronos* is *of* time, but it is not time, which is always and everywhere an eternity of duration. In a sense, one may say that clock-time as the measure of Time characterizes *false* time. Clock-time is the place where the quotidian surges up and vanishes only to surface later partially as recollection. Robert Jordan and Maria are first together as the movement of "the hand on the watch" becomes "unseen." The miraculous entrance into eternity as "now" begins, as the consciousness of clock-time is attenuated and ebbs away. The adverb *then* in the passage serves as the fulcrum of that radical temporal change from chronos to *kairos*.

Clock-time intimates to us our finitude. We experience finitude as a constant intimation of our death and our disappearance. Clock-time as intimation of oblivion resonates in the unconscious as fantasies of eternal death and destruction: the Freudian death-wish. Clock-time is the domain of irretrievable loss. In Faulkner's *The Sound and the Fury*, Quentin Compson's father calls the watch that he gives his son "the mausoleum of all hope and desire . . . the reducto absurdum of all human experience" (95). "I give it to you," he tells Quentin, "not that you may remember time, but that you might forget it now and then for a moment and not spend all your breath trying to conquer it" (95). As we relentlessly rush toward the future in conceptualized, mechanical time, the eternal present, which is all we have, races away from us toward a past that is no more except in memory. In this sense, clock-time marks a double loss. "One day you'd think misfortune would get tired, but then time is your misfortune Father said" (123). As Quentin unhappily discovers, as we all discover to our dismay, Father speaks the truth. And it is in this "mausoleum of all hope and desire" that Robert Jordan and Maria had initially found one another, that is, in the measured time of immeasurable eternity of the now.

THE NOSTALGIC MODE OF BEING AND BEING-TOGETHER

"Then they were *together* so that as the hand on the watch *moved unseen now* they knew that nothing could ever happen to the one that did not happen to the other" (my emphasis). As chronos ebbs and *kairos*, the inner time, which is always now, eternal duration, starts to flow, a *marvelous* mode of being emerges: "being-together" (Heidegger's *Mitsein*). In its deepest sense, being-together opens onto the nostalgic land of the "marvelous" for Robert Jordan and Maria. I use the adjective *marvelous* in its etymological sense here. The marvel of nostalgia is perhaps ultimately an *inexplicable, unthought*, perhaps even *unthinkable* phenomenon; yet its existence is experientially confirmed.

Being-together, union in the act of making love, spiritual oneness, they all characterize an "availability" (Gabriel Marcel's *disponibilité*) to and participation in the experience of the marvelous that makes the earth move from under you. When the earth shifts away as an anchor, it allows the body and the psyche to become coexistent in the interstices of space itself as the void, as "nowhere." "Nowhere" is a cosmic realm and is no doubt another way of indicating everywhere. On a certain level of conceptualization of space, everywhere and nowhere coincide. When the earth moves, one partakes of mysteries—Christian (*les merveilleux chrétiens*) or otherwise—and becomes part of them. The movement of the earth finds its correlative movement in the skyward thrust of the psyche. The earth's falling away reverberates in the psyche as its *boundlessness*. The psyche is no longer earth-bound.

On the level of the mystery of Christian love, one apprehends its boundlessness by participating in it. Love transforms the mundane into the wondrous and the wonderful. Being-together in *For Whom the Bell Tolls* establishes the union of two separate beings within the closure of paradise lost and the disclosure of paradise regained. This union, halfway between the heaven and the earth, demarcates the primordial home of the mystical oneness of Being. Oneness manifests itself then as *omnipresent* and extends itself eternally so that one may be able to say, "this was all and always" or "this was what had been and now whatever was to come." Time as eternity reveals itself as *presence* in this fashion. It makes a seamless whole of the immemorial past, the eternal present, and the infinite future. Thus we arrive in the miraculous realm of nostalgia whose spatio-temporal coordinates are the eternity of time and the infinity of space.

In this context, the nostalgic consciousness coincides with mystical consciousness, with what Maria calls "la gloria [Joy]" (379), or ecstasy, in its rich and dense religious sense of it. Through the clairvoyant mediation of Pilar, Maria's sexual intercourse with Robert Jordan alleviates her sorrow. The English psychoanalyst Donald W. Winnicott specifies this type of profound sorrow as "primitive agonies," (176) a term that designates a psychic phenomenon far more painful than anxiety. In that sense, the experience of nostalgia as ecstasy in sexual love is profoundly healing or, to use a more technical term, therapeutic for Maria. What she has lost in violence and despair she finds intact again in the nostalgic experience of being present in peace and love to oneself, to the other and the world. The nostalgic present offers Maria and Robert Jordan a *present*: a gift of the fulfillment of the dream of perfect unity. Their perfect union is only seemingly extrinsic (genital sex), fundamentally intrinsic or both. In any case, the union finally takes root within themselves, each serving as a spiritual catalyst for the other. Its nature is reminiscent of Saint Augustine's words: "Thou wert within and I abroad [outside], and there I searched for Thee.... Thou wert with me, but I was not with Thee" (195). As E. B. Daniels has put it in more psychoanalytic terms, "there will be no psychotherapy without confronting the problem ... raised by nostalgia: How to come to terms with a desire constituted in the space and time of my own body to return to intimacy with the world—a world of people, of things." (81). Maria fully recognizes the curative powers of the ecstasy of sexual union as nostalgia, of going back to a point when all is sweetness and light and then move from that point forward. The whole experience "is in Greco and San Juan de la Cruz," thinks Robert Jordan (380). "I am no mystic," he adds, "but to deny it is as ignorant as though you denied the telephone or that the earth revolves around the sun or that there are other planets but this" (380).

Nostalgia elevates genital sexuality in this novel to the spiritual self-abandonment that the Sufi whirling dervishes experience in their hypnotic dances and chants. As such, it proffers a state of grace upon Robert Jordan and Maria because, as he states, "this that they were not to have, they were having," against all odds and through no *apparent* merit of their own. Perhaps Maria's merit abides in her young suffering as a victim of gang-rape and the irredeemable sorrow of the loss of her parents. Similarly, Robert Jordan's purity of heart in willing one thing, as Soren Kierkegaard might have put it, the winning of the war against the Fascists, prepares him for the saving grace of love. Robert Jordan's purity is as authentic and poignant in the novel as Maria's young sorrow. "Do you know that until I met thee I have never asked for anything?" he tells Maria. "Nor wanted anything? Nor thought of anything except the movement and the winning of this war? Truly I have been very pure in my ambitions" (348). Since it may indeed be true that "the riddle of what is lost is the riddle of what we shall find" (Daniels 87), Maria, too, finds what she considers to have been lost in her brutal gang-rape: her sense of unmolested womanhood and the possibility of intimacy and love. This regained spiritual purity opens up a miraculous terrain to both Maria and Robert Jordan within whose boundaries the potentials of being as having and as loving intermingle and establish a paradise of limitless blessings. Mircea Eliade tells us, "I rediscover precious things through such [joyful] nostalgia. And in that way I feel that I never lose anything, that nothing is ever lost" (101). This is so because nostalgia is the dream of a cosmos where the sorrow of what is lost is the precondition of the happiness of what is to be found.

THE NOW AS THE DEFINING TEMPORAL DIMENSION OF NOSTALGIA

The eternal present, the "now," appears to define concretely the temporal dimension of nostalgia. The love that Maria and Robert Jordan share has to make up for its brevity in intensity. Robert Jordan is painfully conscious of this brevity. He tells himself, "you had better love her very hard and make up in intensity what the relation will lack in duration and continuity" (168). The striking feature of this intensity for Robert Jordan is the discovery of the nostalgic ever-presence of the "now." First, he reminds himself that "all the life you have or ever will have is today, tonight, tomorrow, today, tonight, tomorrow over and over again" (165–166). He then further refines this temporal notion of his life by commenting that "if there is not any such thing as a long time, nor the rest of your lives, nor from now on, but there is only now, why then now is the thing to praise and I am very happy with it. Now, *ahora, maintenant, heute.* Now, it has a funny sound to be a whole world and your life" (166). For a much fuller treatment of the ever-presence of the "now," as certain expanses of narrative discourse suggest it in the novel, let us examine the rest of the passage from Chapter 39, which brings Robert Jordan and Maria together in sexual union for a second time:

They were having now and before and always and now and now and now. Oh, now, now, now, the only now, and above all now, and there is no other now but thou now and now is thy prophet. Now and forever now. Come now, now, for there is no now but now. Yes, now. Now, please now, only now, not anything else only this now, and where are you and where am I and where is the other one, and not why, not ever why, only this now; and on and always please then always now, always now, for now always one now; one only one, there is no other one but one now, one, going now, rising now, sailing now, leaving now, wheeling now, soaring now, away now, all the way now, all of all the way now; one and one is one, is one, is one, is one, is still one, is still one, is one descendingly, is one softly, is one longingly, is one kindly, is one happily, is one is goodness, is one to cherish, is one now on earth with elbows against the cut and slept-on branches of the pine tree with the smell of the pine boughs and the night; to earth conclusively now, and with the morning of the day to come. (379)

It is obvious that the "now" as a temporal dimension appears in this passage as *sacramental time*, as a temporal axis of spiritual ascension in mutual having and being. The "now" prompts a new ontological premise. The repetition of the "now" in the passage rises to an incantatory level of dizzying, hypnotic intensity. The experience of the "now" resembles the act of taking communion. It is parallel to incorporating into oneself the body and blood of what one may call the *cosmic* Christ and, therefore, becoming a part of all that exists. Such an act of communion serves as a portal to the universe of "now always one now," of the integrative calculus of "one and one is one, is one, is one, is one, is still one, is still one," to the end of time. Fittingly enough, the formulation of "there is no other now but thou now and now is thy prophet" comes very close to the Moslem credo: "There is no God but *Allah* and Muhammad is His prophet."

The sacralization of the "now" is the site of fulfillment of all our longings in universal communion and its time is the ever-present—the sum of all time past and future. This temporal totality is the signal trait of nostalgia, as we have seen. The "now" heals the division of time and provides a glimpse of the eternal. The "now" mends the psychic rift of time that is our "misfortune." As a spiritual phenomenon, nostalgia dwells in the now. The "now" of nostalgia renders whole the fabric of our psyche that was rent asunder. As Ralph Harper explains, "nostalgia is regenerative and requires the starting of life all over again" (28). Nostalgia is regenerative for the simple reason that "it is a return ... to what has been known and loved" (Harper 29). Nostalgia is the inviolate land of hope, the inexhaustible horizon of psychic search for an unbroken world in the "now." Through its intensity the lost paradise of the psyche, whose traces are unerasable, is regained. This regeneration takes place on the plane of great, widening circles of *unities* of the instinctual, the sensuous, the perceptual and the conceptual. These unities unfold perpetually in the "now" as the drama of human life. Only in the oneness of the nostalgic consciousness can one claim that one and one "is one longingly, is one kindly, is one in goodness, is one to cherish" and then find oneself again in the midst of earthly life of the senses "with elbows against the cut and slept-on branches of the pine tree with the smell of pine boughs and the night" (379).

The question is: Would one ever recognize the appearance of nostalgic consciousness in the "now," as yearning in its deepest sense, if one in some way did not already have an intimation of it in the chaos of human existence and did not anticipate it? Harper assures us that "not only is the longing familiar, but fulfilment [*sic*] is also" (20). This question and its affirmative answer, in turn, lead us to another question: *How* is this "longing familiar" in the "now" and *why*? Beyond the notion of Platonic ideas of an other-worldly perfection, I speculatively formulate the answer to the "why" of the question as residing in a demonstrable human tendency toward *epistemophilia*. The quest of this love for knowledge is the apprehension of the potential realization of paradise on earth, at least on the plane of the spiritual. Perhaps nostalgia is the most acute expression of such an epistemophilia.

I ascribe to the "how" of the question the enormous effect that the narrative discourses of nostalgia exert in world mythology, in fables, in fairy tales as well as poetry and prose. Nostalgia is born of the narratives of nostalgia into which we ourselves are born as our spiritual patrimony. As Harper reminds us, "Nostalgia is neither illusion nor repetition; it is a return to something we never had. And yet the very force of it is just that in it the lost is recognized, is familiar" (26). In the context of the argument that I have just presented, Harper's contention amounts to maintaining that nostalgia is that *absence* that constitutes the presence known in the deep structures of mythology in all cultures. Perhaps one may consider mythology as the repository of nostalgic forces within human societies.

Jordan and Maria's first sexual union exemplifies the stylistics of nostalgia as a particular category of stream-of-consciousness technique:

Then there was the smell of heather crushed and the roughness of the bent stalks under her head and the sun bright on her closed eyes and all his life he would remember the curve of her throat with her head pushed back into the heather roots and her lips that moved smally and by themselves and the fluttering of the lashes on the eyes tight closed against the sun and against everything, and for her everything, was red, orange, gold-red from the sun on the closed eyes, and it all was that color, all of it, the filling, the possessing, the having, all of that color, all in a blindness of that color. For him it was a dark passage which led to nowhere, then to nowhere, then again to nowhere, once again to nowhere, always and forever to nowhere, heavy on the elbows in the earth to nowhere, dark, never any end to nowhere, hung on all time all ways to unknowing nowhere, this time and again for always to nowhere, now not to be borne once again always and to nowhere, now beyond all bearing up, up, up and into nowhere, suddenly, scaldingly, holdingly all nowhere gone and time absolutely still and they were both there, time having stopped and he felt the earth move out and away from under them. (159)

What are the stylistic consequences of such a nostalgic-stream-of-consciousness passage? The overall effect is that of the fusion of seemingly disparate sensuous and perceptual elements into an indivisible linguistic entity. This linguistic entity comprises a symphonic passage of great contrapuntal harmony and efficacy. It pulls together strands of nostalgic melodies into what the German language so aptly and cogently calls *Sprachgestalt* [language-form]. *Sprachgestalt* here both unifies, and, at the same time, "defamiliarizes" the language of the passage, to borrow from Victor Shklovsky's terminology (756–755). This contrapuntal, symphonic approach, therefore, "deautomatizes" our perception through stylistic qualities of prose-poetry. Incantatory repetitions and accumulations of words, verbs and adverbs render the sentences in these narrative passages increasingly complex, dilatory, lyrical and supple. The exigencies of nostalgic-stream-of-consciousness make the syntactic and grammatical structures of the sentences in these passages deviate radically from the norm of the "standard language." They progressively violate even Hemingway's own usual descriptive narrative style. These passages come close to the repetitive patterns of hymns and prayers. In a certain sense they *are* hymns and prayers. They are not greatly different from Joaquin's (321) Maria's (450) and Anselmo's (327) prayers.

Consequently, nostalgic-stream-of-consciousness passages in the novel are more *stylized*. Their greater stylization enables them to express the transformative experience of nostalgia. These passages yield an ensemble of devices and structures of their own that pave the way toward the release from the restriction of denotative language. The language of the nostalgic-stream-of-consciousness in *For Whom the Bell Tolls* moves from the necessary univocal, realistic prose to multivocal prose-poetry. The metonymic images in the nostalgic-stream-of-consciousness create an aggregate of new polysemy signifying structures. These signifying structures, in turn, draw the borderlines of what I have defined as nostalgia in distinction to memory. The polysemous nature of the nostalgic-stream-of-consciousness passages surfaces as ungrammaticality and obscurity. That obscurity as a signifier is in itself commensurate with the multi-layered signification of nostalgia that it signifies.

THE POLITICS OF NOSTALGIA

Nostalgia as a psychic and spiritual phenomenon arises from a primary source of human existence to which French philosophers Jean-Paul Sartre and Louis Althusser have assigned the term *le vécu* (lived-experience). Lived-experience signifies approximately the "life-world" (*Lebenswelt*) in Husserlian phenomenology. Lived-experience is no more than the quasi-conscious apprehension of life in action or *praxis*. The flux of everyday experiences, as the individual lives it in its opacity, subliminally alters and guides individual human life. One may then say that lived experience, however opaque, is always subconsciously *directive* and *corrective*. I call this essentially semi-conscious directive and corrective experiential knowledge ideology. Ideology covers considerable stretches of narrative in the arts and literature. I would even assert that ideology constitutes the ground of emergence of all the arts and sciences.

As I have already indicated, nostalgia is located within the vast territory of lived-experience. Nostalgia makes itself known to us as a universal phenomenon within the specific terrain of ideology. If one defines politics as *ideology conceptualized*, as I have done, what will then issue as politics from the nostalgia? This question leads to another: What are the consequences of considering the temporal dimension of nostalgia as regressive-progressive phenomenon in the eternal continuum of the "now"? I would suggest that the regressive-progressive dimension of nostalgia finds its parallel in the retrospective-prospective political *praxis* that guide Robert Jordan in *For Whom the Bell Tolls*.

One may state that Robert Jordan's thought never reaches the level of a fully developed political theory. "What were his politics then?" Robert Jordan asks himself, "He had none now, he told himself. But do not tell anyone else that, he thought. Don't ever admit that" (163). Politics is not Robert Jordan's strong point, even though he is a political militant. As a dynamiter, he is a man of action. However, even political *action* falls into the ideological category in its unfolding. Political science as theory and the pragmatics of action do not coincide. Politics, as a rigorous science rather than ideology, always precedes or proceeds political action on the plane of the theoretical and is never quite identical with it. Robert Jordan remains in the domain of action, that is, the domain of lived-experience and has to devote his time mostly to grappling with its imperatives. If that is so, how can Robert Jordan act as an authentic and believable political militant in the Spanish Civil War? I would situate the answer within the regressive-progressive boundaries of nostalgic consciousness as ideology. Here, I need to go back to a quotation I cited earlier in a different context: "He [Robert Jordan] fought now in this war because it had started in a country that he loved and he believed in the Republic and that if it were destroyed life would be unbearable for all those who belived in it." Thus to be able to look forward, Robert Jordan has to look *simultaneously* backward. For him, to progress is to regress. It is tantamount to a paradoxical movement that only nostalgia as ideology can justify. The past as well as its antipode, an anticipatory activity of the mind that projects itself toward the future, are intensely at work here. Remembering Republican Spain and yearning for it set up one pole of a dialectical truth that shapes Robert Jordan's singularly individualistic ideology: *remembrance of things future*.

Even though Robert Jordan admits that "he was under Communist discipline for the duration of the war" (163), he is not a Communist. His reason for conforming to Communist discipline is that "Here in Spain the Communists offered the best discipline and the soundest and sanest for the prosecution of the war" (163). So what is the difference between Robert Jordan's vision of the future of Spain and that of the Communists? It would seem to me that the Communist Utopia, based upon Karl Marx's dream of a future working-class paradise, offers us nostalgia as political theory *imprisoned* in a mythical future. Nevertheless, nostalgia provides the foundation of the possibility of dreaming the future, Utopian or otherwise. Marx's Communist society is no exception to this assertion; to the contrary, it is a reaffirmation of the primordial power of nostalgia. Communist society is not a dream of regaining paradise lost but of constructing a working-class paradise unprecedented in the history of mankind. Robert Jordan's vision of the future of Republican Spain differs from the Communists' view to the extent that for him this future paradise is already a part of the past and the present through which he has been living. That notion of future as identifiable with the present and the past puts Robert Jordan's thought and action squarely within the category of ideology as nostalgia. Such a future offers a parallel construct to the Christian belief in the resurrection of the body. Both notions incorporate time as an indivisible unity. I must point out that such ideology carries nothing whatsoever of the reactionary about it. Indeed, it establishes itself as the opposite pole of reactionary tendencies of any type. Nostalgic ideology does not idealize the past and does not offer itself as a possible access to it in fantasy. Nostalgia is always headed toward a realization in the future; otherwise, it sinks into a fugue of past memories as a fantasy of regression.

Into this nostalgic future flow all the reminiscentia and wistfulness of lived-experience, all directed toward a future realization. The memory of the future is already embedded in the body and psyche along with all the mnemonic devices that consciously or unconsciously make it active. As such, the future is a project that realizes itself in a unified temporal field that includes the past and the present. Robert Jordan militates in the Spanish Civil War against the enemies of Republican Spain because the country evokes in him a feeling of mystical oneness he has already experienced for it in nostalgia. Nostalgia envelops him as the originary field of all progressive ideals within the eternal now. He is a "nostalgia hecha hombre" as Hemingway himself has expressed it (SS 237).

Nostalgia as a primary ontological phenomenon in *For Whom the Bell Tolls* brings forth specific patterns of thought and action that offer us rare insights. Its attendant stylistics and politics also yield extensive fields of opportunities for Hemingway studies. In the concept of nostalgia, among *unlimited* other notions and concepts, *For Whom the Bell Tolls* offers us lessons never too late for mediating upon or for the learning.

NOTE

1. My formulation of the definition of nostalgia and its connection with presence is inspired by Ralph Harper's *Nostalgia: An Existential Exploration of Longing and Fulfillment in the Modern Age*. Press of Western Reserve, 1966. Harper, in turn, has himself been influenced by the concept of presence in the works of French philosophers Gabriel Marcel and Louis Lavelle.

11

"You Sure This Thing Has Trout in It?" Fishing and Fabrication, Omission and "Vermification" in *The Sun Also Rises*

H. R. Stoneback

"It's too far to go and fish and come back the same day, comfortably."
—Ernest Hemingway, *The Sun Also Rises*

This essay is concerned with the fishing passages in *The Sun Also Rises*, with the hike that Jake and Bill take from Burguete to their fishing site, and with related details of what Hemingway described as "a fishing expedition in the Pass of Roland." I am not concerned here with symbolic or analogical readings of fishing idyll, nor will I treat the relation of this interlude to the rest of the novel. These matters have been treated exhaustively in hundreds of essays and books, and I have discussed in some detail these aspects in earlier essays. Rather, it seems about time, since we are approaching the 70th anniversary of one of the most discussed novels in American literature, to stop worrying to death some of the larger negotiable *truths* of the novel, and, at last, to get the *facts* right.

Jake Barnes and Bill Gorton, contrary to that dearly held axiom of Hemingway studies, *do not fish the Irati*—at least not in the rendered action, not on the day of their walk in Chapter XII. It has been universally assumed that they do fish the Irati River on that day. From the earliest published studies of the novel to the latest, no one has proposed that they fish anywhere but the Irati. Even those studies that putatively project as much expertise about the lay of the land as they do about the texture of the fiction, such as Edward Stanton's recent *Hemingway and Spain*, mutter the old platitudes about the "cooling, cleansing, and healing" waters of the "Irati River" (85).

Long before the first time I took the hike, following Jake's footsteps as precisely as possible, I thought there was something funny, something fishy, something Hemingway wasn't telling us about in this scene. And it is more than just a matter of chronological and topographical exactitude that is at stake here, for the omissions and fabrication of the text do indeed signify beyond time and place. Thus I propose, with text in one hand, a good topographical map in the other—the Roncesvalles Quadrant which shows every detail down to the smallest brook and building—and the landscape under our feet, to reconstruct as precisely as possible the day of Jake's walk.[1]

In spite of all the critical discussion of this chapter, certain key questions have not even been asked, let alone answered; for example, what time is it when Jake and Bill leave Burguete (or Auritz)?[2] How much time elapses on their walk? How far do they walk? What, exactly, is the route they follow? Where do they fish? When Jake wakes up that morning, it is fairly early, but it is not first light. It's clear and there are "no clouds on the mountains" (SAR 112). He says that it's "early morning." He goes right outside to dig worms and notes that "the sun had not yet dried the dew." So it is sometime after sunrise; in that place, at that time of year, sunrise would be at about 7:00 (although the sun does not hit the village until much later). Jake hunts around in a shed, finds a mattock, walks down to the stream behind the inn, digs "carefully" for worms and puts "a good many" in his tobacco tins. (The stream that he is digging by in this scene, which he notes does "not look trouty," is the Ansobi, which runs just west of and roughly parallel with the main road through Burguete. It may not look trouty to Jake, but it is full of trout now.) After the worm-digging episode, Jake goes back into the inn, sees the woman in the kitchen, asks her for coffee and a packed lunch. At this inn, the Hostal Burguete, in the 1970s and 1980s, and still in 1992, coffee and breakfast were available after 9:00. (In the 1920s, the present owner suggests, breakfast may have been available as early as 8:00.) Back in the room, there is some banter with Bill, still in bed, while Jake gets the tackle together. Then Jake goes downstairs to breakfast, leaving Bill in the room, singing: "Oh, Give them Irony and Give them Pity." Finally, Bill comes down to breakfast, and they have at least two "big bowls" of coffee with their toast and jam. Over breakfast, they have three pages worth of joking conversation. The point is that none of this, from the time Jake went outside to dig for worms through the lingering breakfast sequence, is rushed or hurried. Thus it would seem that they get away from the inn sometime between eight and nine, probably not much before nine.[3]

They leave the inn, walk north toward Roncevaux on the main road (Route C.C.-135) about a half-kilometer, then turn off on the trail, heading east-northeast, to their fishing venue. The text indicates that they cross two streams at the beginning of the walk; these are the Rio Urrobi, or the Barranco de Arranosina, which flows down from Roncesvalles and joins the Urrobi at precisely the spot where Jake and Bill cross the first stream;

the second, "faster-flowing" steam they cross is the Bco. de Soralucea. (The Arranosina, Soralucea and Ollarboru, three small streams, converge just outside Burguete to form the Rio Urrobi.) Many of the details Hemingway notes—tadpoles spotting the sand of the first stream, the fields and woods and beech trees, the cattle bells in the woods—are precisely the same today. The road goes up hill—"sometimes it dipped down but rose again steeply"—steadily. We note that Hemingway's text and the topographic map agree precisely that this is a dirt "road," a *camino* that they follow, not a *senda* or *itinerario de ascension*. "Finally," Hemingway writes, "the road came out on the top of the hills. We were on the top of the height of land that was the highest part of the range of wooded hills we had seen from Burguete" (117). Here, they are at the Collado de Nabala; they have ascended 123 meters from Burguete, and covered a little over four kilometers. Hemingway describes with verifiable precision the route that follows "along the shoulder of the ridge of hills," and the fields of yellow gorse and wild strawberries that Jake sees are still there to be seen. It is at this point that we get our distant—*very* distant—prospect, not of the Irati, but of the topographical features that indicate the Irati Valley. Hemingway writes: "Way off we saw the steep bluffs, dark with trees and jutting with gray stone, that marked the course of the Irati River" (117). And he means "*way* off," at least eight to ten miles as the crow flies. Jake explains to Bill: "We have to follow this road along the ridge, cross these hills, go through the woods on the far hills, and come down to the Irati valley." Bill says "that's a hell of a hike"; and Jake replies: "It's too far to go and fish and come back the same day comfortably." Bill is, of course, absolutely right to note that "comfortably" is a "nice word": "We'll have to go like hell to get there and back and have any fishing at all." This is the first clear indication in the text that they do not fish the Irati. For never has there been a more "comfortable" fishing-reading-eating-talking-sleeping afternoon than Bill and Jake are about to have.

The second indication that they do not fish the Irati follows immediately: "It was a long walk and the country was very fine, but we were tired when we came down the steep road that led out of the wooded hills into the valley of the Rio de la Fabrica" (118). That is to say, having walked about ten or eleven uphill-downhill kilometers from Burguete to the valley of the Fabrica, a walk that local inquiry in Burguete and Fabrica indicates is "about" three hours, a walk that has taken more than three hours when I walked it, they are indeed tired. They are not about to walk another twelve to fifteen kilometers to the Irati. The description of the river valley that is in the text—all the detail—is the valley of the Fabrica.[4]

At this point some skeptical reader, unwilling to relinquish the long-cherished notion that Jake and Bill fish the Irati, is likely to raise the objection that novelists are not bound to chronological and topographical precision. Of course they are not and Hemingway is chronologically and topographically imprecise elsewhere in *The Sun Also Rises*. However, if that is presumed to be the case here, I will simply ask three questions: (1) Why has he been absolutely precise about all the other details of the walk if he is suddenly going to transport Jake and Bill an extra twelve kilometers or so in a flash? (2) Why do all the descriptive details indicate the Fabrica, not the Irati? (3) Why does Bill look at the river in question, the river they actually fish, and ask: "You sure this thing has trout in it?" (118). Let me ask my hypothetical objector, especially if he or she has ever done any serious trouting, who would look at a broad, handsome celebrated trout river and ask if the "thing" had trout in it? Who would look at the upper Delaware, the Beaverkill, and ask such a question? No fisherman would, not even Bill, who *is* somewhat of a joker, on certain matters. But indeed many fishermen would look at the Fabrica, a rather small stream, and ask if there were trout in "this thing." (In fact, local inquiry and observation confirm that there are still many 8-to-10 inch trout in the Fabrica.) For that matter, if this is the broad Irati, how is it that Jake is able to toss "the insides, gills and all . . . over across the river" (119)? I try to picture this, at any point of the Irati I have seen (except for the headwaters of the Irati in France), and I come up with an image of an Olympian shotput delivery necessary to reach "across the river"—and still they wouldn't reach. But on the Fabrica this is exactly what you would do, easily and naturally. No, they do not fish the Irati.

All the details confirm it: they leave the inn sometime between eight and nine o'clock, they take the standard three-hour walk to Fabrica, they're tired, they fish. Then, after "a little while" (119), Jake quits fishing, and settles down in the shade of a tree to read A.E.W. Mason at "a little past noon." When Bill comes back they have a long, leisurely, talky lunch. Then they go to sleep, until "late in the afternoon" (124). It's all very comfortable, it's not the Irati. Finally they take their three-hour walk back, arriving with great precision, chronologically and topographically, in Burguete at nightfall.

There are other details that point with sufficient exactitude to the precise spot where Jake and Bill fish the Fabrica. For example, there are the sites on the Fabrica where there used to be dams, some of them, as the government ranger in Fabrica says and as Hemingway said, "built to provide a head of water for driving logs" (119). There are springs along the Fabrica where Jake could cool two bottles of wine. One, just above the point on the Fabrica where the Itolaz and the Txangoa converge, seems to fit Jake's description best: it's ice-cold water, flowing "out of an iron pipe" into a basin deep enough to hold two bottles of wine, and, in the 1920s (and until recently) the locals say, there was indeed "a board over the spring" (119). *The Sun Also Rises*, then, provides an exact map we can still follow: Jake fishes the Fabrica (the Itolaz branch) just down from the spring, the *fuente* of Fabrica which *is* another landmark, which was and is indicated on old and new maps of the area, and just above the confluence of the Itolaz and the Txangoa. Bill most probably (since he fishes downstream, since he fishes longer than Jake, and since he catches bigger trout) works his way down past the Txangoa-Itolaz confluence to the deeper holes, to the bigger water. In brief, I am so certain that the fishing scene we have all always loved takes place on the Fabrica that I offer this challenge to Hemingway scholars who resist being disabused of their Irati-dreams: demonstrate, with map and text in hand, and, preferably, the Spanish earth underfoot, that it is the Irati, not the Fabrica, and I will buy you a fine Navarrese Trout dinner. That's a Pascalian wager.

> "We were tired when we came down...into the valley of the Rio de la Fabrica."
>
> —*The Sun Also Rises*

Why has everyone assumed that Jake and Bill fish the Irati in Chapter XII of *The Sun Also Rises*? Because to the end of Chapter X, in Pamplona, Bill says: "We're going trout-fishing. We're going trout-fishing in the Irati River." (102). Because at the end of Chapter XII, after the hike, Jake says that Harris "went with" them "twice to the Irati River" (125). Because at the beginning of Chapter XIII, Jake says to Harris: "You want those big ones in the Irati" and Harris acknowledges he wants those "enormous" Irati trout (127). But there are many streams in *The Sun Also Rises, all* the streams they fish, and that stream with a swimming hole, and all the others: the Urrobi, Ansobi, Arranosina, Soralucea, Ollarburu, Itolaz, Txangoa— and the only stream where we witness any rendered fishing—the Fabrica.

Perhaps in addition Hemingway scholars have assumed that Chapter XII is an Irati-fishing scene because they know his letters, and the facts of Hemingway's multiple excursions to the Irati, and the biographical fallacy makes the Irati the inevitable river of *The Sun Also Rises.* But if we read the novel and the letters more carefully, we will know that Jake does not fish the Irati in Chapter XII. Consider, for example, Hemingway's letter to Howell Jenkins (9 November 1924):

The wildest damn country in the Spanish Pyrenees in from Roncevaux. The Irati River.... You leave the car at Burguete and go in fifteen miles by foot. Even the mules pass out on the trail. It is in there where they fought the Carlist wars.... Water ice cold and virgin forests, never seen an ax. Enormous beech forests and high up, Pines. We'll camp in at the headwaters of the Irati for a week and then go back to Burguete. (Baker, *Ernest Hemingway: Critiques* 130)

As Hemingway says here, it's at least thirty very hard miles round-trip from Burguete to his favorite place on the Irati, and if you go in on that trail that even the mules pass out on, you camp overnight. The other details in this letter, the romantic projection of the Irati headwaters and the country around, the overstated emphasis on wildness (it's not terribly wild now, and some locals say it was even *less* wild in the 1920s)[5], the oversimplification of the Carlist Wars, reducing them to a guerrilla action in the Irati country, and the celebration of the cold clean waters and the virgin forests, lead into another point, which has implications for most critical studies of *The Sun Also Rises*.

Hemingway critics have often remarked on the disappointing reality of Hemingway's actual fishing trip in 1925—how the logging had spoiled the countryside and ruined the fishing in the Irati. Then they have made the leap from the biographical fact to the composition process and stressed that Hemingway creates, *fabricates*, the idyllic setting of the novel, that he avoids describing the ruined Irati for novelistic reasons. Frederic Svoboda, for example, writes: "A purely journalistic description of the events of June 1925 would be far different from the idyllic week of relaxation that Hemingway described"; Svoboda and others attribute this evasion, this calculated non-mention of the ruined Irati countryside to Hemingway's artful construction, to the aesthetic and symbolic demands of the novel (15). However, all such critical views are now beside the point, since Hemingway did not even purport to describe the Irati, ruined or non-ruined. What he actually describes, more or less exactly as it was (and is), is the country between Burguete and the Valley of the Fabrica, country *far* from the Irati that Hemingway loved, country that was not ruined by logging, streams where the fishing was not spoiled. He never tells us what the Irati-country was like in *The Sun Also Rises*. He just says they went there twice, and nothing else.

I have said that Hemingway describes the Valley of the Fabrica exactly as it was in 1925. This is true except for the most astounding omission of all: he omits an entire village that Jake and Bill walk through (or to), where they *must* go, given their clearly defined route.[6] Known variously as Fabrica, Fabrica de Orbaiceta or Orbaizeta, and referred to locally as just "Fabrica," it is the most striking feature of the Valley of the Fabrica where Jake and Bill walk and fish. There are abundant ironies and complexities in all this. Fabrica, of course, means factory. And when they fish the River of the Factory, they are at the hamlet called Factory: a distinct village, with a number of houses (in Fabrica proper and in the adjacent Barrio Larraum), an old hostel, an old church, government buildings where the forest ranger lives, and the like. But most striking of all are the extensive ruins of a large nineteenth-century factory on the Fabrica, sprawling more than 400 feet along the river—the factory that gives the village, the valley, and the river its name, the factory that dates back to the early years of the Carlist Wars. And yes, it was a *Carlist* factory, an important site for the manufacture of firearms and munitions to supply the Carlist guerrillas. (The topographical map supplement, the booklet that accompanies the *Editorial Alpina* publication cited above, identifies it as follows: "Fabrica de Orbaiceta, antigua fabrica de fudicion de armas de fuego hoy dia en ruinas." Local inquiry elicits the answer that it was a *Carlist* munitions factory.) Jake fishes in the shadow of these ruins, and it is simply impossible to be there and miss the ruined factory. More than two decades ago, when I asked a priest at the church in Burguete, a priest who said he had read *The Sun Also Rises*, where the fishing scene was located, he told me to go "over the hills to the ruined Carlist factory." I had no idea what he was talking about then; like everybody else, I thought Jake fished the Irati. The priest, I thought then, was confused. I didn't find the factory then; I didn't even look for it. Everybody knew there wasn't any factory in the mountain idyll of *The Sun Also Rises*— no factory, no village, no ruins.

So what is Hemingway up to? Why this calculated omission, this Fabrication (and I mean by such a coinage as, let us say, Pamplona-fication). Let me suggest several possibilities: (1) He fabricates, he omits all this, for obvious aesthetic reasons, to avoid the intrusion in his mountain idyll of civilization, a village, a *factory* village at that. This seems a reasonable view, yet it *feels* wrong or limited, given the way Hemingway constructs the entire scene, given the fact that he tells us exactly where they are, and he *names* the river and the valley of the Fabrica—after all, the scene would work well without the jarring, counter-idyllic mention of the River and the Valley of the Factory. Thus, it seems like more of a "theory of omission" fabrication, a deletion intended to make the reader feel more than is understood; (2) Another possibility, given Hemingway's view that Jake and Bill are "in there where they fought the Carlist wars," is that the attentive reader is required, by Hemingway, to engage the actual country here, to read the landscape historically and symbolically. Of course, the Carlist wars, from the first in the 1830s to the last in the 1870s were immensely complicated; and they were not fought just "in there" in the backcountry Hemingway speaks of— but, briefly put, this is symbolic terrain in the sense that the last stand of the Carlists took place in this remote Navarrese hill-country. The Carlists were—among other things—Catholics and Conservatives; and their more or less heroic, underdog resistance in these hills may have appealed to a very young Hemingway who was capable of very romantic feelings about the "real old" Spain, about the courageous last stands of proud outnumbered heroes (such as that other valiant Catholic warrior, Roland, who made his last stand just over the hill from Fabrica—at Roncevaux). So it does indeed signify that Jake fishes the River-of-the-Factory-That-Made-Munitions-For-the-Carlists: Jake and Hemingway are both more engaged by history, are more Catholic and conservative, than has generally been recognized; (3) My last suggestion is this: nothing is more appropriate, and more resonant with the novel's deepest patterns of meaning, than the fact that Jake as Fisher King, Jake as wounded war-veteran, should fish, read, sleep, talk, eat, ponder his Catholicism and his love for Brett in and by the banks of the river flowing through and by the ruined war munitions factory. It is neither accidental nor incidental. It is somewhere near the base of Hemingway's "iceberg"; it is the very stuff of the ultimate "alchemy" of *The Sun Also Rises*. Such things, as Hemingway said, may not be "immediately discernible" in what he writes, but eventually they will be seen, will be understood. That sufficiently covers the fishing and the fabrication and the omission indicated in my title; now, for the "vermification."

> "Your worms."
>
> —Bill to Jake, *The Sun Also Rises*

Recently, I both read and heard for the umpteenth time an old chestnut that I thought had been banished to the outer darkness of Hemingway studies decades ago: to wit, the argument that Jake is somehow diminished as a man, somehow a failed code-hero or Hemingway-hero, somehow anti-exemplary because he fishes with worms; and the flip side of the argument, that Bill is some kind of true code-hero, some kind of valid tutor or exemplar because he fishes with flies, because he scorns Jake's worms. Well, well, well: What are we to make of such vermiphobic nonsense? If Bill is the exemplar because he fishes with flies and scorns worms, then he is an ever-so-flat character, and the argument reads like a synopsis for an episode of a television drama, "Jake and the Flat Man," shall we say, or "Jake and Super-Fly"? One does not go gladly down this road, this *Sendero Luminoso*, where the Shining Path school of literary terrorism searches out and destroys all those who are not piscatorially correct, but go we must, once more unto the breach. Maybe, to keep things on the cheerful side, we can begin with a chorus and dedicate it to Bill, that *tourist* from New York who just might be the worst kind of cultic urbanite L. L. Beanified fly-snob: "Oh Give him Irony and Give him Pity. Oh, Give him Irony, When he's feeling fishy."

Just the other month, at the opening of trout season in New York, a trouty-gent neighbor of mine observed to me in passing that he did not care for "The Big Two-Hearted River" or the fishing scene in *The Sun Also Rises* because of all that detestable bait-fishing; he allowed as how Nick, and Jake, and Hemingway, too, were "mere wormers." I responded: So was Izaak Walton, so was Dame Juliana, so was Charles Cotton. Let me clarify this situation: This yuppie (I almost said guppie) neighbor is a Wall Street stockbroker who first fished at the age of 44; now after several politically correct lessons at elite fly-fishing schools and an investment of several thousand dollars in tackle and gear, he is an expert on trout; this expert has fished two streams in his life and caught three ten-inch browns in the past two years; he does not know the difference between a night crawler and a heller (or hellgrammite); he has purchased 16 expensive books on fly-fishing but he does not own nor has he ever read those immortal fishing classics, Dame Juliana, Izaak Walton and Charles Cotton; he has never heard of the art of clear-water worm-fishing; in sum, he is the perfect type of a certain kind of trout-seeker-cum-literary-critic who is very insidious indeed, especially when unleashed in the full regalia of the vermiphobe on such a classic fishing scene as Jake's worm-fishing in *The Sun Also Rises.*

Let us reconsider, then, Jake's fishing in the shining light of the most recent characteristic study of the question. David C. Ward, in a piece entitled "Poor Sports: Hemingway, Jake Barnes and the Sporting Life in *The Sun Also Rises*,"[7] sets out to prove that Jake is a "hollow man" who is "the least passionate of characters." Ward's primary evidence for this assertion is the lowly worm: "The problem," Ward says, "is the way Jake fishes." If that's not enough to identify the kind of Hemingway criticism we are dealing with here, consider that is his opening sentence Ward establishes his research credentials by praising "Kenneth S. Lynn's brilliant reassessment" of Hemingway, which Ward says is rooted in "critical, scrupulous attention" to the fiction. Alas, would it were so, and alas for Ward, who seems to be one of the three readers in the Western World to take seriously Lynn's mishmash of pseudo-biography and pseudo-criticism. Perhaps we should not be too hard on Ward, since he seems to have discovered Lynn before he discovered Hemingway. In any case, the heart of the problem is the worm, that worm which gnaws at the heart of Ward, of every vermiphobe; since his argument about Jake's "hollowness" (and thus about the novel's ultimate meaning) pivots on the fishing scene, I will just list here his main assertions about Jake's fishing, together with my interlinear response: (1) "In a style that the British call coarse fishing, Jake uses worms"; referring to Jake's fishing as "coarse fishing" is questionable, at best. British angling writers generally use the term "coarse fishing" to refer to the pursuit of fish other than trout—that is, "coarse" fish, not fishing. In any case, what is known as the art of clear-water worming, which is the art Jake is practicing, is not, by any definition, coarse fishing. On these matters, Charles Cotton's classic seventeenth-century treatise may be consulted, or such standard twentieth-century British angling writers as Alexander Mackie, James Robb and Sidney Spencer. Clear-water worming, as they have it, is as sportsmanlike, as difficult and as scientific as fly-fishing. (2) After Jake finishes what Ward sneeringly refers to as his "dredging for trout," he further confirms his slothful, unsportsmanlike character when he "lies down on the bank of the stream, reads and . . . falls asleep." Since Ward says this twice in less than one page, and he oddly associates it with what he imagines to be Jake's apathetic, "uncaring" character, it is clear that Ward has something against reading and sleeping, as well as worms. (3) "The point is," Ward writes, "that the ethics of trout fishing demand that the fisherman cast an artificial fly using the lightest tackle possible. Bill does fish correctly." The point is that in fact the ethic of trout fishing demands no such thing; the cult of fly-fishing makes the demand. (4) "It cannot be accidental that Hemingway, the outdoorsman whose father drilled into him the correct ways of fishing and hunting, depicts Jake fishing in a way that would be anathema to any sportsman." The most charitable response here is "no comment." But it is necessary to point out that the anathema here may be found in Ward's prose, his analysis, his views of Hemingway, of fishing. (5) "Jake's fishing subverts the ethic of the outdoorsman as it reinforces Lynn's contention that Jake is a person adrift, disconnected from both people and beliefs." No, Jake's fishing subverts nothing but the "ethic," if we must call it that, of the egregious fly-cultist. Nor is there one shred of evidence in the fishing scene, or anywhere else in the novel, to support the bizarre view that Jake is "a person adrift, disconnected from both people and beliefs." All the evidence argues forcefully to the contrary, if we read the novel, not the fly-book. (6) Finally, Ward concluded that because "Jake does not fly fish" he is "a man past caring," a lazy, debilitated character who lacks passion. Repeating for the third time his favorite point, and echoing Lynn again, Ward adds that Hemingway, too, "like Jake, after uncaringly catching his limit of trout as quickly as possible... wanted only to lie under a tree, to read, to sleep." What *are* we to do with such pure driven nonsense? First of all, Hemingway is not Jake. Jake is not Hemingway. Second, we see again Ward's heartfelt bias against sleep, against reading. It is obvious that Ward does not want his fishermen to read, for if Ward had read *The Sun Also Rises* with any care, instead of worming his way through one scene, he would see that Jake is anything but "a man past caring," passionless and adrift; if Ward would put away his fly-book, he might even come to see that Jake is the committed, engaged, ethical, moral, spiritual and passionate center of the novel.

It is curious, given his aversion to sleep, that Ward fails to notice that old slugabed Bill sleeps late, while Jake gets up early to dig the worms. It is even more curious that Ward and the many other vermiphobes who berate Jake for fishing with worms, fail to note that they are fishing with Jake's tackle, Jake's flies, and, since Jake is the host here, bringing a friend to one of his sacred fishing places; it is a function of his decency, civility, generosity, that he gives his tackle and his fly-book to his friend on that first day of fishing. (Would Jake be redeemed for the vermiphobes if we knew that he fly-fished on all the other days?) Moreover, Jake knows, and the vermiphobes apparently do not know, that it is standard fishing wisdom, and every well-instructed trout fisherman knows, that the art of clear-water worm-fishing is practiced from mid-June to mid-August, that time of the year when other methods are at a discount. Finally, Jake knows where he is going to fish, and that brings us back to why it matters that this is the Fabrica, not the Irati. The Fabrica is a much smaller stream with much more shoreline growth, and many more obstacles for the fly-fisherman than would be encountered on the Irati. The Fabrica is ideal for clear-water worming. Jake knows this, Hemingway knows this; nobody else, vermiphobe or not, has ever noticed.

The truly disturbing thing, the profoundly disconcerting matter in Ward's diatribe against Jake is not so much that, yet once more, he raises this old chestnut about Jake's use of worms, as that in doing so he plays into the hands of the 60ish view, the then fashionable but now quaintly dated mode of denigrating Hemingway as man and sportsman, and in the process he completely misses what the *writer*, what the fiction, was about. And the saddest thing of all is that he is led down this logy path by some Beanie-weenie Orvis-nervous niggling view of the lowly worm, the noble worm. No, Hemingway was not, Jake is not, a "mere wormer"; they were bait *and* fly fishermen, sportsman of the highest order, aficionados with a disciplined and passionate code, with sufficient amplitude and wisdom to include the noble worm in the codification. Fishing, we remind ourselves, is a spiritual exercise related in some fashion to Saint Ignatius of Loyola's technique of the "composition of place"; fishing is not the nitpicking technical drill of the ill-informed, ill-tempered, ideologically and piscatorially correct cultist. So, the next time we hear that patronizing song and dance, that silly up-tilted tonality, that fly-on-the-nose (and in the head) sneer— Hemingway, or Jake: "mere wormers"—as I have heard it all too many times—you'll know where to find me: digging worms, with Jake, in the sacred earth of Roncevaux.

I should not bring this worm-cankered homily to a close without noting one other property of worms that is more literary and spiritual than piscatorial—that is, the traditional image of the work as an elegant and eloquent *memento mori*. Fly-tying and fly-fishing may sometimes be an intricate and elegant imitation of life; make it worms, however, for those who wish to think on death. Fly, if you will, fly-fish if you wish to avoid meditation. But *we* may choose to "talk of graves, of worms and epitaphs"; *we* may join Jake and Richard II in saying "For God's sake, let us sit upon the ground / And tell stories of the death of Kings—" (*Richard II*, III, ii, 145–156). *We* may choose to remember what Jake knows, what Hamlet knew: "A man may fish with the worm that hath eat of a king, and eat of a fish that hath fed of that worm" (*Hamlet* IV, iii, 28–30). And before we dismiss this "convocation of politic worms" (*Hamlet* IV, iii, 21), which may or may not be trying Jake's "long preserved virginity," we should recall that even old Poe, that Virginia fisherman, knew "That the play is the tragedy, 'Man', / And its hero the Conqueror Worm" (*The Conqueror Worm*). Still, I prefer to go with old Izaak, that wise wormer, that complete Angler, who tells us joyfully: "I love any discourse of rivers, and fish and fishing" (*Complete Angler* Ch. 18). This, then, has been a discourse of rivers, a necessarily vermicentric discourse, the best kind for the banks of the Fabrica. And if some vermiphobic fly-fishing Hemingway purist has been hereby deprived of his or her Iratic-dreams, if such a reader objects to my pervasive unorthodoxy in the matter of rivers and fishing in *The Sun Also Rises*—well, then, as some fine old bishop said, "Orthodoxy is *my* doxy, heterodoxy is another man's doxy." So we have come full circle, back to Hemingway's precisely ordered landscape, and we must seek, and we will find, Jake fishing worms in the Fabrica. As for all the rest? It's sort of what we have instead of worms.

NOTES

1. The information presented here is based on three sources: the text of *The Sun Also Rises*, the Mapa Topografico Excursionista of the Roncesvalles quadrant published by *Editorial Alpina* (Barcelona), and the writer's first-hand knowledge of the area dating back some three decades; this includes extensive walking in the country here discussed, local inquiry in the various villages of the area, tours of some back-country trails with the local forest ranger, and so on. However, it should be noted that the conclusions reached here can be confirmed by any good map-and-text reader without ever leaving home—that is, the essential geographical conclusions.

2. Auritz is the Basque name for Burguete. In this region of Spain, as in all the Basque provinces on both sides of the French-Spanish border, the reader and scholar-traveler may at times be confused by current signage practices and by directions given during local inquiry. Presently, both the Spanish and Basque names of places and villages are given on most signs in the region. However, in some places, the Spanish names have been blacked out, painted over; and, if you inquire locally, you may be given only Basque place-names. This does not seem to be the practice in Burguete, however; local inquiry there suggests that Auritz is a name for the village that never has been much employed, and it is only rarely used now, even with the heightened political consciousness of the Basque community in recent decades. Burguete, of course, is the diminutive form of *Burg*; and the ancient name of Burguete was *Burgo de Roncesvalles*, a fact in which some locals take pride. In fact, Burguete was the first, the original place that bore the name Roncesvalles. This fact may have no direct bearing on the argument of this essay, but it will serve to remind readers that Burguete is not a randomly chosen venue for Jake's fishing trip and mountain idyll. Jake is there very much by design, not accidentally, not incidentally, not because Burguete is "cheap," not because the best fishing near Pamplona is around Burguete—reasons which are often advanced—and not because it is close to the Irati. Actually, it is a good distance from the Irati. Rather, as I have argued elsewhere in some detail, Jake stays at Roncevaus-Burguete for one reason: he sojourns there, in this great pilgrimage center, in this "capitale spirtuelle de L'Europe (Burgo 7), because he is a historically and religiously engaged pilgrim, a fact that is central to the novel's overall spiritual design.

3. Over the years, many of my students—as well as many literary critics who discuss this scene without close attention to the text—have assumed that Jake and Bill head out on their walk more or less at "the crack of dawn." Clearly, given the details Hemingway presents, this is not the case. Of course, it might be argued that fiction-time is not clock-time, and that Hemingway is free to move the real-time clock backward and forward as he pleases. Certainly this is true (though it may more likely be a sign of sloppy fiction-technique), if it serves some narrative purpose. However, there is no apparent purpose here; indeed it is precision that dictates the presentation of other details of the walk to the fishing site. The time that they set

out from the inn does signify, then, for it has a direct bearing on whether they fish the Irati or the Fabrica; in the rime-scheme of the novel—with Jake finished with his fishing and settled down under a tree to read by "a little past noon"—it is clear that not enough time has been allowed for them to walk all the way to the Irati.

4. Obviously, regarding the duration of the walk from Burguete to the Fabrica, a good many variables could be factored into any calculation. For example, when a large group recently took this walk, under my direction, the elapsed time was much better than three-and-a-half hours. But that included certain diversions and delays, such as a break at the Collado de Nabala and the sudden appearance of an enraged bull in the midst of the group of walkers. To be sure, a walker in good shape and concerned only to cover distance in the shortest time could probably do this walk in two-and-a-half hours. But, as per local tradition—the view of farmers, shepherds, the government rangers who patrol this country, and the residents of both Burguete and Fabrica, all of whom I have queried on this matter—it is normally a walk of "about three hours." As for other textual details which confirm that they fish the Fabrica, it might be noted that the "white house under some trees on the hillside" (118), which Jake sees just after he says they were "tired" as they came "into the valley of the Rio de la Fabrica," is still there, through not visible today (from Jake's trail) because the trees have grown up. The government ranger at Fabrica, who agrees with my conclusions about the site of Jake's fishing, who has studied the text of *The Sun Also Rises* in the light of his deep and detailed knowledge of the local terrain, pointed this out to me, adding that this "casa blanca" was as much of a firm location-determinant as all the other details in the text. It should be noted here, for the reader with access to a topographical map, that the site pinpointed by Hemingway, by Jake, as the place of their fishing, is in the immediate area of the confluence of the Barranco de Itolaz and the Barranco de Txangoa, at the hamlet of Fabrica. Although Jake, technically, is fishing what the maps designate as the Itolaz, local usage refers to this stream as the Fabrica. As for the additional twelve-to-fifteen kilometers to the Irati, this kilometrage of course refers to Hemingway's favorite place on the Irati (see, e.g., the Nov. 1924 letter cited in the text); to get there, Jake and Bill would have to walk many more hours, through truly difficult terrain, beyond the Barrio Larraun, over the Collado Orion, past the present site of the Embalse de Irabea to somewhere in the neighborhood of the Casas de Irati and the Ermita de Nuestra Senora de las Nieves—that is, to the headwaters of the Irati, at the point where it flows into Spain from France and the true Foret d'Iraty. As Hemingway says in the letter, you cannot do that walk and return in one day. It is possible, however, to follow the Fabrica on down to its confluence with the Irati, an additional four-plus kilometers from the place where Jake and Bill stop to fish the Fabrica. This would add another eight-plus kilometers to the round-trip walk. Diehard students and Irati-aficionados, determined to assert, against all the evidence, that Jake and Bill do fish the Irati will have to settle for this spot as the only site on the Irati where Jake and Bill could even conceivably have fished in the rendered action. But, if we know how to read the text, where all the details say they did *not* fish the Irati and they *did* fish the Fabrica, even this fond and forced conception must yield to the precisely rendered geography, to the *facts* of the novel. One other point, which may address the subtextual or extratextual concerns of some readers: it is somewhat amusing to hear people belligerently insist that no "true trout fisherman" would stop to fish at the Fabrica when the celebrated Irati "is only

fifteen minutes away." There are several answers to such bemused nonsense. First of all, there is the reason the text explicitly gives; they are "tired" when they hit the Fabrica, so they stop there and spend a most pleasant day. Second, it takes more than "fifteen minutes" to cover the four-plus kilometers to the confluence of the Fabrica and the Irati. Round-trip, at least an extra hour, an hour that Jake and Bill do not have, as demonstrated above. Moreover, and most importantly, it is patent absurdity to suggest that "true trout fishermen" always prefer the broad famous rivers to the lesser-known, less-fished smaller waters. In fact, the reverse is more likely to be the case. On this account, I'll settle for the wisdom of an 88-year old fishing friend, a native of the Catskills, who stopped fishing the famous trouting-shrine rivers like the Beaverkill more than fifty years ago, preferring the smaller creeks and the feeder streams: "Why would a man want to work through them crowds around them famous pools and rivers? All them trouty city-folk fools—what do they know about feeder streams, about real trouting? Not a damn thing, if you ask me."

5. Even to the casual observer, the number of abandoned farm buildings—in fact abandoned villages or hamlets—in this area will suggest that Hemingway's romantically designated "wild country" was really well- developed pastoral country. As the booklet that accompanies the Editorial Alpina map of the region reminds us, these days "la transhumancia esta en decadencia" (9). But not too long ago, in fact when Hemingway was there in the 1920s, there were about five times as many sheep and more than twice as many cattle as there are today—with, of course, far more shepherds to tend them, and more farms and villages to serve the transhumant economy.

6. It should be said, given my exact delineation of the place where Jake fished, where he put the wine in the spring, and so on, that this spot is just at the edge of the village of Fabrica, about a hundred yards upstream from where the stonework of the factory begins. Thus it would be possible for a precisionist to argue that Jake doesn't see the factory, or the village. Hardly likely, however. Jake is wounded, but he's not blind; and he's been there before, so he knows very well that he's fishing in the village and the valley of the factory.

7. David C. Ward, "Poor Sports: Hemingway, Jake Barnes and the Sporting Life in The Sun Also Rises," Aethlon 6 (Spring 1989): 21–25.

IV

Getting It Right

12

Reading the Names Right

Miriam B. Mandel

"Names go to the bone—"

The Garden of Eden

In *To Have and Have Not*, the novelist Richard Gordon announces that "A writer has to know about everything" (140). In a 1952 letter to Malcolm Cowley, Hemingway made a similar claim: "Ideally," he wrote, "a man should know everything." But, he added, "Erudition shouldn't show."[1] Elsewhere, as we all know, Hemingway indicated that as much as seven-eighths of his material doesn't show.[2] The search for this alarmingly large mass of absent materials has energized generations of scholars work—in biography, psychology, geography, and manuscript studies—has produced many and valuable insights. While welcoming all these methods of enriching our reading, I would propose that the most primary of our materials—the published texts themselves—have not yet been fully exploited. Excited, inspired and sometimes intoxicated by extratextual information, we should not lose sight of that which is, like Poe's purloined letter, in plain view.

In creating his fiction, Hemingway drew on his considerable arsenal of knowledge, although only a fraction of it is apparent on the surface of the text.[3] But that material which is present in the text can, if we look at it as steadily as Nick looked into the pools of the Big Two-Hearted River, reveal "the big trout" that are not visible "at first." In particular, the proper names that appear in the novels and stories guide us to the facts, rumors, and feelings that attach to the names but that the text does not provide. By retrieving some of that absent erudition, "the part that doesn't show," we can clarify our understanding of Hemingway's characters, of his central concerns, and of his methods of composition.

As a posthumously edited and published novel, *Islands in the Stream* (*IS*) is particularly difficult to evaluate. But our attention need not be directed exclusively at the problems—and the ensuing horrors—of the editing. Characters in this novel, as in any novel, are defined by what they know, what they say, what they notice. As a painter himself, Thomas Hudson of course knows a great deal about painting, and we are not surprised at his mentioning Cezanne, Eakins, Gris, Masson, Picasso, and several other painters—20 in all. Living in Cuba, he is also familiar with well-known contemporary Cubans, like the dictator Fulgencio Batista, the baseball player and manager Adolfo Luque, and the boxing promoter and sports commentator Pincho Gutierrez. But these are not the only names he knows.

As Hudson is driven from his home to the city of Havana, the narrator records the thoughts that drift through Hudson's mind, among them a brief reference to a minor event in Cuban history: "Ahead now beyond the lines of stalled cars and trucks was the hill with the Castle of Atares where they had shot Colonel Crittenden and the others when that expedition failed down at Bahia Honda" (*IS* 246). Who was Crittenden and why does Hemingway allow Hudson to mention him?

William L. Crittenden, born in 1822, was a professional soldier, trained at West Point and graduating in 1845. He served for a year in Texas, fought in the War with Mexico from 1846 to 1848, and resigned from the U.S. Army in March 1849. In 1851 he sailed to Cuba in the second of two expeditions organized by Narciso Lopez, the Venezuelan-born freedom-fighter who was anxious to liberate Cuba from Spanish rule. On the night of 11–12 August 1851, their boat, the *Pampero*, unloaded about 550 troops, mostly Americans, near Bahia Honda, Cuba.[4] The men were, of course, attacked by the colonial authorities. Lopez had expected the local citizenry to support his attempt to liberate them, but they preferred to stay out of the fight, and Lopez and his troops were soon defeated by the colonial leadership. Crittenden and his contingent of men were among those who were captured, tried, condemned to death, and executed. Crittenden himself was shot on August 16, 1851, at the Castle of Atares, Havana Harbor, shortly after his 28th birthday.[5] Not only are Hudson's facts accurate, but he connects them to himself (and thus reveals his birthdate) when he notes that "the expedition failed ... forty years before he was born" (*IS* 246).

Hudson gives other evidence of familiarity with matters unrelated to his profession as painter. In Part III, during the sea chase in which he will lose his life, Hudson notes differences between actual conditions at sea and what the navigation charts describe. He concludes that "many things have happened since the U.S.S. *Nokomis* had boats sounding in here" (*IS* 454). The *Nokomis*—a real boat—was a converted 243-foot private yacht that saw service in World War I and did in fact survey Mexican and Caribbean waters. With the U.S.S. *Hannibal*, the *Nokomis* surveyed the north coast of Cuba in the years from 1924 to 1930. The results were published in the official Hydrographic Office Charts, Nos. 1311, 1417, 2625, and 5162.[6] When Hudson navigates the cays off the northern coast of Cuba, he is using charts that are about 15 years old. He notices that "There was plenty of water although no such water showed on the chart" (*IS* 454). His remarks indicate not only that Hudson has read the charts carefully but that he is interested enough to notice and remember when and by whom they were prepared—information that is not relevant to his needs as a sailor.

Taken together, Hudson's remarks about Crittenden and the *Nokomis* offer an entry to critics interested in evaluating Hudson's personality and his ability to make commitments. Hudson has been accused of drifting through life, of using his work as an escape from the reality around him, of being unwilling or unable to commit himself to people or places. But these seemingly throw-away remarks—about Crittenden and the *Nokomis*—round out the character. They indicate that Hudson has invested time and study in the history of Cuba and its waters. It's not surprising that he mentions public figures like Batista, Luque or Gutierrez. But his knowledge of Cuba is deeper than that, and it shows his commitment to the place where he lives.

In other novels as well, the names that the author allows into his character's thoughts and speeches can help the reader determine the character's interests, education and values. *Across the River and Into the Trees* (*ARIT*) is sometimes called Hemingway's *Othello* novel, or his Venetian, or Italian, or Dantean, or "calculus" novel, but seldom a military novel. Its main character, Colonel Cantwell, is usually considered in terms of his creator, his accidents and illnesses, his ego, his age, his wounded heart, head, and hands, or his relationship to his beloved. But during the 300 pages of *Across the River and into the Trees*, more than 30 historical military figures occur to Richard Cantwell's mind, far more than the four military figures Frederic Henry thinks of in the similarly sized *A Farewell to Arms*, and only 6 fewer than the 37 with whom Robert Jordan shows himself to be familiar in *For Whom the Bell Tolls*, which is half again as long. Frederic Henry and Robert Jordan are often, and rightly, evaluated in terms of their relationships to military activity. So should Richard Cantwell who is, after all, a career officer.

Like Robert Jordan, Cantwell mentions many military figures from the American Civil War. He also refers to military leaders from the two World Wars, references that would come naturally to Americans of his generation. But Hemingway also has Cantwell refer to two eighteen-century Europeans, Frederick the Great, king of Prussia (1740–1786), and Maurice de Saxe, the French soldier (1696–1750), both of whom Cantwell correctly identifies as authors: Frederick the Great wrote *Anti-Machiavell* and Maurice de

Saxe's *Mes Rêveries* was published posthumously. Cantwell is also familiar with the work of the Chinese philosopher and military strategist T'Sun Su (more commonly transliterated as Sun Tzu), whose work *The Art of War*, written over 2,000 years ago, is a classic of Chinese military history and theory. These three brief and bookish references (*ARIT* 135) are quite appropriate to Cantwell, emphasizing his education at the Virginia Military Institute and the College des Maréchaux (*ARIT* 272, 290).

In addition, Cantwell mentions another, less familiar military figure, Colonel du Picq, whom he describes as the last of the French military thinkers (*ARIT* 27). Who was this man, and why does Cantwell admire him? Du Picq—whose family name was actually Ardant du Picq—is indeed regarded as one of the most original and influential of the French military theorists. In the mid-nineteenth century he shifted French military thinking away from the traditional, romantic, heroic view of combat that relied on massive military formations and on the top ranks of leadership to inspire its armies to victories—that is, the star system. Before Ardant du Picq, lower- and middle-echelon officers were not expected to provide much leadership, and the troops were therefore largely unsupervised and undisciplined. The infantry suffered great losses under this plan, and the untrained foot soldiers tended to decamp in disorder when exposed to fire. Ardant du Picq's own combat experience, as well as his understanding of human psychology, led him to develop a less romantic, more realistic attitude. In two books about combat, *Etudes du combat d'après l'antique* (published in 1868) and in *Etudes sur le combat* (published posthumously in 1880), he argued that an army's success depends on meticulous cooperation among all sections of the military machine, on the initiative and intelligence of commanders at all ranks and, more importantly, on the psychological state of the individual soldier.[7] Although Cantwell mentions Ardant du Picq only once and then very briefly, the reference indicates his grasp of military history and theory, and shows us how his mind works. He understands, approves, and remembers Ardant du Picq's theories because, like him, Cantwell's main concern is the infantry, the troops, and not the reputations of their leaders. Cantwell sneers at contemporary leaders—stars like Montgomery and Eisenhower who, he says, were primarily interested in their careers and reputations. Because Cantwell's criticism of these generals is so crude, it can make us reject him rather than them, and it may obscure the fact that Cantwell does mourn the loss of his men more than he mourns the loss of his own rank. Ardant du Picq appeals to him because he was the first French military thinker to value the infantry soldier and to downplay the grandiose leader. His admiration of du Picq is one with his rejection of "those jerks" and with his unvoiced remark, "Christ, I am opposed to the excessive butcher bill" (*ARIT* 188).

Other names in the novel reinforce this theme of concern for others that the reference to du Picq suggests. Characters in this novel are more prone to gift giving than are most of Hemingway's other characters. The nature, number, and quality of gifts, both actual and intended, mark gifts as a central motif. The aristocratic Renata, for example, gives Cantwell three elegant gifts: an inscribed silver flask, a portrait of herself, and a fistful of antique emeralds. Like the priest in *A Farewell to Arms*, Cantwell chooses gifts carefully to please and honor the recipient: sausage for the dog Bobby, a jeep engine for the boatman, wild ducks for Arnaldo the waiter and, for Renata, a jeweled pin. He would also like to give her "all my worldly goods," which consist of his books, his medals, his uniforms, and "two good shot-guns" (*ARIT* 290–291). More important than these are the things he does not have but would like to have made to order for her: a hand-sewn, down-filled jacket, "double-breasted with no pocket on the right and . . . a chamois shooting patch so the gun butt would never catch" (*ARIT* 189), and guns: "a good Purdey 12, not too damn light, or a pair of Boss over and unders. She should have guns as good as she is. I suppose a pair of Purdey's" (*ARIT* 290). Compared to the emeralds Renata gives him, Cantwell's offerings seem mean—unless we know something about the pedigree and quality of the Boss and Purdey guns.

The Boss family of gunmakers can trace its expertise back to the great eighteenth-century gunmaker Joseph Manton, who trained William Boss, who then trained his son Thomas Boss (1790–1857), who in 1812 founded the company still known as Boss & Co., Ltd. (current address: 13 Dover Street, London). Ranked among the best in the field, the Boss company produces fine guns in limited editions and will refuse orders if there is any risk of pressuring their skilled workers and thus compromising quality. They provided guns for Czar Nicholas and for Queen Victoria and much of her large family. The double-barreled over-and-under model Boss & Co. intro-duced in 1908 or 1909 "represents probably the acme of over-and-under development." In 1950, the year *Across the River and into the Trees* was published, a pair of Boss over-and-unders cost about $1,000.[8] Cantwell wants to give Renata a "pair of Boss over and unders." That would certainly be an elegant and generous present, expressive of Cantwell's nature and of his regard for her.

The equally famous Purdey family began making guns in 1814. The founder of the company, James Purdey (1784–1863), also learned his trade from the famous gunmaker Joseph Manton. He is known to his descendants and admirers as James the Founder, and his son, who took control of the firm in 1858 and died in 1909 at the age of 81, was and is still referred to as James the Younger. Like the Boss company, Purdey's firm also built guns for European royalty. Among their famous customers was Charles Darwin, who in 1831 acquired from Purdey the weapons, spare parts, ammunition, and other equipment he needed for his historic journey on the *Beagle*. The firm, which moved from Oxford Street to its current location on South Audley St., London, in 1862, has maintained its reputation for fine workmanship throughout its 180-year history. Its customers are carefully measured, the guns are individually made and, like all fine handcrafted goods, they are registered and numbered.[9] A year or two before Hemingway began writing *Across the River and into the Trees*, the King of England was casting about for a suitable wedding present for his daughter Elizabeth's fiancé, Philip Mountbatten. Because only the best would do for the future husband of the future queen, King George ordered a couple of guns from Purdey for Philip. And only the best, thinks Cantwell, is good enough for Renata: "She should have guns as good as she is. I suppose a pair of Purdey's" (*ARIT* 290).

Although far from rich, Cantwell is well acquainted with fine guns. In fact, there is a Purdey gun in Cantwell's family, which Cantwell's older brother inherited from their grandfather (*ARIT* 92–93). If we look at the names Purdey and Boss, then, we can learn something about Cantwell's family background, his generous spirit, and his attitude toward his beloved.

Even the well-explicated and much admired *The Sun Also Rises* presents names whose potential has not been fully exploited. Familiar as we are with this novel, how many of us include Jake's reference to Lenglen when we assess his attitude to and presentation of Robert Cohn? Tennis buffs know that Suzanne Lenglen (1899–1938) was the French women's singles champion in 1920 to 1923 and that in 1925 and 1926 won both the French singles and doubles crowns. She was the Wimbledon singles champion from 1919 to 1923 and won both the singles and doubles championship (with Elizabeth Ryan) in 1925. She was a feisty, combative player who argued with referees when the call went against her. Her "high emotion and fierce desire for victory" made her performances exciting and dramatic.[10] She appears in the text when Jake attempts to show "Robert Cohn clearly" (*SAR* 45). Jake tries, or pretends to try, to be fair but, tortured by jealousy of Robert, he is consistently unfair. He writes of Cohn that "he loved to win at tennis. He probably loved to win as much as Lenglen, for instance. On the other hand, he was not angry at being beaten" (*SAR* 45). By describing Cohn's temper as milder than a woman's, Jake offers an insult similar to the "steer" remarks made by Mike Campbell (*SAR* 141). Because Jake is more subtle than Mike, his insult is more likely to be overlooked. It is expressed in only one word: Lenglen.

Among the many insults hurled at Robert Cohn are those included in Frances Clyne's tirade, early in the novel, when she sneers at him: "You're not a young writer. Are you, Robert? You're thirty-four." She goes on to compare him unfavorably to two literary giants: Thomas Hardy, who was then in his mid–80s, and Anatole France, who had died in 1924 at the age of 80. At 34, Frances tells Cohn, he is a failure as a writer. What Clyne probably does not know is that Anatole France was 35 years old when his first volume of stories, *Jocaste et le chat maigre* (1879), was published, and 37 when his first novel appeared (*The Crimes of Sylvester Bonnard*, 1881).

At 34 Robert is already working on his second novel, his first having been "praised... pretty highly" in New York (*SAR* 8).[11] Frances Clyne's patently unfair comparison actually shows Cohn to advantage—and Frances to disadvantage—when we look at it more closely.

Another overlooked name is that of the very minor figure of the bullfighter Algabeno. Algabeno is mentioned twice in *The Sun Also Rises*, first as an example of a bullfighter ruined by the flattery of foreigners, mostly women, and again to report that he has suffered a hand injury (*SAR* 172, 185). These two details point to two different bullfighters, father and son. The reference to the hand wound and the nickname suggest Jose Garcia Rodriguez (1875–1947), the elder Algabeno, a serious man who often suffered hand injuries. This matador retired from the bullring in 1912. The dates of the action (the appearance of Belmonte indicates the San Fermin fiesta of July 1925) and the weak personality of the bullfighter suggest his son, Jose Garcia Carranza, known variously as el senorito Pepe, Pepe Algabeno, Algabeno, or Algabeno II. Born in 1902, this bullfighter was at the height of his career in the mid–1920s. Hemingway would have seen or heard about him during his visits to Pamplona for the 1923, 1924, and 1925 Sanfermines, as Algabeno fought in Pamplona on 12 and 13 July 1923, and again the next year, on 11 and 13 July 1924, performing so well that in 1925 he was contracted to appear on 11 July at the *gran corrida extraordinaria*, sharing the bill with the great Juan Belmonte and Marcial Lalanda. On the preceding day, however, he was injured in Madrid, at a special *corrida* in benefit of the Red Cross: He was hurt in the hip and arm and had to cancel his Pamplona engagement. Hemingway altered the facts when he had his fictional Algabeno suffer a hand injury in Madrid. The change has the effect of recalling the elder Algabeno.[12] The two references to Algabeno join the physical weak point of the father with the psychological weakness of the son.[13] Not only the name but also the characteristics of the fictional Algabeno point simultaneously at a flawed father and his flawed son.

We all know that in creating Pedro Romero, Hemingway also conflated two real matadors, in this case two heroic figures: the young prodigy Cayetano Ordonez Aguilera (1904–1974), who replaced the injured Algabeno on 11 July 1925, and the legendary eighteenth-century Pedro Romero (1754–1839), reputed to have killed all the bulls of his long career in the most honorable and dangerous way: *recibiendo* (standing still to receive the charging bull).[14] Both these matadors came from Ronda. In creating the fictional Pedro, Hemingway chose a name and a birthplace that would connect the present to the past.

The seamless, patrilineal joining of generations that the names of Algabeno and Romero bring to our attention emphasizes the absence of fathers among the British and American characters. None of the main characters ever mentions a father. Mothers are more prominent than fathers—Mike, Brett, Frances and Bill all seem to have one—but they are mentioned only to be mocked and dismissed as irrelevant. We know most about Cohn's family—his parents, ex-wife, and three children—but even Cohn wastes his patrimony and is separated from his children, who will grow up with a stepfather. There is no continuity. The present generation of British and American characters is totally estranged from its forebears, male and female; they are unmarried, childless and likely to remain so.[15] Their isolation is an important thematic concern in the novel. But the enormous distance that separates them from their parents and their past does not exist among the Spaniards, whose very names are a testimony to tradition and continuity.

"Names," Hemingway wrote in *The Garden of Eden*, "go to the bone" (*GE* 141). Hemingway's texts present a great many historical names: about 70 in *The Sun Also Rises*, more than 100 each in *Islands in the Stream* and *Across the River and Into the Trees*. Because most of these names are offered without adjectival adornment or narrative pointing, it is all too easy to dismiss them as background details or even to mistake them for fictional constructs that have no significance other than the solidity that proper names bestow upon the text. Names mentioned only once or twice may even be overlooked entirely. My work has convinced me that these historical names—all of these names—are potentially helpful and that recontextualizing them is a necessary exercise. It enables us to retrieve the erudition that does not show, and thus gives us information that can help us to define character, to examine compositional tactics, and to clarify important motifs, themes, ideas and ideologies.

We know that Hemingway took a great deal of trouble to get his words right. In particular he valued the concrete detail, the specific noun—the proper name. He was a great artist, and, mostly he did get the names right, even the background names. It behooves us, who hold his reticent texts in our hands, to read those names right.

NOTES

1. To Cowley, Hemingway explained that if "everything" is included in the art the results can be disastrous: "You know Ezra [Pound] can't leave any erudition true or false out of a poem and what the results are sometimes. . . . Erudition shouldn't show" (qtd. in Brasch 222–223). Twenty years earlier, in 1932, Hemingway had made a similar remark: "A writer who appreciates the seriousness of writing so little that he is anxious to make people see he is formally educated, cultured or well-bred is merely a popinjay" (*DIA* 192).

2. Hemingway presented his iceberg theory in *Death in the Afternoon* (1932):

If a writer of prose knows enough about what he is writing about he may omit *things that he knows* and the reader, if the writer is writing truly enough, will have a feeling of those things as strongly as though the writer had stated them. The dignity of movement of an iceberg is due to only one-eighth of it being above water. A writer who omits things because he does not know them only makes hollow places in his writing. A writer who appreciates the seriousness of writing so little that he is anxious to make people see he is formally educated, cultured or well-bred is merely a popinjay. (192, emphasis added)

Interviewed by George Plimpton, Hemingway elaborated:

I always try to write on the principle of the iceberg. There is seven-eighths of it underwater for every part that shows. *Anything you know* you can eliminate and it only strengthens your iceberg. It is the part that doesn't show. If a writer omits something because he does not know it then there is a hole in the story. (*Writers at work: The Paris Review Interviews, Second Series*, [New York: Viking, 1963] (125, emphasis added)

Hemingway claimed to have developed this principle early in his writing career. When writing "Out of Season," he "had omitted the real end of it which was that the old man hanged himself. This was omitted on my new theory that you could omit anything *if you knew* what you omitted and the omitted part would strengthen the story and make people feel something more than they understood" (*A Moveable Feast* 75, emphasis added).

    3. Although unschooled in the formal sense—he never went to college—Hemingway was erudite. As Michael Reynolds, James D. Brasch and Joseph Sigman have shown, he read a great deal in a variety of fields and in several languages. He was no "dumb ox."

    4. According to some reports, Crittenden led the assault and, when it failed, he and his men attempted to abandon Cuba in launches. Other reports indicate that Crittenden and a small contingent of about 50 men had stayed aboard the *Pampero* to wait for reinforcements and organize supplies and that, when they began to suspect that the incursion had been unsuccessful, went ashore to investigate.

    5. The loss of life was considerable, only 170 of the 548 men surviving: see "Cuba" *Enciclopedia Universal Ilustrada* XVI (1913): 836. Crittenden's brief career is summarized in Cullum II 249, Item 1271; see also "Crittenden [*sic*], Guillermo" in *Enciclopedia Universal Ilustrada* XVI (1913): 411–412. Narciso Lopez's first expedition to Cuba, in July 1851, had also been unsuccessful.

    6. Nelson 86–88, 98; *Dictionary of American Naval Fighting Ships* V: 102. Additional information about the *Nokomis* was supplied by R. P. Dinsmore, of the Woods Hole Oceanographic Institution, Woods Hole, MA (letter to author and enclosures, 11 February 1991); by A. J. Booth, Deputy Director of Naval History, Department of the Navy, Washington, DC (letter to author and enclosures, 4 February 1991), and by R. M. Browning Jr., Historian, U.S. Coast Guard, Washington DC, and Lysle B. Gray, Executive Director of the American Boat and Yacht Council, Inc., Millersville MD (letters and enclosures, 22 January 1991). The *Nokomis* was retired from the Navy Hydrographic Office in 1934 and decommissioned in 1938. Early in World War II, she was acquired by the U.S. Coast Guard, renamed the *Bodkin*, and slated for renovation to make her fit to fight U-boats in American waters. Her condition was poor, the U-boat threat abated, and work on the boat was suspended in July 1943. She was scrapped a year later.

    7. See "Ardant du Picq, Charles-Jean-Jacques-Joseph" Balteau III 441–442; "Ardant du Picq, Charles" *Grand Dictionnaire Encyclopédique Larousse*, 1982; "Ardant du Picq" Carrias 257–259. Ardant du Picq was born in 1821 and died in 1870.

    8. My thanks to Mr. D. J. Penn, Keeper of the Department of Exhibits and

Firearms at the Imperial War Museum, London, for information on the Boss and Purdey firearms companies. Mr. Penn explains that Cantwell would want to give Renata two guns because "two shotguns are required for formal, driven game shooting when birds are put up by a line of beaters and driven over the standing 'guns,' who each have a loader (usually a game keeper, servant or chauffeur) who unloads and reloads the second gun while the first is in use. Competently performed, this partnership allows virtually continuous shooting for the brief duration of each drive" (letter to author, 29 July 1991). Mr. A.J.W. Lokatis, Director of Boss & Co., provided detailed information about the Boss & Co., their guns and their prices (letter to author, 3 October 1991). The records of Boss & Co. do not list Hemingway "as an account of order" but Lokatis suggests that Hemingway may have been given a Boss or perhaps purchased one second-hand. According to Carlos Baker, Hemingway shot himself with "a double-barreled Boss shotgun with a tight choke. He had used it for years of pigeon shooting." That gun was cut into pieces, which were buried "in a secret place" (714, 936).

9. Serial No. 1 was produced in 1814 and in 1983 they registered no. 28,600. The present chairman of the board at Purdey's is Richard B. Beaumont, author of *Purdey's: The Guns and the Family* (London: David & Charles, 1984).

10. In 1926, after a quarrel with a Wimbledon referee, Lenglen turned pro, but her career as a professional was short. Like Robert Cohn, she had written one book before the beginning of the novel's events: *Lawn Tennis* (1925). She published two more books: *Lawn Tennis for Girls* (1930) and *Tennis by Simple Exercise* (1937). See "Lenglen, Suzanne" in the *New Columbia Encyclopedia, Encyclopedia Americana*, and the *Oxford Companion to Sports and Games*.

11. Even the jealous Jake must admit that Cohn's first novel "was not really such a bad novel as the critics later called it" (*SAR* 5–6).

12. Bullfighters are often known by nicknames that, if the bullfighter becomes famous, are often used by several members of the family. Nicknames may indicate ethnic origin (e.g., *el qitanillo*, the gypsy) or a salient physical feature (e.g., *el gordito*, the fat one). Most often, they indicate the bullfighter's birthplace: "el Algabeno" refers to Garcia's hometown, La Algaba (Seville). The best source for information about bullfighters is Cossfols monumental encyclopedia *Los Toros*. For the elder Algabeno, see "Garcia Rodriguez, Jose," cossfo III 331–333, and "Algabeno," Silva Aramburu 257. For the son, see "Garcia Carranza, Jose," cossfo III 329–331, and "Algabeno II," Silva Aramburu 280. The younger Algabeno's Pamplona performances are reviewed in the local daily *El pensamiento Navarro*, 13 and 14 July 1923, and 12 and 15 July 1924. The Saturday issue (11 July 1925) announced the arrival of Belmonte and the expected arrival of Algabeno for that afternoon's *gran corrida extraordinaria*. The Madrid Red Cross *corrida* is also reviewed in this issue, including the fact that Algabeno had been injured by both the bulls he had fought on 10 July. The injuries were not seen as serious then, but the Madrid daily *ABC* explained that Algabeno had had to cancel Pamplona because his arm (*brazo*)—not his hand (*mano*)—was inflamed (*ABC* 12 July 1925, 31:1). Algabeno II was killed in the first year of the Spanish Civil War.

13. In *Death in the Afternoon* (1932), Hemingway distinguished clearly between these two matadors, describing the elder Algabeno as "one of the best killers who ever came out of Andalucia" and his son as "the worst faker of them all" (*DIA* 158, 271).

14. For information about Cayetano Ordonez, see "Ordonez y Aguilera, Cayetano," cossfo III 684–688, IV 611, and VI 204. For the legendary bullfighter after whom the fictional Romero is named, see "Romero, Pedro," cossfo III 825–834; "Pedro Romero y lo rondeno," Cossio IV 866–870; and "El coloso del siglo: Pedro Romero," Silva Aramburu 233–235. Ordonez's performances on 11 July 1925 was not overly impressive; the honors of that afternoon went to Marcial Lalanda, who was awarded an ear for his first bull and both ears and the tail for his second. Lalanda clearly outperformed both Belmonte and Ordonez on this afternoon. On the next afternoon, in the last *corrida* of the San Fermin fiesta, Ordonez did earn an ear for his first bull, the only ear he was awarded in the Pamplona Sanfermines of that year. See the reviews of these corridas on the front pages of the Pamplona daily, *El pensamiento Navarro*, 12 and 14 July 1925, and in the Madrid daily *ABC*, 14 July 1925, 14:1. Cayetano Ordonez is the father of Antonio Ordonez Araujo (b. 1932), the bullfighter whom Hemingway extolled in *Dangerous Summer* (1959).

15. Jake, of course, cannot have children. Brett realizes that although Mike Campbell is "my sort of thing," she "can't even marry Mike" (*SAR* 243, 242). Bill Gorton is unattached, both back home and throughout his European travels. Frances Clyne is divorced, bereft of Cohn, and fully convinced that "now I don't think I could get anybody" (*SAR* 47). They are in their mid–30s.

13

Who Wrote Hemingway's *In Our Time*?

Paul Smith

There was a time when I thought I knew the answer to the question in this title, back in the early 1980s when most of us assumed the obvious: It was Ernest Hemingway, of course, although we recognized the intricate web linking him with his character, Nick Adams, and we had been instructed by a number of persuasive studies of the various narrative points of view in the 1925 collection, *In Our Time*.[1]

Between then and now, a decade later, that seemingly simple question has been asked again, and asked in a way that makes the answer a good deal less obvious. A new generation of critics has returned to the issue of the unity of *In Our Time* and, with some of the evidence from Hemingway's manuscripts, has argued for the hypothesis of *a* Nick Adams as the implied author of the stories in that book, and not only those that concern *another* Nick Adams, the character from "Indian Camp" to "Big Two-Hearted River."[2] That's my concern here, and in particular, the evidence for that hypothesis and the consequences for the interpretation of the crucial story, "Indian Camp."

The several arguments for Nick Adams as the implied author of *In Our Time* are complex, so for time's sake I will depend on the one that ranges the farthest and dares the most: Debra A. Moddelmog's 1988 essay "The Unifying Consciousness of... *In Our Time*."[3] And with an apology for summarizing, I take this to be its general structure.

First, the importance of Moddelmog's hypothesis. Reading Nick Adams as the "author" of the *In Our Time* stories may resolve confusions about the book's "unity, structure, vision, and significance," and cast "new light on Nick Adams as a character, both separate from and an extension of Ernest Hemingway" (592).

Second, an admission that although at the time of writing these stories Hemingway did not plan to "attribute any of them to Nick," he realized—sometime in the summer of 1924, one presumes—that since "Nick shared so much of [his] personality and experience that turning him into the author of the stories *ex post facto* required very little work. All Hemingway had to do was supply Nick with the relevant background, specifically a writing career and some post-war history" (594).

Third, the evidence for Hemingway's intention to give Nick a career as a writer in the post-war period is there in the story's original conclusion, later published as "On Writing" in *The Nick Adams Stories* (*NAS*, 1972). It begins with the remark from "On Writing" that, "Nick in the stories was never himself" (*NAS* 238); that is, Nick-as-author was never Nick-as-character in the Nick Adams stories; but since he cites "My Old Man" and refers to only one of the Nick Adams stories ("Indian Camp"), those "stories" might include any or all of those alluded to in the "On Writing" conclusion in addition to those that have Nick as a character. To count: first, the Nick Adams stories "The End of Something," "The Three-Day Blow," "Cross-Country Snow;" and "The Doctor and the Doctor's Wife." Those without Nick as a character but with linking allusions or thematic similarities are "A Very Short Story," "Soldier's Home," "Mr. and Mrs. Elliot," "Cat in the Rain" and "Out of Season." That list includes all of the 1925 edition of *In Our Time*, with the exception of the Nick Adams story "The Battler," written after "Big Two-Hearted River," and "On the Quai of Smyrna," and substituted as an "introduction" in the winter of 1926–1927.[4]

Here the argument deserves a review and a comment on its evidence.

First, it interposes between the reader and the conventional narrator an implied author named Nick Adams. That implied author is, in his own words, *never* the character he creates, whether that character bears his name or not.[5] Thus everything that happens to the character Nick, or anything he thought or imagined, would seem to be un-attributable to the narrator Nick, with the exception of those in "On Writing" in which he claims or implies authorship.

To evaluate this assumption, consider Nick's claim to have written a story called "My Old Man" and then his offer to prove his fine and prescient eye with the remark that "the next week Georges Parfrement was killed at that very jump [where the jockey Butler was killed] and that was the way it looked" (*NAS* 237).

Here, at the outset, we must make a decision. The argument maintains that "we cannot pin down the precise date when Nick wrote any particular story in *In Our Time*" (595). However, we can "pin down" the precise date "Nick Adams" wrote "My Old Man" with a fact discovered by Michael

Reynolds—Reynolds reads the papers, all of them. There was a Georges Parfrement who was killed on or about 18 April 1923, which might place Nick's "composition" of the story in early April of that year, at least six months after Hemingway wrote his version (Reynolds 1989, 105).

Now this may be a trivial fact of history, but I note it since we are told later of our inability to discover the implied author's "actual history . . . because we lack the biographical evidence (letters, memoirs, interviews) that usually fill the gap between an author's life and his fiction, [and] we are left wondering where we might find the real Nick Adams" (596). To speak of an implied author's "actual history" or of him as the "real Nick Adams" is to suggest a rather curious ontology. An "implied author" is, one would suppose, a fictive figure, whether he "exists," so to speak, in the text or not, or has been inferred from evidence in a manuscript, rejected by its "other author with the not uncertain term, 'shit' "(*LTRS* 133). What's troubling is to be asked to imagine what sort of documents would serve as "biographical evidence" of that "real" Nick Adams: a letter from him, but to whom; one of his memoirs, but of what; an interview, but where and when and, indeed, how?

If Nick Adams wrote Hemingway's "My Old Man" and cited Georges Parfrement's death as evidence of "the way it looked" a week or two later, then either Parfrement is a fictive construct, or he is not. If he is, then everything the implied author claims (including, by the way, his writing a story called "My Old Man") is, at most, as fictive as that hapless rider. If, however, the name Parfrement refers to a French jockey who really died in April 1923, then everything else Nick Adams recalls is, at least, as suspect as that evanescent fact from a defective memory.

But for this argument, such questions are quibbles—and, perhaps, rightly so, for neither Hemingway nor his manuscripts suggest that either ontology or epistemology were much on his mind. So the argument moves from matters of "biographical evidence" to the next point.

Since "our main interest is Nick's psyche, we need not worry too much about our inability to sort reality from imagination [for by] looking for repeated patterns and by studying the subjects that Nick chooses to develop as well as his manner of presenting those subjects, we should uncover those fixations of his imagination that reveal his basic outlook on life" (596).

Here, another comment is warranted, for this is the crucial point of the argument. Relieved of the burden of sorting "reality from imagination," we are free to consider those epistemic choices that reveal Nick, in the role of implied author, through his imaginative obsessions and to discover his vision of life.

And that seems fair enough, if only because it has been done before with Joyce's *Dubliners* and Anderson's *Winesburg, Ohio*, two story collections that laid influential hands on Hemingway's. But it seems just as fair to observe that to raise the distinction between "reality and imagination" (whatever those terms mean) in an argument for an implied author of *In Our Time*, and then to dismiss it, is to work both sides of the critical street. If that distinction is troubling, it should be resolved; if it is not, it should not be raised. But since it has been raised, we should recall that the critical concept of an "implied author" was not originally meant to be fleshed out with a life, a wife, or whatever.[6]

These are troubled waters, and not easily bridged; nor, I suspect, will they be until we understand why we want to cross them. It was tried briefly at the 1990 International Hemingway Conference in Boston with a panel discussion gathered to consider the topic of "Nick as Narrator of *In Our Time*." Debra Moddelmog introduced the discussion with these questions: "Why should we want to find . . . self-reflexivity in Hemingway's fiction? Are we trying to make him 'one of us'? . . . [And] do the conceptions of Nick as a novelist of Hemingway as a meta-fictionist make the fictions more complex and interesting; and if so, are we perhaps being New Critics with a vengeance?"[7]

I was on that panel and mumbled, mainly; yet I do not recall any precise answers to those questions. But now, armed with a script, I bring them up again, with my own, I trust, more audible answers.

First, yes, we are trying to make Hemingway "one of us," as every critical generation has, and *has* to, to earn its critical stripes.

Second, yes, the conceptions of Nick as novelist make the fictions more complex and interesting, but only in the way that we, with our meta-fictional bent, define complexity or interest.

And third, yes, the aesthetic criteria the New Critics assumed half a century ago still underlie the assumptions of the meta-fictionist generation. Once again, the intent of the hypothesis that Nick Adams is the implied author of the *In Our Time* stories is to resolve "many confusions about the book's unity, structure, vision, and significance" (592). *Unity* and *structure* are old formalist terms, and they beg the same questions they did 50 years ago: What is so sacrosanct about *unity*? Why do we fix our gaze on the structure of the collection rather than on the individual structures of the stories? Would the force of each of those stories be diminished if each was read as randomly as they were written, as most of us do? And how does their cumulative "vision and significance" differ from a set of stories written by an "implied author," or even an incipient novelist?[8] That's a raft of questions—surely too many even to contemplate here—so I will consider one matter in a crucial case, the enigmatic ending of "Indian Camp."

For such a mysterious story, there is a remarkable unanimity among its commentators: with varying emphases, all recognize it as an initiation story. And all but a few see that initiation as a failure, for Nick's certainty that he "would never die" is patently illusory, innocent, romantic, or all three.[9]

With the publication of the story's original manuscript's first eight pages, given the title "Three Shots," the two manuscript halves were joined by most readers to mark the ending as doubly ironic, for Nick seems to regress to his state of innocence before he fired the three shots.[10] But one critic, agreeing that Nick only sensed death "in the abstract" in "Three Shots," and then came to "know its reality," saw something more: When Nick comes to realize his father's love, "that love reinforces his sense of being, and of immortality. Thus the ending is neither illusory nor ironic" (Penner 202).

Each of these interpretations assumes that the story is told by an *undramatized narrator*—again, Booth's term. The narrator is familiar with events of the past three days and remarks four times on the characters' emotional states before the ending: once on Nick's, once on the Indian wife's, and twice on Nick's father's; but in each instance the remark does not depend on much more than what is apparent in the character's behavior of speech—indeed, they seem almost redundant.[11] But it is precisely that redundancy that suggests a narrator, however undramatized.

Very little of what I have summarized from earlier critics is necessarily incompatible with the later position of those who argue that Nick Adams is the implied author of "Indian Camp." That argument simply interposes Nick Adams between the reader and the story's narrator, and makes the younger Nickie Adams his own fictional projection. But that authorial Nick Adams is a far from simple figure, and what is attributed to him radically changes our reading of the story.

The invention of Nick as the implied author begins with the remark in "On Writing" that he "had never seen an Indian woman having a baby [but that] he'd seen a woman have a baby on the road to Karagatch and tried to help her"; and it adds that the sentence in chapter 2 of *In Our Time*, "Scared sick looking at it" describes Nick's reaction (596). This conflation of the two texts transfers the authority and something of the event in the *In Our Time* chapter to the memory in "On Writing"; but in chapter 2, there is no engaged narrator who "tried to help" the woman in labor, and the person "scared sick looking at it" was the young girl holding the blanket (*SS* 97).[12]

From this it is concluded that Nick, in writing "Indian Camp," changed the "witness of the delivery from an adult immersed in war and evacuation to a child involved with family life and night-time adventures." Furthermore, this implies that "the older Nick views his meeting with the woman on the road to Karagatch as an initiation of the innocent," and then projects himself as a young boy present at a difficult childbirth "[who] is both victimized by the exigencies of the adult world... [and has] a lingering inability to accept suffering and dying." This leads to the conclusion that the story Nick Adams wrote is permeated with a "strong degree of self-pity" in his projection of himself as its victim; but that "self-indulgence" is then repudiated with "self-irony [in] the child's denial of his own mortality, a denial that he, a war veteran and a writer, now knows to be a lie" (596–597).

Whether as author or implied author, the older Nick Adams interposed between the reader, the narrator, and the younger Nick Adams, reduces the boy's feeling "quite sure he would never die," first, to a youngster's lie; second, to an authorial projection's self-delusion; and finally, to a fictive author's ironic dismissal of that self-delusion.

This strategy to explain a boy's lie as an older person's self-delusion to be repudiated by an author's ironic honesty certainly satisfies a meta-fictional need, but in so doing it trivializes the immediate, profound, and enigmatic question of how that boy could lie, how he could have "felt quite sure that he would never die."

Most of our explanations of Nick's final certainty explain it away with something between indulgence and sanctimony. We wink at his feeling as a childhood fantasy, an understandable delusion, a romantic impulse, for we know—don't we?—that he will die, as will we—or *because* we will. Or from our superior position we say that he lied. But what Nick feels is not a lie. Neither we nor any fictive author can invoke any truth-conditions to deny the boy's feelings, any more than you can tell me that I do not feel quite sure that most critics of this story are dead wrong. *What* I feel may be wrong, but *that* I feel it is incontestable. Not, of course, that I do.

Finally, imagine for a moment that what Nick felt was a truth of a sort that is strange to us. In "The Art of the Short Story"—that rough, suspect, and self-serving memoir—there is a mysterious remark, only part of which has raised comment. Hemingway maintained that the title "Big Two-Hearted River" was substituted for the Fox River, the setting of the story, because "Big Two-Hearted River" is poetry, and because there were many Indians in the story, just as "the war was in the story, and none of the Indians nor the war appeared" (3). "Indian Camp" begins the *In Our Time* collection and "Big Two-Hearted River" ends it, and both are set in the same locale, a morning's train ride west from St. Ignace in Michigan's Upper Peninsula. The last story is so resonant with rituals linking Nick Adams to the natural world—like his offering of the trout's offal to the mink, the local spirits of the tragic swamp—that although there are, indeed, no Indians in the story, there is no need for them, or perhaps there is only one. They are there in "Indian Camp"; and although some have hinted at it, no one has yet wondered whether the initiation we all agree Nick Adams has endured follows an Indian ritual, the end of which, if he survives it, rewards the young initiate with the profound and undeniable feeling that "he will never die."

If it turns out that some native American ritual is closer to the informing source of "Indian Camp," we may well seem to be so engaged in our reasonable world, with its logical laws, that we have forgotten, as Hemingway once said, "what mysteries were in the woods . . . that we came from" (*FWBT* 176–177).

NOTES

1. The most accessible collection of these is *Critical Essays on Ernest Hemingway's "In Our Time,"* ed. Michael S. Reynolds (1983). It includes Robert M. Slabey, "The Structure of *In Our Time,*" *South Dakota Review* (August 1965): 28–52; Clinton S. Burhans, Jr., "The Complex Unity of *In Our Time,*" *Modern Fiction Studies* (1968): 313–328; Jackson J. Benson, "Patterns of Connection and Their Development in Hemingway's *In Our Time,*" *Rendezvous* (Winter 1970): 37–52; Linda W. Wagner, "Juxtaposition in Hemingway's *In Our Time*" *Studies in Short Fiction* 12 (1975): 243–252; and David J. Leigh, S. J., "*In Our Time:* The Interchapters as Structural Guides to Pattern," *Studies in Short Fiction* 12 (1975): 1–8; see also David Seed, "The Picture of the Whole: *In Our Time,*" in *Ernest Hemingway: New Critical Essays,* ed. Robert A. Lee (1983).

2. Of those critics who have entertained this hypothesis, the two most challenging have been Elizabeth Dewberry Vaughn and Debra A. Moddelmog; I focus on the latter article since it offers a practical example of its theoretical position with an interpretation of "Indian Camp."

3. Debra A. Moddelmog, "The Unifying Consciousness of a Divided Conscience: Nick Adams as Author of *In Our Time,*" *American Literature: A Journal of Literary History, Criticism & Bibliography* 60 (Dec. 1988): 591–610.

4. Yet the argument includes "The Battler" to demonstrate Nick's learning "about the cruelty of society ..., a lesson which ends ... in confused escape" (598) and "On the Quai...," as evidence of Nick's obsession with "the violence and senselessness of war" (599).

5. Note that the argument begins with Nick identified as an "implied author" on p. 592; on p. 594 Hemingway "surrenders authorship to Nick"; and from there to the end there are eight overt references to Nick as author, although on p. 609 Nick becomes a "fictional persona." On Nick as author and Nick as character, the argument opens with the distinction between the two, but thereafter it attributes details of the life of the character to that of the author. Near the conclusion of the essay, after we are told that Nick was "writing about himself" in "Cross-Country Snow," we are warned to be "careful not to confuse Nick the writer with Nick the character" (606).

6. As noted earlier, Moddelmog begins with the term *implied author,* continues with *author, writer,* and *fictional persona;* and I, perhaps too assiduously, have assumed that the latter terms were shorthand references to the first. In *The Rhetoric of Fiction* (1961) Wayne Booth was, I believe, the first to consider the concept of an "implied author" systematically and at length. He defined it as the author's "implied version of himself," as a "presence," a "second self," that is always distinct from both the "real" author and the narrator and that will differ in different works. "Our sense of the implied author includes not only the extractable meanings but also the moral and emotional content of each bit of action and suffering of all the characters. It includes, in short, the intuitive apprehension of a completed artistic whole; the chief value to which *this* implied author is committed" (70–73, 151).

7. Undated letter from Debra Moddelmog to the panelists, which was read in part at the conference, 10 July 1990.

8. Booth used the term *self-conscious narrator* to distinguish between those

conscious of their roles as writers and those narrators who seem unaware that "they are writing, thinking, speaking, or 'reflecting' a literary work" (155). One or another of those terms might be more appropriate in this discussion.

9. For Joseph DeFalco, Nick's certainty is "illusory and childlike" (32); for Arthur Waldhorn, Nick, like the newborn, is still protected by the "caul of innocence" (54); and several suggest that when Nick trails his hand in the morning lake there is at best the potential for a later recognition of "renewal and reassurance" (Waldhorn 55). Yet they all consider this a romantic, even Wordsworthian, response to experience (DeFalco, Waldhorn, and Oldsey [217–218]). Some interpret Nick's feeling in rather more narrow or conditional ways: having witnessed only a suicide, Nick feels he will never die *that* way (Monteiro 155); or that *only* in the early morning *and* on the lake *and* sitting in the stern *and* with his father rowing could Nick feel "*quite* sure that he would never die" (Smith 39).

10. Larry Grimes ("Night Terror and Morning Calm: A Reading of 'Indian Camp' as sequel to 'Three Stories.' " *Studies in Short Fiction* 12 [1975] 413–415), for example, argues that "Three Shots" dramatizes Nick's fear of death, common to a child's "fantasy life," and that Nick's experience of the "raw and grotesque" evidence of death can be ignored only "in the reassuring presence of his father" adds to the story's concluding irony (414).

11. They occur when the narrator notes that Nick's "curiosity had been gone for a long time," the Indian wife "did not know what had become of the baby or anything," and Nick's father "was feeling exalted and talkative as football players in the dressing room after a game" and, later, "all his post-operative exhilaration [was] gone" (*SS* 93–94).

12. That it was the girl who was "scared sick" is explicit in Hemingway's *Toronto Daily Star* dispatch of 20 October 1922, titled "A Silent Ghastly Procession," the source for chapter 2 (*Dateline Toronto*).

14

Beginning with "Nothing"

Frank Scafella

When it functions as a symbol in a Hemingway text, "nothing" points beyond itself in two directions simultaneously: to an event in a person's life, on the one hand, and on the other to an *absolute* origin (or beginning) of consciousness. The event, whether past or future, actual or imagined, deepens reflexively into an experience of "nothing" when a Hemingway protagonist makes his way in words into the interior of his own memory where the event becomes present, accessible to thought, and amenable to formulation and expression as symbol. In "nothing," conceived and formulated in this way, the Hemingway protagonist participates apperceptively in the event to which the symbol points. The symbol thus constitutes an absolute origin for the apperceiving consciousness and opens up levels of reality as it unlocks dimensions of the soul otherwise hidden from and closed to him and us.

Nick Adams, for example, reflects apperceptively on the loss and recovery of his soul, conscious at once of the event itself and of his *consciousness* of it:

[of my body] and I told him it went out like a red silk handkerchief; and felt that way floating. "How did it feel when it came back?" he asked. "Like nothing at all," I said. (Item 638, JFK)

Frederic Henry formulates his consciousness of a similar event in a similar way:

I felt myself rush bodily out of myself and out and out and out and all the time bodily in the wind. I went out swiftly, all of myself, and I knew I was dead and that it had all been a mistake to think you just died. Then I floated, [hesitated and instead of going on I felt myself slide back as though there was a long thin wire through the center of my soul. The me that was gone out slid down that wire *through nothing* and the wind twice it caught and stood still and once it turned completely over on the wire] and then jerked and stopped and I was back. (Item 588, JFK; quoted in Reynolds, *Hemingway's First War* 30; words in brackets deleted by Hemingway; emphasis added)

In recollection that places the event squarely in the mind's field of vision, Nick and Frederic Henry become conscious of their *consciousness* of their souls going out of their bodies: "It went out like a red silk handkerchief; and felt that way floating," says Nick. "I felt myself rush bodily out of myself," says Frederic. "I knew I was dead and that it had all been a mistake to think you just died." Neither man aims merely to describe what happened. Each aims instead to become conscious of his consciousness of what happened, in words to descend article by noun by adjective by verb to that level of memory where recall of emotion and fact reveals experientially what each had truly known and felt. Consciousness in fact originates in the images of the red silk handkerchief and floating bodily in the wind.

But there at the center of his consciousness of the event, each man also experiences a sudden and total lapse into unconsciousness. The soul coming back into Nick felt like "*nothing* at all," and Frederic Henry felt himself return bodily through "*nothing* and the wind." Through a lapse in consciousness, the symbol, "nothing," emerges in each man, a sudden salience on the surface of his reverie, a palpable presence and undisclosed mystery from the dark interior of each man's psyche.

As a symbol, "nothing" participates in the unconsciousness to which it points. Consequently, neither Nick nor Frederic can distance himself philosophically from "nothing" by categorizing it as the cipher of a meaningless void or abyss of consciousness, nor can they, either one, reconcile themselves psychologically to "nothing" by resigning themselves to having to live with this impenetrable mystery at the very core of their being. The symbol itself moves each of these men consciously beyond either categorization or resignation in the direction of a place where, in Nick Adams's words, "Nothing could touch him" (*SS* 215). Neither Nick nor Frederic can go on saying nothing about "nothing." In "nothing" each experiences an end to the old and an absolutely new beginning of self-consciousness.

Moreover, as a symbol personifying a dimension or element of the unconscious soul, "nothing" points to the special quality or character of a future event as readily as to one past. For example, Harry lies dying in Africa in "The Snows of Kilimanjaro":

And just then it occurred to him that he was going to die. It came with a rush; not as a rush of water nor of wind; but of a sudden evil-smelling emptiness and the odd thing was that the hyena slipped lightly along the edge of it.

"What is it, Harry?" [his wife] asked him.

"Nothing," he said. (*SS* 64)

Not death itself but *consciousness* of death as an "evil-smelling emptiness," a "nothing," comes to Harry with a rush wholly from within him, its coming like no bodily sensation he can recall. The notion fills the whole of his consciousness just as, a little while earlier when the native boy came to his cot to enquire of Harry's needs, the notion had slipped lightly across the background of his mind:

"Memsahbib's gone to shoot," the boy said. "Does Bwana want?"

"Nothing." [Harry answers] (*SS* 59)

Notice the same ominous and foreboding consciousness in Francis Macomber:

"What's the matter, Francis?" his wife asked him.

"Nothing," Macomber said.

"Yes, there is," she said. "What are you upset about?"

"Nothing," he said. (*SS* 12–13)

And there it is, too, at the center of consciousness in most of the people of *Islands in the Stream*. Thomas Hudson asked Roger Davis, "What was it last night?" "Nothing," Davis responds" (84). Eddy asks Davy, "What's the matter with you?" "Nothing," Davy says" (88). Davy asks Thomas Hudson, "What can I do, Papa?" 'Nothing,' he answers" (112). And Thomas Hudson decides to "lie down and think about nothing" (383).

In "Out of Season," "The young gentleman and his wife understood nothing" (*IOT* 130). "I was acolyte," says the thin little Mexican to Mr. Frazer in "The Gambler, the Nun, and the Radio." "Now I believe in nothing" (*Winner Take Nothing [WTN]* 139). The doctor in "A Natural History of the Dead" consoles the artillery officer: "We dispute about nothing. In time of war we dispute about nothing" (*WTN* 106). "What's the matter with you? You seem all worked up over something?" Robert Cohn asks Jake Barnes. "Nothing," Jake answers (*SAR* 21). Brett sits "looking straight ahead at nothing" and Pedro Romero, just before the bullfight, "was looking at nothing" (178, 212). Pilar looks into Robert Jordan's hand: " 'What did you see in it?' Robert Jordan asked her. . . . 'Nothing,' she told him. 'I saw nothing in it' " (*FWBT* 33).

But our purpose is not to catalog examples. We want to grasp and understand "nothing" as a symbol. To this end, nothing seems more reasonable than to follow Hemingway's lead in his epigraph to *Winner Take Nothing*.

"Unlike all other forms of lutte or combat the conditions are that the winner shall taking nothing; neither his ease, nor his pleasure, nor any notions of glory; nor, if he win far enough, shall there be any reward within himself." The epigraph tells us two things. First, that the lutte or combat with which we have to deal in a Hemingway story is "unlike all other forms" of combat. This rules out war, hunting, boxing, horse racing, motorcar racing, football, and "all other" forms of competitive sport as resources for understanding, analogically, who the winner is or the nature of the "nothing" that he takes. Second, the epigraph says a very curious thing about winning. It says of the winner, "If he win *far enough*." This simple phrase enchants me, for if a man wins he wins, doesn't he? There should be no near or far about it. Yet there at the heart of Hemingway's notion of winning lurks the metaphor of distance, the suggestion that winning involves one in the opening of an adventure, quest, or journey. Then what does winning "far enough" entail if the winner takes nothing?

For Phil, the brown young man in "The Sea Change," winning entails settling consciously into "something new" so completely that he no longer knows who he is. The "lutte or combat" of his tale pits him conceptually against himself and against the brown young girl, whom he loves. The girl, drawn to a sexual liaison with another woman, wins far enough against Phil to take her pleasure with his consent, so she cannot be the "winner." Phil consents to her affair because he understands her attraction; deep within himself he knows, as she points out, that both he and she are "made up of all sorts of things." Yet consciously, conceptually, Phil also knows that her proposed affair is a "vice" and a "perversion." So here is precisely where the metaphor "far enough" comes in. Can Phil win "far enough" against the conceptual prohibitions of "vice" in himself not only to consent to her affair, but to take her back not knowing what she *or* he will be when she returns? Our answer comes in the very strangeness of the voice that speaks Phil's consent:

"Go on," his voice *sounded strange* to him. He was looking at her, at the way her mouth went and the curve of her cheek bones, at her eyes and at the way her hair grew on her forehead and at the edge of her ear and at her neck. "Not really. Oh, you're too sweet," she said. "You're too good to me."

"And when you come back tell me all about it." His voice sounded very strange. He did not recognize it. She looked at him quickly. *He was settled into something.*

"You want me to go?" She asked seriously.

"Yes," he said seriously. "Right away." *His voice was not the same*, and his mouth was very dry. "Now," he said.

She stood up and went out quickly. She did not look back at him. He watched her go. *He was not the same*–looking man as he had been before he had told her to go. He got up from the table, picked up the two checks and went over to the bar with them.

"I'm a different man, James," he said to the barman. "You see in me quite a different man."

"Yes, sir?" said James.

"Vice," said the brown young man, "is a very strange thing, James." He looked out the door. He saw her going down the street. As he looked in the glass, he saw he was *really quite a different-looking man.* . . . The young man saw himself in the mirror behind the bar. "I said I was a different man, James," he said. Looking into the mirror *he saw that this was quite true.* (WTN 42–43; emphasis added)

Phil wins "far enough" against the notion of vice in himself to take nothing but the beginning of an absolutely new self-consciousness. His consent is given in a voice not his own until the very moment *it* speaks *him*. So the lutte or combat of "The Sea Change" occurs entirely within Phil. It is a combat wholly intra-psychic—head versus heart, mind over/against soul, intellect in a struggle with feeling, the powers of light in opposition to the powers of darkness.

The sympathetic older waiter in "A Clean Well-Lighted Place," caught up like Phil in a lutte or combat between conflicting dimensions of his own sensibility, wins far enough in "conversation with himself" to grasp intellectually something he had only known intuitively before. He was always for letting the deaf old man sit late at the table in the cafe with his stack of saucers in the shadows of the leaves. Yet the older waiter does not know why he indulges the old man until the younger waiter challenges him to make conscious that which motivates him to do so. Then the older waiter, nudged into a conversation *with himself* in which he thinks through his motivation, justifies the indulgence by articulating, intra-psychically, his reluctance to close the shutters at two o'clock in the morning:

Turning off the electric light he *continued the conversation with himself.* It is the light of course but it is necessary that the place be clean and pleasant. You do not want music. Certainly you do not want music. Nor can you stand before a bar with dignity although that is all that is provided for these hours. What did he fear? It was not fear or dread. It was a nothing that he knew too well. It was all a nothing and a man was nothing too. It was only that and light was all it needed and a certain cleanness and order. Some lived in it and never felt it but he knew it all was nada y pues nada y nada y pues nada. Our nada who art in nada, nada be thy name thy kingdom nada thy will be nada in nada as it is in nada. Give us this nada our daily nada and nada us our nada as we nada our nadas and nada us not into nada but deliver us from nada; pues nada. Hail nothing full of nothing, nothing is with thee. He smiled and stood before a bar with a shining steam pressure coffee machine.

"What's yours?" asked the barman.

"Nada." (WTN 17)

Now the older waiter stands *conscious* of what he has for a long time known only unconsciously: "It was all a nothing and a man was nothing too," and light (the light of conscious thought) was all it needed.

Hence the winner *takes* nothing. He takes no reward within himself for a man is nothing, too; but knowing this by putting it into words is something, isn't it? And if a man should win "far enough" in words to see, as Roger in "The Mother of a Queen" sees, that "you can't touch" a Queen because "nothing, nothing can touch them" (*WTN* 67), then you *have* touched this Queen and "nothing" has become "something," hasn't it? And if, as in every instance above, the winner "takes" nothing, then he grasps or lays hold intellectually of something latent within himself—an image, an idea, an emotion, a memory—to which he must give thought above all else. He *takes* "nothing" in the sense that an emotion or idea grasped as image demands thinking through; it becomes something symbolic when it is given to recollecting thought. And thinking itself, regarded in this way, involves one in coming to know imaginatively, by action of the soul, rather than through the exercise of intellect in analysis of something previously known.

To put it another way, winning "far enough" to "take" nothing signals the opening of an adventure in consciousness. "Adventure" indicates the kind of re-collective thinking and writing that Harry in "The Snows of Kilimanjaro" calls "work(ing) the fat off his soul"—fat signifying the cutting edge of his imagination blunted by laziness, sloth, snobbery, pride, and all those "betrayals of himself" with which he had "destroyed his talent" in his life with the rich:

You kept from thinking and it was all marvelous. . . . You made an attitude that you cared nothing for the work you used to do, now that you could no longer do it. But, in yourself, you said that you could write about these people; about the very rich; that you were really not of them but a spy in their country; that you would leave it and write of it and for once it would be written by some one who knew what he was writing of. But he would never do it, because each day of not writing, of comfort, of being that which he despised, dulled his ability and softened his will to work so that, finally, he did no work at all. (*SS* 59)

Yet if Harry has kept from thinking throughout his life with the rich, he does not keep from thinking on his deathbed there at the foot of Kilimanjaro. Devotedly thinking back through all that he had stored in memory for writing, he recollects and thereby destroys the destruction of his own talent. In re-collective thought he works the fat off his soul. And by doing what he can do in thinking back over all he has not done, he does the very thing he avoided when he bragged to the rich of what he could do.

On his deathbed, therefore, Harry chooses to make his living by writing and thereby prepares himself for death, this new adventure of consciousness that awaits him. Strongly against "nothing" in him comes the desire to write, to "put it all into one paragraph if you could get it right" before you go. And who wins? Does "nothing" take Harry or does Harry "take" nothing? Most certainly, death takes Harry:

Death had come and rested its head on the foot of the cot and he could smell its breath. . . . It moved up closer to him still and now he could not speak to it, and when it saw he could not speak it came a little closer, and now he tried to send it away without speaking, but it moved in on him so its weight was all upon his chest, and while it crouched there and he could not move, or speak, he heard the woman say, "Bwana is asleep now. Take the cot up very gently and carry it into the tent." He could not speak to tell her to make it go away and it crouched now, heavier, so he could not breathe. And then, while they lifted the cot, suddenly it was all right and the weight went from his chest" (SS 74–75)

Harry dies.

A break in the narrative symbolizes this transition in Harry's conscious life. Yet the next segment of the narrative, a passage in itself separated from the main text, forms a flight in thought by Harry toward the top of Kilimanjaro. Harry's soul, trimmed down and active in recollection of all that he had saved to write, takes flight in this final realization of imaginative possibility into the East and light of the morning sun. A man was nothing too, and light was all he needed. As in Francis Macomber, the soul passes *consciously* in Harry and elsewhere in Hemingway not only as a surge of "pure excitement," like a "dam bursting," but as a "new wealth" of life and a tremendous "feeling of happiness about action to come" (SS 33) at the top of the mountain.

Unlike all other forms of lutte or combat, then, in the intra-psychic combat of a Hemingway story a man, usually a writer in full consciousness of his action, of necessity stands firmly against some dimension or element of himself—vice, excruciating memories and pain, fear, the destruction of talent, a soul that feels like "nothing." In the ensuing intra-psychic struggle, the winner always *takes* nothing by winning far enough against it to lose himself to a new possibility for thought and action, consciously laying hold of a new idea of order for his life, or grasping a "new wealth" of feeling that rejuvenates imaginative possibility in him. He finds himself, like Harry of "Snows" or Phil in "The Sea Change," in a new direction of thought (or at least, like Mr. Frazer in "The Gambler, the Nun, and the Radio," under a new obligation for thinking) which may promise nothing more substantial, or less symbolic of majesty of vision and soul, than high, white Kilimanjaro itself.

15

Opiates, Laughter, and the Radio's Sweet Lies: Community and Isolation in Hemingway's "The Gambler, the Nun, and the Radio"

Ann L. Putnam

"The Gambler, the Nun, and the Radio" was first published in *Scribner's Magazine* as "Give Us a Prescription, Doctor" in 1933, then retitled as we know it in the collection *Winner Take Nothing*, published the same year. It is based on an autobiographical incident that Hemingway was later to describe in *Green Hills of Africa*:

That day of watching the camel flies working under the horse's tail.... gave me more horror than anything I could remember except one time in a hospital with my right arm broken off short between the elbow and the shoulder.... Alone with the pain in the night in the fifth week of not sleeping I thought suddenly how a bull elk must feel if you break a shoulder and he gets away and in that night I lay and felt it all."[1]

But the facts are wonderfully transformed into a rich tapestry woven of many characters and moods, making "Gambler" one of Hemingway's most interesting, yet most difficult stories. The story is set in a hospital—rooms within rooms and corridors from which come whispers, screams, and the occasional sound of laughter. In its tonal mix of humor and bleakness, it is one of the darkest, most perplexing stories Hemingway ever wrote, made bearable only by its comedy. It is a fascinating yet frustrating study of hope and despair whose meanings continually invert, come to focus and fade away. The story contains a certain surface brilliance—dazzling juxtapositions of character, scene, and dialogue—but, as a number of readers have suggested, perhaps little else.[2] Perhaps too much has been buried beneath the dazzling surface. Do we know enough about the protagonist's dilemma, for example, to connect it with some universal significance? Does the story finally turn on itself in an orgy of despair? Idealism, religion, luck, hope, revolution, music, all human pleasures—each in turn are examined under the stark lights of the hospital and rejected. The story seems to be about the search for some constant value; yet what if any value survives the ruthless scrutiny that Frazer, the despairing protagonist of the story, subjects them to?

What then is the point of a story that is despairing of so much and seemingly offering so little? Where is the narrative tautness, the tension between hope and hopelessness? Has the story gone slack, just like Mr. Frazer who in the end turns toward the wall? The belief that there is *nothing* of value becomes, in the final analysis, narratively uninteresting.

"Gambler" becomes a study in the art of winning, the choreography of holding steady. It is a posture central to many of Hemingway's finest stories, stories in which the principal action is the activity of waiting, of holding in suspension the equal claims of hope and despair.[3] They dramatize the failure of action to materialize in any paraphrasable form and thus are often characterized by their lack of seeming coherence, depicting as they do a world that is chaotic, brutal, and utterly capricious. In a world such as this, the best one can do is learn strategies for holding steady with some dignity and pride.[4] But in a clean, well-lighted place of one's own making, created through repetition and ritual, such waiting can occur. "Gambler" is the story of one such attempt to hold steady against the "horror" of unremitting pain in the fifth week of not sleeping.

As he does in so many short stories, Hemingway employs a *pair* of characters to tell what is essentially a single story, a *pair* of characters whose relationship determines the form and effect of the stories in which they appear. In this story, the function of one character's story is to provide an objectification of the untold story of the other, suggesting what in the surface story is withheld. Regardless of whatever else it has become over the years, Philip Young's isolation of a pair of characters (the Hemingway hero/the code hero) has been useful in illuminating what is a *structural* device as much as a thematic one.[5] For Hemingway, it became an immensely useful technique for creating the oblique telling essential to the construction of the lyric story, as well as a device for controlling sentimentality.

In this story, Hemingway links a pair of protagonists, the gambler, Cayetano Ruiz, and the writer known only as Mr. Frazer, through the metaphor of the blow each has received. It is a blow at once literal and symbolic that links them through their communal pain and the strategies they employ for bearing it. The gambler has sustained an abdominal gunshot wound that has severed the nerves to the leg, causing a paralysis; Frazer's leg has been badly broken in a horseback riding accident.[6] In an autobiographical sense, it is clear that Hemingway has split his own nightmarish experience with a badly broken arm between both characters, for he saw Cayetano and

Frazer as parts of a single story. Hemingway's broken arm became Frazer's broken leg, an arm that was broken so badly, the damaged "nerves" caused a paralysis of Hemingway's writing hand.[7] The tricky "nerves" Frazer experiences in the fifth week shares with Cayetano the damaged "nerves" that have paralyzed his leg.

In the opening scene of the story, Hemingway brings this pair of characters together. The scene not only establishes their commonality but establishes the dominant tone of the story as well—comedy strangely mixed with darkness. Brought to the hospital after being shot during a card game, the gambler, Cayetano, is interrogated by a police detective, through a Mexican interpreter. Mr. Frazer is in the room too, and as he can speak Spanish, he is soon asked to do some of the interpreting. Not wishing to name his assailant, Cayetano claims he was shot by accident.

"An accident that he fired eight shots at you and hit you twice, there?" asks the police detective.
"An accident that he hit me at all, the cabron," the gambler says through the interpreter.
"What happens if after shooting you, this man shoots a woman or child?"
"I am not married," Cayetano says.
"He says any woman, any child," Frazer now interprets.
"The man is not crazy" Cayetano answers, then confesses to Frazer that he has understood all along (355–356).
"You are of the great translators. I speak English, but badly, I understand it all right."[8]

The opening scene is wonderfully farcical, but it is comedy tinged with darkness, for Cayetano may very well die. It is a tonal mix sustained throughout the story by stretches of vaudevillian comic dialogue, comic juxtaposition, and broad ironies—the nun prays in the hospital chapel for the victory of her favorite football team; the citizens want the hospital to shut off their x-ray machines because they interfere with their radio reception; when the doctor moves Frazer's bed toward the window for a better view, the bed lamp falls on his head and knocks him out; friends of the man who shot Cayetano are coerced by the police into serenading him. It is slapstick played on the edge.[9]

Soon it is apparent that Frazer has had some sort of setback and is now confined to bed, a detail that initiates the movement from outer to inner. It is in this context that the idea of the radio is introduced. By evening the radio signal could be picked up and "all night it worked beautifully and when one station stopped you could go further west and pick up another" (358). This way Frazer can get through the night if he can stay ahead of the fading radio signals, if he can win this special "pursuit race."[10] It becomes an emblem of the pattern of the lives of both the gambler who must begin all over again with each new town, and the writer who is once again "forced to repeat the same experiment" (363). The scene establishes the ritual of the radio with its infinitely repeatable and repeating sequence of Minneapolis to Denver to Seattle, a ritual enacted in the clean well-lighted place. Here Frazer's private room develops a rhetoric of its own in contrast to the rhetoric of the ward. Thus it introduces the key dichotomy of the story, the community of the ward on the one hand, and the isolation of the private room on the other. The private room is "cool" and clean, and infinitely preferable to the "hot rooms" of the ward. It is a room that Frazer fashions into a "clean well-lighted place" out of what is at hand, for "[i]f you stay long enough in a room the view, whatever it is, acquires a great value and becomes very important and you would not change it, not even by a different angle" (358–359).[11]

The only outsiders to visit either of the two protagonists are three Mexicans, friends of neither, who are coerced into coming by the local police at the behest of the nun. The three Mexicans introduce values that Frazer will consider one at a time near the end of the story. "I distrust all priests, monks and sisters," says the thin, serious Mexican, who is the revolutionary (362). When the Mexicans come again, Mr. Frazer "did not feel like talking and when they went he knew they would not come again" (363). His nerves are beginning to get "tricky," and he turns to the radio, which he has learned to play so quietly that he can "listen to it without thinking" (480).

But we get the strange sense, or, so it seems, that Mr. Frazer is the protagonist of another story altogether, one about which we know little. "Mr. Frazer had been through all this before," and "he resented being forced to make the same experiment when he already knew the answer" (363). Yet it becomes clear that in telling Cayetano's story, Hemingway is telling Frazer's story as well. The nun brings Cayetano into Frazer's room, and what is apparent is that this scene reverses the postures of the opening scene that put Frazer in Cayetano's room. "What about the pain?" Frazer immediately asks. It is their bond and their subject. "I thought the pain alone would kill me," Cayetano says. But Frazer pushes on. Cayetano explains that of course he couldn't cry out with so many other people in the ward, then asks "What class of pain do you have?" (365). Frazer confesses that although clearly his pain is not as great as the gambler's, he is fast losing control and often cries. Cayetano tells him that "if I had a private room and a radio I would be crying and yelling all night long" (365). The contrast developed between the private room and the ward suggests the polarities that emerge at the story's conclusion—the isolation of the private room and the community of the ward. It was a theme Hemingway was slowly coming to, even here in this story written in the desperation of 1933.

Frazer continues. How does he continue, going as he does from one small town to the next? Cayetano reveals that his illusions are what enable him to persist—that, and his ability to laugh, to undercut his own beliefs with irony. ("I am a poor idealist, I am the victim of illusions.") He confesses that although he is a "professional gambler," he "like[s] to gamble. To really gamble" (365). It is here that Cayetano's professionalism and dedication to craft suggest parallels with a writer's life—and what this strange life does to one's human attachments. Frazer asks him about women. A gambler is "too concentrated," Cayetano explains. "When he should be with the woman" he is busy working. This detail resonates against the story of Mr. Frazer for whom no visitors have come, who has no loved one present. So one wonders what there is about Mr. Frazer *the writer* that finds such strange correspondences with this small-time gambler whose unsettled life is ruinous to love.[12]

In "The Gambler, the Nun, and the Radio," as with the other pairs stories, two characters are brought together by the accident of proximity.[13] Their relationship, though intensely symbolic, remains strikingly casual in terms of the action of the story. Here, Cayetano is a function of the surface story whose subject is the bearing of physical pain. He acts as the beginning of Frazer's story, which we do not see—the early days when the pain was very great. He acts as the middle of Frazer's story too, when he tells us of the long, endless cycle of his life, living from one small town to the next, to win finally, only to lose everything and begin the sequence all over again. It becomes the metaphor for whatever Frazer means when he tells us that he had "been through all this before"—that he was again "forced to make the same experiment when he already knew the answer." He functions as Frazer's past, just as Frazer functions as Cayetano's future, should he ever lose the ability to hold hope and despair in absolute tension. So Hemingway has fit Cayetano's story into the larger story of the writer with the broken leg, and then both into an even greater story that tells of the pain of all humankind. It is a house of pain they inhabit, an emblem of the world of betrayal and violence from which no one in 1933 was spared.[14]

Hemingway uses the title of the story to establish the parameters of belief[15]—the nun with her breathless idealism ("Oh I hope I get to be a saint!"), the gambler whose hope is in hope itself, and the writer who has lost hope altogether. But which of these perspectives does the story itself affirm? The nun's naive idealism is sweetly, humorously undercut—Cayetano can believe in illusions knowing they are illusions as a strategy to keep on believing.[16] Frazer, on the other hand, cannot sustain the tension between hope and despair, cannot sustain both the illusion and the knowledge that it is an illusion.[17] The final scene of the story firmly establishes the progression set into motion from the beginning and clarifies the narrative perspective. The scene takes place the night the Mexicans come into the ward with their bad beer and their "fatal" music. It imitates the movement of the entire story as we see it progress from an outward posture to a closed, inward one. The point of view, which until now has been almost synonymous with Frazer's, shifts to an objective camera view, which pulls away from Frazer and becomes a roving eye that looks down upon them all. It drifts down the corridor into "hot rooms" that hold the rodeo rider with the broken back, the carpenter who had fallen from a scaffold, the farm boy whose broken leg had been badly set and was to be rebroken, a gambler named Cayetano Ruiz now with a paralyzed leg, and down the corridor a man named Frazer, who lies listening to the singing and the laughter. The view is epic, the prose eloquent, as it catalogues the world of accident and chance, and the pain of all those who have one way or the other been broken by the world. This brief shift in point of view validates a perspective other than Frazer's and sits in judgment upon it. Despite inescapable pain, there is also movement and action in the ritual of communist laughter coming from the ward, which stands in sharp contrast to the paralysis of the sequence of Minneapolis to Denver to Seattle.

The Mexicans enter Frazer's room to ask for his request, which is for the Cucaracha. He thinks he would like to hear this music with its "sinister laughter" that "men have gone to die to" (367). He keeps thinking of the thin, sour Mexican who dreams of revolution, who would "operate" on the people "without an anesthetic." Thus begins Frazer's own catalogue of the best of the world's opiums. He then systematically demolishes every value save one—religion, patriotism, politics, sex, drink, a radio (perhaps), gambling, ambition in any form, and revolution. But what, he asks, is the "real, the actual, opium of the people?" (367). Here, as many readers have noted, the story, in its turning toward, then away from resolution, becomes a puzzlement. Mr. Frazer thinks it is bread that is the actual opium of the people. Reread. Life itself is the ultimate illusion. This he claims he knows in the "well-lighted part of his mind that was there after two or more drinks in the evening, that he knew was there (it was not really there of course)" (367). He calls for the Mexican revolutionary and makes a plea for the value of all opiums. But the Mexican does not follow him. "Many times I do not follow myself," Frazer tells him. Frazer is fast losing control. Even the revolutionary looks at him "worriedly." "You want to hear the Cucaracha another time?" he asks. "Yes," he says, "it's better than the radio." He seems to embrace, for this one confused, slippery moment, the value of revolution—then he rejects this too. "They would go now . . . and they would take the Cucaracha with them" (367–368). Afterwards, he would have a "spot of the giant killer" and turn toward the radio, playing it so he "could hardly hear it," playing it so quietly he could dream other people's lives, dream every life but his own. The story has exposed and undercut the "opiums," the illusions, of both the gambler (his belief in luck will one day crucify him), and the nun (her belief in the possibility of sainthood depends upon a cosmic design that the story shows to be glaringly absent). Everyone—the gambler, the nun, the writer, the men in the ward—are hostages of fate, victims of the practical jokes of the cosmos. Yet for all their illusions, the nun and the gambler are able to *act*. The nun goes about her quotidian duties at the hospital, perhaps believing in sainthood, perhaps not; the gambler is able to go from town to town, hoping for a change of luck but knowing it probably will not come. And Frazer—is he to be admired because he has shown the intellectual daring to look at life emptied of all illusions save for the radio? Does he win a victory through this act of awareness that no one else in the story dares attempt? Frazer in the end is thinking so "clearly" he destroys all sense of humanity, humor, joy, indulging in an orgy of despair. The "horror" of this story is the image of a man turned toward the wall. And of what value, finally, is Mr. Frazer's radio played in his private room so low he can hardly hear it?

At the conclusion of the story, all the others have joined together in their commonality and their pain and sung the songs that Frazer has chosen to hear on the radio. In the end, the radio represents escape not involvement, retreat, not commitment, control not risk. It plays "Little White Lies" all night long. The real world is in the "hot rooms" down the corridor. Our Frazer's private room, his "clean well-lighted place," has become a tomb, and his ritual of holding steady has become the long slide toward death. The final progression of the story confirms its theme. Beginning in the real world, in the ward of common humanity, the story traces Frazer's movement from the corridors of the hospital to his private room, and finally to a turning away from all people. The story shrinks to a tiny pointed light in the image of a man turned toward a radio, an image so precise that it expands even as it narrows. Only humor gives the characters some distance from their pain and some control. At the end, the one true value, which has been laughter all along, has been silenced by the whispering hiss of the radio's sweet lies.

NOTES

1. Ernest Hemingway, *Green Hills of Africa* (New York: Scribner's, 1935), 147–148.

2. See Marion Montgomery's article "Hemingway's 'The Gambler, the Nun, and the Radio': A Reading and a Problem," in *The Short Stories of Ernest Hemingway: Critical Essays*, ed. Jackson Benson (Durham: Duke University Press, 1975), 210. Montgomery points to a criticism often levied against Hemingway fiction, that Hemingway leaves out too much, that the ending is ultimately unsatisfactory because we never do "understand what pain the opium of the radio helps him bear.... But Mr. Frazer—the writer(?), bronco-buster(?), revolutionary(?)—has whiskey and radio to help him bear what pain?" Yet if one reads the story of the *pair* of characters as a single story, Frazer emerges as a fuller character, refracted as he is through the circumstances of the gambler, Cayetano Ruiz. See also for comparison Frank O'Connor's reading of "Hills Like White Elephants" in his study of the short story, *The Lonely Voice* (Cleveland: World, 1963) where he negotiates the same issue—a story with great surface brilliance, but ostensibly too much left out.

3. Here are included such stories as "Hills Like White Elephants," "A Day's

Wait," "Now I Lay Me," "A Canary for One," "The Killers," and "A Clean, Well-Lighted Place," to name only a few.

4. As Hemingway explains in the story "Get a Seeing-Eyed Dog," the best one may hope for is that he may eventually "get good" at the waiting, for often that is "all there is." Ernest Hemingway, "Get a Seeing Eyed-Dog," *The Complete Short Stories of Ernest Hemingway*, The Finca Vigia Edition (New York: Scribner's, 1987), 491.

5. Philip Young, *Ernest Hemingway: A Reconsideration* (University Park: Pennsylvania State University Press, 1966).

6. What led Hemingway to give Frazer a broken leg rather than a broken arm was perhaps not so much a distancing device, as the result of Hemingway's self-consciousness that just a broken arm could have incapacitated him so long. He wrote (Pauline's dictation) to Guy Hickock that the *Billings Gazette* had sent a reporter up "to find out what this fellow Hemingway was still doing in the hospital with nothing more than a fractured arm." See *Ernest Hemingway: Selected Letters*, ed. Carlos Baker (New York: Scribner's, 1981), 334.

7. "Certainly I can't write anything now, nor for some time," Hemingway had written to Archibald MacLeish three weeks after the accident. See *Letters*, 330. "The doctors are talking six months now before the nerve may come back. If it shouldn't come back, it can be relieved by an operation. It may come a lot quicker, of course, but there is still complete paralysis of the wrist." *Letters* 335. Also see Carlos Baker's description of how the injury to the writing arm affected the writing process, given Hemingway's dependence upon longhand. Baker comments that "anything meant to be read by the eye, said he, must be written out by hand and checked by the ear and the eye in process. His busted arm made this a physical impossibility." *Ernest Hemingway: A Life Story* (New York: Scribner's, 1968), 279. This physical fact, "a break in his chief professional tool, the right arm" (Baker, 278), which halted work on *Death in the Afternoon*, no doubt led to the general despair of Frazer the writer as Hemingway created him.

8. Ernest Hemingway, "The Gambler, the Nun, and the Radio," *The Complete Short Stories of Ernest Hemingway*, The Finca Vigia Edition (New York: Scribner's, 1987), 355–356. All subsequent references to this and every Hemingway story are to this edition.

9. It is a trick like the major's wink in "In Another Country," a trick like Catherine Barkeley's wink at the end of *A Farewell to Arms*: "[major] winked at me and said: 'And will I too play football, captain doctor?'" And, "'Please go out of the room,' the doctor said. 'You cannot talk.' Catherine winked at me, her face gray. 'I'll be right outside,' I said." *A Farewell to Arms* (New York: Scribner's, 1957), 331. In both cases the protagonists wink at their fate, grasp irony from inevitable defeat.

10. "In a pursuit race, in bicycle racing, riders start at equal intervals to ride after one another ... and if they slow their riding another rider who maintains his pace will make up the space that separated them equally at the start. As soon as a rider is caught and passed he is out of the race and must get down from his bicycle and leave the track." Ernest Hemingway, "A Pursuit Race," 267. In this story, Hemingway has fashioned a striking metaphor from the world of cycling to portray humankind's position in a world that may "catch" one at any moment. "To stay in the race, one must keep moving on a track that goes round and round, with no

beginning and no sure end—an endless middle, endlessly repeated . . . an apt meta-
phor for . . . meaningless activity that rarely if ever coheres into significant action."
See Ann L. Putnam, "Waiting for the End in Hemingway's 'A Pursuit Race' " in
Hemingway's Neglected Short Fiction: New Perspectives, ed. Susan F. Beegel (Ann
Arbor: UMI Research Press, 1989), 186–187.

11. The room with the changeless view and the controls for temperature represents not so much a statement of political conservatism as the familiar security in
the changeless ritual of the clean well-lighted place.

12. It is a theme treated in full in *The Garden of Eden*, a novel that examines
the high cost of art in terms of the effects of the "enforced loneliness" of the artist
on those most loved. Part of David's difficulty in the novel is the cautery he must
perform in order to leave his human attachments and enter the "high country" of
his work. Ernest Hemingway, *The Garden of Eden* (New York: Scribner's, 1986),
14.

13. In a finely argued essay entitled "Levels of Irony in Hemingway's 'The Gambler, the Nun, and the Radio'," *Studies in Short Fiction* 7 (Summer 1970): 439–
449, Paul Rodgers analyzes the relationship between Cayetano Ruiz and Mr. Frazer.
He states that "Cayetano is not important to Frazer," though he adds that "in
admitting this, we are not necessarily denying Cayetano's importance to the story"
(Rodgers 445). Yet Rodgers undercuts the positive value Cayetano may seem to
represent by examining the split in the narrative point of view, coming finally to
the conclusion that the narrative split Rodgers notes confirms that the *narrator* of
the story is even more pessimistic than Mr. Frazer, if that is possible. Rodgers's
reading is much like the story itself, as it examines every possible value presented
and rejects them all.

14. A very fine article which discusses the historical context of the story is Edward
Stone's essay, "Hemingway's Mr. Frazer: From Revolution to Radio," *Journal of
Modern Literature* (March 1971): 375–388. Stone makes a good case for Frazer's
(and Hemingway's) awareness of and response to the cataclysmic events of the early
1930s. Indeed, in the letters from the period of Hemingway's stay in the Billings,
Montana hospital, he makes references to the economic collapse and links his own
"unemployment" with the general economic collapse. "I see where his organs [Pres-
ident Hoover's] are beginning to refer to the unemployed as the idle. Well, your old
friend Hem is among the unemployed, or the idle." See *Letters*, 336.

15. It is much the same technique Hemingway employs in "A Clean Well-Lighted
Place," in the tripartite structure of the old man, the young waiter and the older
waiter, three points on a continuum of belief.

16. See Frederick Murolo's essay, "Another Look at the Nun and Her Prayers,"
Hemingway Review 4 (1984): 52–53, for a look at the nun's actual track record.
Her naive faith is re-examined in light of the actual outcomes of the events she prays
for: the victory of Notre Dame over Southern California, the Philadelphia Athletics
over the St. Louis Cardinals in the 1930 World Series, and also the recovery of
Cayetano, the subject of much prayer during the story, victories all of which provide
"a refreshing, ironic twist to an otherwise devastatingly pessimistic story" (Murolo
53).

17. The story "A Pursuit Race" is structured much like "Gambler" in its use of
two protagonists who compose a single story. William Campbell says to William
Turner, "Listen, Silly. . . . I want to tell you something. You're called 'Sliding Billy.' "

That's because I never could slide at all. I can't slide, Silly. It just catches. Every time I try it, it catches. . . . It's awful when you can't slide." That is, William Turner can "slide"—can maintain the illusion that there are cures to be had. But when Silly Campbell tries to "slide," the truth "catches," and he must get off his bicycle and quit the race. Frazer cannot keep up with this special "pursuit race," for like William Campbell, reality "catches" every time. Yet at the story's conclusion, and it is the reader's epiphany, the two men are revealed to be brothers after all, in the same way we recognize the brotherhood of the older waiter and the old man in "A Clean Well-Lighted Place" and the brotherhood, too, of Cayetano the gambler and the writer Mr. Frazer. See "A Pursuit Race," 269.

16

Hemingway on Sexual Otherness: What's Really Funny in *The Sun Also Rises*

Wolfgang E. H. Rudat

In his 1985 article on "What's Funny in *The Sun Also Rises*," a ground-breaking article in that it both demonstrated the need for and offered new approaches to close-reading Hemingway's text, James Hinkle made the following observation: "Occasionally a passage needs to be read aloud for us to realize what is funny" (Hinkle 37). Hinkle illustrated his point by citing the speech mannerisms of the gays in whose company Brett had entered the *bal musette* in Paris, speech mannerisms that the narrator reports as follows:

One of them saw Georgette and said: "I do declare. There is an actual harlot. I'm going to dance with her, Lett. You watch me."
The tall one, called Lett, said: "Don't you be rash."
The wavy blond one answered: "Don't you worry, dear." And with them was Brett. (20)[1]

Hinkle's particular point in discussing this part of the *bal musette* scene was that "Hemingway and Jake do not care for homosexuals" (37). I wish to question Hinkle's determination of the ideology of Hemingway's narrative in this context. Can we really say that Hemingway is using Jake as a mouthpiece to voice his own dislike of gays? And is it really true that, as Linda Wagner-Martin has argued in a 1991 article "Racial and Sexual Coding in Hemingway's *The Sun Also Rises*," the *bal musette* scene insults "the male homosexual culture" (41)?[2] As I will attempt to show, in order for us to fully realize just *how* "funny" the homosexuals scene is, and how important that scene is for our interpretation of the entire novel, we have to bear in mind in what context Jake Barnes will use the word "funny": Jake will use it in his agony-packed talk with Brett in the cab, when he tries to make light of his sexually disabling war injury by claiming that it is "supposed to be funny" (*SAR* 26)—although to him the injury is not funny at all.

After making his point about the gays' initial dialogue, Hinkle observed that if we "continue reading aloud we discover that [Robert] Prentiss too must have been part of Brett's [homosexual] entourage" (Hinkle 37). A dialogue develops between Jake and Prentiss, who, Jake informs us, is a "rising new [American] novelist [speaking with] some sort of an English accent" (*SAR* 21). The dialogue makes Jake so angry that he gets up and walks toward the dance floor. *Why* does Jake get angry—simply because an American putting on an English accent irritates him, or because Jake associates Prentiss with a speech mannerism that American homophobes have customarily attributed to gays? Let us listen to the conclusion of the dialogue:

"Do you find Paris amusing?" [Prentiss asked]
"Yes"
"Really?"
I was a little drunk. Not drunk in any positive sense but just enough to be careless.
"For God's sake," I said, "yes. Don't you?"
"Oh, how charmingly you get angry," he said. "I wish I had that faculty." (21)

When Jake gets up and walks away toward the dance floor, Mrs. Braddocks follows him, which leads to the exchange between the two that Hinkle quotes in an attempt to prove his point that "Hemingway and Jake do not care for homosexuals." Mrs. Braddocks is trying to calm Jake down:

"Don't be cross with Robert," she said. "He's still only a child, you know."
"I wasn't cross," I said. "I just thought perhaps I was going to throw up." (21)

I wish to argue that it is part of Hemingway's irony here that there is nothing in the text to indicate that Prentiss is gay. On the contrary, there are two facts that strongly suggest that Prentiss does not belong among what Hinkle calls "Brett's entourage." First of all, Mrs. Braddocks, who is among the circle of Jake's acquaintances in Paris, identifies "Robert" as a fairly close acquaintance of hers, and Jake himself is sufficiently familiar with Prentiss to know that he is a "rising new novelist." Second, Prentiss says that "they" have told him Jake is from Kansas City: It seems unlikely that the word "they" refers to Brett's homosexual companions, a group Jake apparently is not acquainted with since the only group member he mentions by name is Lett, whose name had been announced by "[t]he wavy blond one." In any case, when Hemingway refrains from telling us explicitly whether Prentiss is gay, the author is indicating that his point is in Jake's *reaction* to Prentiss's speech mannerism. Jake automatically *concludes* that Prentiss is homosexual,[3] and having barely recovered from the annoying effect that Lett and his friends had on him earlier, Jake again becomes angry.

However, I would argue that what makes Jake the most angry in his exchange with Prentiss is Prentiss's frivolously conciliatory remark, "Oh, how charmingly you get angry...*I wish I had that faculty*" (emphasis added). Prentiss's rejoinder is meant to poke fun at Jake for his angry outburst, but then the speaker has no idea how painful that remarks is to Jake. Since Jake assumes that Prentiss is homosexual, he also assumes that Prentiss is baitingly implying that due to their psychological makeup gays lack the supposedly "manly" faculty of becoming seriously angry in the manner in which Jake had become angry—seriously angry because Jake, possibly even without Prentiss himself being aware of it, was giving expression to a serious case of homophobia. Like the gays who are making a show of dancing with Georgette, Jake does not have sexual intercourse with women and therefore thinks that Prentiss is referring to his so-called manly business of heterosexuality and, unknowingly of course, is reminding him that Jake no longer has the "faculty" for that kind of business.

This reminder is more than Jake, who is "a little drunk" but "not drunk in any positive sense," that is, not sufficiently anesthetized, can tolerate. Jake is telling Mrs. Braddocks the truth: Since Prentiss could not know how painful his remark would be to Jake, Jake had no reason to be "cross" with him personally but, instead, "just thought [he] perhaps was going to throw up." Prentiss's unintentional blow quite literally was more than Jake could stomach. Yet what makes Prentiss's unintentional blow even worse is that the suspected homosexual is reminding Jake that he lacks something more than the physical ability to have intercourse. Jake is reminded that he lacks the spiritual quality that would have enabled him to come to terms with the physical loss, which after all had occurred seven or eight years earlier. Jake thinks he may have to throw up, not so much because the gays and/ or Prentiss personally make him sick but because he is sickened by his own lack of spiritual mettle. In fact, there is the irony that the narrator had, at an earlier point in the context of his voiced displeasure with Lett and his friends, attributed some such spiritual quality to the gays, namely a "superior ...composure" of sorts. Armed with the knowledge of what it really is that makes Jake think that he may have to throw up, let us take a closer look at the scene that immediately follows the narrator's attempt to ridicule the gays by reporting their dialogue but that precedes Jake's dialogue with Prentiss:

And with them was Brett.
I was very angry. Somehow they always made me angry. I know they are supposed

to be amusing, and you should be tolerant, but I wanted to swing on one, any one, anything to shatter that superior, simpering composure. Instead, I walked down the street and had a beer at the bar at the next Bal. The beer was not good and I had a worse cognac to take the taste out of my mouth. (20)

Jake admits that he knows that "[one] should be tolerant" of gays, but Jake is incapable of that kind of tolerance because, in his view, the gays he had just encountered waste the capability of which he himself has been deprived—the physical capability to have sexual relationships with women. Worse yet, "with them was Brett," an observation with which the narrator frames his statement, "she was very much with them." The gays are consuming time that Brett could bestow on worthier men, that is, on men sexually appreciative of her—or, if Brett is *not* in the mood for sexual intercourse, the gays are usurping the company that Jake thinks he himself deserves because he at least loves Brett. This thought literally and metaphorically puts a bad taste in Jake's mouth—so that he leaves the *bal musette* for a short while to get himself under control. The situation gets worse for Jake when he returns to the *bal*. Mark Spilka made a sexo-culturally telling comment about this scene in 1958, in an article whose content as well as title—"The Death of Love in *The Sun Also Rises*"—I would call a case of socio-moral overkill.[4] Spilka observed: "Jake Barnes' honest anger has been aroused by the appearance of a band of homosexuals, accompanied by Brett Ashley. When one of the band spies Georgette, he decides to dance with her; then one by one they all follow suit, *in deliberate parody of normal love*" ("Death of Love" 243, emphasis added). The portion I italicized in Spilka's comment misses the point since what Spilka meant was that Hemingway himself intended the description of homosexuals lining up to dance with Georgette as a parody of heterosexual love. We have to bear in mind that "one of them," who is left unidentified by the narrator, had publicly declared Georgette "an actual harlot": I therefore admit that from the author's stance this description is not a parody of heterosexual love—it is, instead, a parody of a band of sexually excited males lining up for a quickie with one female prostitute.

The description is a *parody* because Lett and his group are not sexually interested in Georgette. Hemingway's point is that Jake, because, in Robert E. Gajdusek's words, he is "dephallused...[and therefore] cannot wholly relate beyond himself" (Gajdusek, "Elephant Hunt" 16),[5] perceives the gays dancing with Georgette as a parodic reminder of that which a little earlier he himself had been unable to do with Georgette when she offered her services. The reason for what Spilka calls Jake's "honest anger," then, is that in Jake's view the gays freely choose not to do what Jake simply cannot do. In the narrator's own words, "[Georgette] had been taken up by them. I knew then that they would all dance with her. They are like that" (*SAR* 20). Hemingway must have expected at least some readers to examine the narrator's sweeping statement about gays, "They are like that," and query, "They are like what?" Those readers will come up with the following ironic answer. When the gays are courting a woman although they know they will not go to bed with her, the gays are like Jake himself—but there is the big difference that Jake cannot announce the fact that he will never sleep with the woman in the mocking manner in which the gays make such an announcement, namely by displaying what Jake calls "that superior, simpering composure" that he would do "anything to shatter."

Thus, if Jake-the-narrator is trying to give us a satiric portrayal of gays in general, Jake's strategy backfires and the narrator becomes a Satirist Satirized.[6] Whatever Hemingway's own attitude toward gays may have been, the author is giving us a satiric portrayal of his narrator-protagonist, who still has not come to terms with his physical handicap. This is why Jake lashes out at the homosexuals in whose company Brett happens to be when he sees her again. Jake resents the gays because he assumes that they are physically capable of choosing whether or not to sleep with a woman. The main focus of his honest anger, however, is that they are capable of doing to a woman precisely that which Jake, Brett's "standby lover" (Grimes 86), wishes he could do to the woman whom he has been allowing to keep him on an emotional roller coaster: to sexually reject that woman.

If Jake could somehow manage to sexually reject Brett—now, that *would* be "funny." That would be just as "amusing" as, according to the narrator's thoughts about the gays dancing with Georgette, the gays "are supposed to be." Actually, those thoughts are not merely the narrator's but also Jake-the-character's: While Jake is reporting the thoughts that are going through his mind as he is writing these lines, these thoughts concerning gays were in his mind when the event was taking place. Hemingway is employing here a point of view that, as in discussing a different context Sheldon N. Grebstein has put it, "evolves out of the sense of a continuous present, of the narrator's close proximity in time to the events he recounts" (Grebstein 72). Hemingway is employing this point of view here because in the scene where Jake unexpectedly sees Brett again the narrator is *very* close to the events he recounts. The narrator is very *painfully* close to the event because, as the threefold "with them was Brett" attests, the primary subject of what now we can call an interior monologue is not so much the behavior of Lett and his friends as it is the effect that Jake's war injury has on his love relationship with Brett—an injury that Jake places in a perverse linkage with what he considers to be an intrusion into his life by gays. Jake is trying to deny the linkage that in his desperation he has created between his handicap and the homosexuals, but the denial does not get him very far because Prentiss incisively, although unknowingly, reminds him that his anger directed at gays is caused by the loss of a certain "faculty" and his inability to cope with that loss.

In fact, what I consider to be the most "funny" aspect of the homosexuals scene is that Hemingway will be pointing to the linkage when he has Jake echo his interior-monologue statement that gays are "supposed to be amusing" in the very scene in which Jake tries to assure Brett that his sexuality disabling war injury is "supposed to be funny." Jake never tells us why he thinks gays "are supposed to be amusing," but I would argue that Hemingway has Jake establish a self-echo between his pronouncements on what supposedly is "amusing" and on what supposedly is "funny" for the following narrative purpose. Through the self-echo Jake is first of all setting up an ironic equivalence between his supposedly "amusing" physical inability to have sexual intercourse with women on the one hand, and on the other the gays' supposedly "funny" demeanor through which they *show* that they reject that type of sexual relationship and exercise a different sexual preference. As I tried to textually illustrate by exchanging the adjectives "amusing" and "funny," the equivalence is *ironic* because its establishment is not intended by Jake.

Second, through the self-echo Jake, likewise ironically because unintentionally, is already mapping out the road to coming to grips with his physical handicap. When Hemingway has Jake in his interior monologue about the gays observe, "they are supposed to be funny, and you should be tolerant," and then has Jake say about his sexual wound that it is "supposed to be funny," Hemingway is introducing the following idea. In order to be able to tolerate himself as he is with respect to sexual status, Jake will have to learn to tolerate other men who have a sexual preference different from his own. And once readers have become aware of the linkage, they may want to reread Jake's command to himself with the following emphases: "They [i.e., the gays] are supposed to be funny, and *you* [i.e., Jake] should be tolerant." After all, what does Jake, who knows he has in common with Lett and his group a sexual otherness, think he has that makes him superior to gays? When in his interior monologue Jake angrily speaks of the gays' "superior . . . composure," he is conceding that in one sense they are superior to him. Jake is envious of their composure—even if he feels called upon to judge that composure to be "simpering."

Jake does eventually learn to tolerate men who have a different sexual preference. Jake shows this in the most "funny" and the most "amusing" line in the entire novel, in the final line. When during another cab ride Brett says, "Oh, Jake . . . we could have had such a damned good time together," Jake responds, "Yes. . . . Isn't it pretty to think so?" (*SAR* 247). Brett's last words in the novel are a psychological-castration attempt in the sense that she is spelling out to Jake sexual demands that she knows he cannot meet, and that in his rejoinder Jake finally comes to terms with his physical handicap. Jake finally comes to grips with his sexual status when he parries Brett's psychological-castration attempt and exorcises her from his life by imitating the presumably effeminate-sounding language of Lett and his friends—that is, by verbally adopting the position of a homosexual, on whom Brett could not and would not make any sexual demands. Mimi Reisel Gladstein observes that in Jake's rejoinder, "Isn't it pretty to think so?", the word *pretty* is "a woman's word" (Gladstein 62), and I suggest that Hemingway intended Jake's final line to be spoken with an affected English accent much in the manner in which Robert Prentiss, the suspected homosexual, had expressed himself in the scene where Jake has his ill-fated reunion with Brett Ashley.

I said earlier that it would *really* be "funny" if Jake could somehow manage to sexually reject Brett. I will now add that in his rejoinder Jake transcends his physical handicap not only by exorcising Brett as an on-again off-again friend or companion, but precisely by rejecting her *sexually*. When she contends that if it weren't for Jake's war injury the two of them "could have had such a damned good time together," he is replying to her that she is wrong. Jake is telling Brett that the nonexistence of a sexual relationship between them has nothing to do with his injury: Because of the sexual preference that he reveals to Brett in the closing line of the novel, Jake simply would have had no sexual use for her.

By this I do not mean that at the conclusion of *The Sun Also Rises* Jake Barnes turns gay, but I do believe that Hemingway wanted the more adventurously speculative among his readers to at least consider such a possibility. When George Plimpton told Hemingway in their interview for the *Paris Review* that one of the editors of that journal interpreted Jake to have been "emasculated precisely as is a steer," Hemingway indignantly replied: "Who ever said that Jake was 'emasculated precisely as is a steer'? Actually, he had been wounded in quite a different way and his testicles were intact and not damaged. Thus he was capable of all normal feelings as a *man* but incapable of consummating them" (Plimpton 29).[7] Jake is incapable of *consummating* his feelings because he has lost his phallus—his manly "faculty," as it were—which, however, does not mean that somebody else could not consummate these feelings *for* him. After all, in the bedroom scene where Brett sends Count Mippipopolous away to get champagne, Brett gives Jake what in 1971 Chaman Nahal called "a perverted sexual satisfaction" (Nahal 44).[8]

Especially since Nahal did not even bother to talk about the possible mechanics of Jake's sexual satisfaction, I have to object to Nahal's insensitive use—insensitive not only to Hemingway's sexually handicapped or limited protagonist but also to Hemingway-the-artist—of the term "perverted," but Nahal was at least conceding that Jake is capable of experiencing orgasm without the capability of performing penile penetration. The interpretation that offers itself the most readily is that Brett employs a type of manual stimulation involving the testicles.[9] But since Brett refuses to let Jake sexually satisfy *her*, why would Jake want to remain in that relationship? After all, there is a possible alternative to what is in effect a one-way sexual relationship. Jake might be able to enjoy sex, enjoy both giving and receiving sexual satisfaction, through anal homosexual intercourse—that is, through taking what Jake would consider the "female" role during such intercourse. In fact, Jake may well be giving Brett a hint precisely in that direction when in the final line he tries to sound not just like Lett and his friends but actually like a female.

If Hemingway indeed tried to insinuate the possibility that Jake, instead of continuing his painful relationship with Brett, might consider homosexuality, would that mean that Hemingway is presenting Jake as a closet homosexual? There are several elements that suggest that Hemingway may have been thinking in those terms. First of all, even before Prentiss unknowingly rubs in Jake's loss of a certain "faculty," Jake's anger toward the gays is so vehement that he could be overcompensating for guilt feelings, guilt feelings that may have been caused by the recurring thought that he might be able to have mutually satisfying sexual relations if he turned to homosexuality. Jake has been living in Paris, which in the 1920s presumably was the homosexual capital of the world, long enough to have become "hard-boiled" about gays—unless gays in some way affected him personally.

"[H]ard-boiled" is of course what the narrator will later tell us he wishes he could be in his feelings toward the injury that denies him a mutually satisfying sexual relationship with Brett (SAR 34). But especially in light of the interaction between the words that Hemingway has Jake use in reference to sexual status—"amusing" for the gays and "funny" for Jake himself—I suspect that Hemingway is trying to tell us something about Jake when he first has his narrator speak of "composure" as an outward sign of how the gays feel about themselves *and* their sexuality, and later that night has Jake inform us that, in order to feel comfortable about his own sexuality, he would have to be "hard-boiled." Jake is envious of the gays both because they are able to have sex without women and because they seem to feel comfortable about their sexuality.

Since Jake has had his handicap for seven or eight years, his use of the word *hard-boiled* must be an exaggeration that expresses Jake's need to adjust to a situation that has recently developed. There has indeed been a new development that might explain Jake's self-pitying rumination that "it is awfully easy to be hard-boiled about everything in the daytime, but at night it is another thing" (SAR 34). When during their cab ride from the *bal musette* Jake tries to get something sexual started, Brett fights off his attempt to sexually gratify her in a manner that would be possible for him, an attempt that he had unsuccessfully made on an earlier occasion, for Brett pleads, "I don't want to go through that hell again" (26). The most intimate method for a dephallused man who loves a woman would seem to be that of cunnilingus. Thus Jake presumably has tried to assume a lesbian's role, that is, Jake-the-male has tried to play the role of a female homosexual.[10] When Jake is rejected by a woman who would give him sexual satisfaction but would not accept sexual satisfaction from him, Jake has come to the end of the heterosexual line.

The end of the heterosexual line for Jake is being confirmed when in the cab Brett voices agreement with Jake's assessment of their situation: "And there's not a damn thing we could do" (26). At this point Jake, who by his own account is not willing to accept the Catholic Church's "swell advice" (31) to forget about his self and his sexual urges, has to make a choice between celibacy and homosexuality. Until the cab ride from the *bal musette*, Jake had entertained the romantic hope that Brett eventually might be willing to allow him a two-way sexual relationship, and the suddenness of the disillusionment confronts Jake with a new situation and the resulting need for a decision that he perceives to be so dramatic that he has to become "hard-boiled." The decision is whether to turn homosexual—whether to turn to the sexual status that might enable him to gradually develop a measure of "composure." When Jake gets the feeling that he needs to become "hard-boiled," Hemingway is having Jake's contemptuous characterization of the gays' composure as "simpering" come back to haunt his protagonist. It is exactly by putting on the kind of composure that Jake had ascribed not only to the gays but also to the suspected homosexual, Robert Prentiss, that Jake exorcises the woman who had contributed to keeping the obsession with his war injury alive—and thus exorcises that obsession. When Jake parries Brett's reminder of what could have been by responding, "Yes. . . . Isn't it pretty to think so," he is displaying a composure that, while it may or may not be "superior," certainly is "simpering."

Hemingway, then, is poetically punishing Jake for his earlier display of bias against and contempt for people who held a sexual preference different from his own. It could even be argued that, whatever the reader personally may decide will become of Jake's love life, when Hemingway presents Jake as finally coming to terms with his sexual status, Hemingway ironically is making his narrator-protagonist apologize for his earlier bias against otherness in matters of sexuality. At any rate, Hemingway is presenting the acceptance of sexual diversity as instrumental in helping his protagonist find himself. When in the novel's "boy meets girl" scene, or more precisely, "boy meets girl *again*" scene, Hemingway introduced gays, he was bucking the customary contemporary authorial attitude toward homosexuals as marginalized characters.

What makes the conclusion of *The Sun Also Rises* especially "funny" is that, in dealing with Brett's contention about what could have been were it not for Jake's sexual otherness, Jake takes his cue from Robert Prentiss. Jake takes his cue for finding himself from a character whom Jake assumes to be gay but whose sexual orientation Hemingway teasingly withholds from us. All we know from Hemingway's text is that the "rising new [American] novelist" speaks with "some sort of an English accent." We do know that the model for Robert Prentiss was the Midwestern writer Glenway Wescott, whose affectation of a British accent irked Hemingway (Baker,

Ernest Hemingway: Critiques 146).[11] Therefore, was Hemingway perhaps satirizing the habit of stereotyping people according to their sexual orientation—and according to what *we perceive* to be their sexual orientation? Once we suspect that Hemingway may have presented one of his male protagonists as guilty of what I will semi-facetiously call "composure-envy," a thorough re-evaluation of Hemingway's treatment of what in his own time used to be authorially marginalized characters is overdue.

NOTES

1. I am using the 1954 edition of *The Sun Also Rises* rather than the first edition (1926) because it was not until 1953 that Charles Scribner, Jr., reinstated Mike Campbell's "bulls have no balls" (175–176) for the bowdlerized version, "bulls have no horns"; cf. James Hinkle, "Dear Mr. Scribner" 46. Hinkle citations in the following will be from his article "What's Funny in *The Sun Also Rises*," *The Hemingway Review*, 4 (Spring 1985), 37.

2. Let me quote Wagner-Martin in full:

The insult within the text is given to the male homosexual culture—as Jake watches the gay men—but his reference is genderless. On one occasion he says tersely, "This whole show makes me sick is all"; and earlier, more meditatively, "I was very angry. I know they are supposed to be amusing, and you should be tolerant, but I wanted to swing on one, any one, anything to shatter that superior, simpering composure" (21). This phrasing—widened to include *lesbians* as well as homosexual males—is more in keeping with the final "story" in his *A Moveable Feast*, when his "surprise" for Stein's passion for Alice B. Toklas shocks him into breaking with his mentor. ("Racial and Sexual Coding in Hemingway's *The Sun Also Rises*," *The Hemingway Review* 10 [Spring 1991] 21, emphasis added).

To be fair to Wagner-Martin, I will concede that she seems to be attributing "the insult within the text" and "this phrasing" to the narrator, but when she goes on to argue that Hemingway is actually using the *bal musette* episode to attack the lesbian Gertrude Stein (41), Wagner-Martin fails to distinguish between the author and the narrator. Hemingway's feelings toward Gertrude Stein notwithstanding, I see nothing in the text Wagner-Martin quotes that suggests that Jake's phrasing has been "widened to include lesbians." See notes 9 and 10 below.

3. The point about Jake uncritically concluding that Prentiss is gay has been made by me before; I am adding here evidence that Jake has little justification for identifying Prentiss with Lett's group.

4. Mark Spilka, "The Death of Love in *The Sun Also Rises*," *Twelve Original Essays on Great American Novels*, ed. Charles Shapiro (Detroit: Wayne State UP, 1958).

5. As Gajdusek notes in *Hemingway and Joyce*, in a letter to Philip Young Hemingway would "indicate that his model [for Jake] was actually a young man whose penis had been shot away but whose testicles and spermatic cord remained intact." Since the idea of Jake's much-debated wound as a shot-off penis could have been an afterthought on Hemingway's part, we have to find clues in that direction

in the novel itself. See also, Robin E. Gajdusek, "Elephant Hunt in Eden: A New Study of Old Myths and Other Strange Beasts in Hemingway's Garden," *The Hemingway Review* 7 (Fall 1987): 15–19.

6. For the Satirist Satirized idea I am indebted to Robert C. Elliott, author of *The Power of Satire: Magic, Ritual, Art*. Princeton: Princeton University Press, 1960, passim; Elliott does not mention Hemingway in a Satirist Satirized context.

7. *Writers at Work: The Paris Review Interviews, Second Series* (New York: Viking, 1963).

8. Chaman Nahal, *The Narrative Pattern in Ernest Hemingway's Fiction* (Rutherford, NJ: Fairleigh Dickinson UP, 1971).

9. Kenneth S. Lynn has suggested that Brett uses oral sex on a quasi-lesbianized Jake (324). While Lynn's interpretation is an interesting reflection of current critical preoccupation with Hemingway's preoccupation with androgyny (see Spilka's *Quarrel with Androgyny*), it leaves too many physiological questions unanswered. For example, is Lynn suggesting that Jake has enough of a neurologically functioning penile shaft left to give him a clitoris of sorts? *That* would be a thought worth pursuing—and it would be extremely "funny," adding thematic significance to Brett's comment, made in reference to Jake's injury, that "chaps never know anything, do they?" (*SAR* 27). And such a notion of a lesbianized Jake would call into question the validity of Wagner-Martin's rather harsh argument that Hemingway used the *bal musette* episode to attack the lesbian Gertrude Stein.

10. If my reading that Jake has tried to assume a lesbian's role is acceptable, is it still possible to interpret with Wagner-Martin that Hemingway used Jake's characterization in the *bal musette* scene to attack lesbianism? And if Hemingway indeed had Jake widen his phrasing to include lesbians, wouldn't such a widening be satirical toward Jake rather than toward lesbianism?

11. As Michael S. Reynolds noted in his paper on "The *Jimmy Breen* Novel Manuscript" at the "Up in Michigan II" Conference in October of 1991, Wescott's contemporaries considered him to be homosexual. Awareness of this fact can make the *bal musette* scene even more "amusing" and "funny," for in that case it could be argued that Hemingway is toying with his readers by not telling them whether Prentiss belongs to Lett's group.

Selected Bibliography

BOOKS BY ERNEST HEMINGWAY

Across the River and Into the Trees. New York: Scribner, 1950.

By-Line: Ernest Hemingway. Selected Articles and Dispatches of Four Decades. Ed. William White. New York: Scribner, 1967.

Complete Short Stories of Ernest Hemingway, The. New York: Scribner, 1987.

Dangerous Summer, The. Introduced by James Michener. New York: Scribner, 1985.

Death in the Afternoon. New York: Scribner, 1932.

88 Poems. Ed. Nicholas Gerogiannis. New York: Harcourt, 1979.

Ernest Hemingway: Selected Letters, 1917–1961. Ed. Carlos Baker. New York: Scribner, 1981.

Farewell to Arms, A. New York: Scribner, 1929.

Fifth Column and Four Stories of the Spanish Civil War, The. New York: Scribner, 1972.

For Whom the Bell Tolls. New York: Scribner, 1940.

Garden of Eden, The. New York: Scribner, 1986.

Green Hills of Africa. New York: Scribner, 1935.

Hemingway: The Wild Years. Ed. and introduced by Gene Z. Hanrahan. New York: Dell Publishing, 1962.

in our time. Paris: Three Mountains Press, 1924.

In Our Time. New York: Boni & Liveright, 1925.

Islands in the Stream. New York: Scribner, 1970.

Men at War. Ed. and introduced by Ernest Hemingway. New York: Crown Publishers, 1942.

Men Without Women. New York: Scribner, 1927.

Moveable Feast, A. New York: Scribner, 1964.
Nick Adams Stories, The. Preface by Philip Young. New York: Scribner, 1972.
Old Man and the Sea, The. New York: Scribner, 1952.
Spanish Earth, The. Introduced by Jasper Wood. Cleveland: J. B. Savage Co., 1938.
Sun Also Rises, The. New York: Scribner, 1926.
To Have and Have Not. New York: Scribner, 1937.
Torrents of Spring, The. New York: Scribner, 1926.
Winner Take Nothing. New York: Scribner, 1933.

BOOKS ABOUT ERNEST HEMINGWAY

Algren, Nelson. *Notes from a Sea Diary: Hemingway All the Way.* New York: Putnam, 1965.

Allen, Michael J. B., and Robert L. Benson, ed. *First Images of America.* Berkeley: U of California P, 1976.

Arnold, Lloyd R. *High on the Wild with Hemingway.* Caldwell, ID: Caxton Printers, 1968.

Asselineau, Roger, ed. *The Literary Reputation of Hemingway in Europe.* New York: New York UP, 1965.

Astro, Richard, and Jackson J. Benson, ed. *Hemingway in Our Time.* Corvallis, OR: Oregon State UP, 1974.

Atkins, John. *The Art of Ernest Hemingway.* London: Spring Books, 1952.

Baker, Carlos. *Ernest Hemingway: Critiques of Four Major Novels.* New York: Scribner, 1962.

———. *Ernest Hemingway: A Life Story.* New York: Scribner, 1969.

———. *Hemingway: The Writer as Artist.* Princeton, NJ: Princeton UP, 1972.

Beegel, Susan F. *Hemingway's Neglected Short Stories: New Perspectives.* Tuscaloosa: U of Alabama P, 1992.

Benson, Jackson J. *Hemingway: The Writer's Art of Self-Defense.* Minneapolis: U of Minnesota P, 1969.

———, ed. *The Short Stories of Ernest Hemingway: Critical Essays.* Durham, NC: Duke UP, 1975.

Brasch, James D., and Joseph Sigman. *Hemingway's Library: A Composite Record.* New York: Garland, 1981.

Brenner, Gerry. *"The Old Man & the Sea": Story of a Common Man.* New York: Macmillan Co., 1991.

Bruccoli, Matthew J. *Scott and Ernest.* New York: Random House, 1978.

Buckley, Peter. *Ernest.* New York: Dial Press, 1978.

Burgess, Anthony. *Ernest Hemingway and His World.* New York: Scribner, 1978.

DeFalco, Joseph. *The Hero in Hemingway's Short Stories.* Pittsburgh: U of Pittsburgh P, 1963.

Diliberto, Gioia. *Hadley.* New York: Ticknor & Fields, 1992.

Donaldson, Scott. *By Force of Will.* New York: Viking, 1977.

Fenton, Charles A. *The Apprenticeship of Ernest Hemingway.* New York: Farrar, Straus, 1954.

Fetterly, Judith. *The Resisting Reader.* Bloomington: Indiana UP, 1978.

Fuentes, Norberto. *Hemingway in Cuba.* Secaucus, NJ: Lyle Stuart, 1984.

Gajdusek, Robert E. *Hemingway and Joyce*. Corte Madera, CA: Square Circle P, 1984.

Grebstein, Sheldon N. *Hemingway's Craft*. Carbondale: Southern Illinois UP, 1973.

Griffin, Peter. *Along with Youth*. New York: Oxford UP, 1985.

Gurko, Leo. *Ernest Hemingway and the Pursuit of Heroism*. New York: Crowell, 1968.

Hanneman, Audre. *Ernest Hemingway: A Comprehensive Bibliography*. Princeton, NJ: Princeton UP, 1967.

————. *Supplement to Ernest Hemingway: A Comprehensive Bibliography*. Princeton, NJ: Princeton UP, 1975.

Hemingway, Gregory H. *Papa*. Boston: Houghton Mifflin, 1976.

Hemingway, Jack. *Misadventures of a Fly Fisherman*. Dallas: Taylor Publishing, 1986.

Hemingway, Leicester. *My Brother, Ernest Hemingway*. Cleveland and New York: World Publishing, 1962.

Hemingway, Mary Welsh. *How It Was*. New York: Knopf, 1976.

Hotchner, A. E. *Papa Hemingway*. New York: Random House, 1966.

Hovey, Richard B. *Hemingway: The Inward Terrain*. Seattle: U of Washington P, 1968.

Joost, Nicholas. *Ernest Hemingway and the Little Magazines*. Barre, MA: Barre Publishers, 1968.

Kert, Bernice. *The Hemingway Women*. New York: Norton, 1983.

Lewis, Robert W. *A Farewell to Arms: The War of the Words*. New York: Twayne Publishers, 1992.

————, ed. *Hemingway in Italy and Other Essays*. New York: Praeger Publishers, 1990.

————. *Hemingway on Love*. New York: Haskell House, 1973.

Lynn, Kenneth S. *Hemingway*. New York: Simon and Schuster, 1987.

Martin, Robert A. *The Writer's Craft*. Ann Arbor: U of Michigan P, 1982.

McCaffery, John K. M., ed. *Ernest Hemingway: The Man and His Work*. New York: Cooper Square Publishers, 1969.

Mellow, James R. *Hemingway: A Life Without Consequences*. Boston: Houghton Mifflin, 1992.

Meyers, Jeffrey. *Hemingway: A Bibliography*. New York: Harper & Row, 1985.

————, ed. *Hemingway: The Critical Heritage*. London: Routledge & Kegan Paul, 1982.

Montgomery, Constance Cappel. *Hemingway in Michigan*. New York: Fleet, 1966.

Morrison, Toni. *Playing in the Dark: Whiteness and the Literary Imagination*. Cambridge, MA: Harvard UP, 1992.

Nagel, James, ed. *Ernest Hemingway: The Writer in Context*. Madison: U of Wisconsin P, 1984.

Noble, Donald R., ed. *Hemingway: A Revaluation*. Troy, NY: Whitson, 1983.

Oldsey, Bernard S., ed. *Ernest Hemingway: The Papers of a Writer*. New York: Garland, 1981.

————. *Hemingway's Hidden Craft*. University Park: Pennsylvania State UP, 1979.

Penner, Dick. *Countries of the Mind: The Fiction of J. M. Coretzee*. Westport, CT: Greenwood Press, 1989.

Phillips, Gene D. *Hemingway and Film*. New York: Ungar, 1980.

Pivano, Fernanda. *Hemingway*. Milan: Rusconi, 1985.

Raeburn, John. *Fame Became of Him*. Bloomington: Indiana UP, 1984.

Reynolds, Michael S., ed. *Critical Essays on Ernest Hemingway's "In Our Time."* Boston: G. K. Hall, 1983.

———. *Hemingway: The American Homecoming*. Oxford: Basil Blackwell, 1992.

———. *Hemingway: The Paris Years*. Oxford: Basil Blackwell, 1989.

———. *Hemingway's First War*. Princeton, NJ: Princeton UP, 1976.

———. *Hemingway's Reading: 1910–1940. An Inventory*. Princeton, NJ: Princeton UP, 1981.

———. *The Young Hemingway*. Oxford: Basil Blackwell, 1986.

Ross, Lillian. *Portrait of Hemingway*. New York: Simon & Schuster, 1961.

Rovit, Earl, and Gerry Brenner. *Ernest Hemingway*, rev. ed. Boston: G. K. Hall, 1986.

Rudat, Wolfgang. *A Rotten Way to be Wounded: The Tragicomedy of "The Sun Also Rises."* New York: Peter Lang Publishing, 1990.

Samuelson, Arnold. *With Hemingway*. New York: Random House, 1984.

Sanderson, Rena, ed. *Blowing The Bridge: Essays on Hemingway & "For Whom the Bell Tolls."* Westport, CT: Greenwood Press, 1992.

Sanford, Marcelline Hemingway. *At the Hemingways*. Boston: Atlantic-Little Brown, 1962.

Scafella, Frank, ed. *Hemingway: Essays of Reassessment*. New York: Oxford UP, 1990.

Smith, Paul. *A Reader's Guide to the Short Stories of Ernest Hemingway*. Boston: G. K. Hall, 1989.

Spilka, Mark. *Hemingway's Quarrel with Androgyny*. Lincoln: U of Nebraska P, 1990.

Stanton, Edward. *Hemingway and Spain*. Seattle: U Washington P, 1989.

Stephens, Robert O. *Hemingway's Non-Fiction*. Chapel Hill: U of North Carolina P, 1968.

Svoboda, Frederic Joseph. *Hemingway & "The Sun Also Rises."* Lawrence: UP of Kansas, 1983.

Tetlow, Wendolyn. *Hemingway's "In Our Time": Lyrical Dimensions*. Cranbury, NJ: Bucknell UP, 1992.

Wagner, Linda W., ed. *Ernest Hemingway*. East Lansing: Michigan State UP, 1974.

Watts, Emily S. *Ernest Hemingway and the Arts*. Urbana: U of Illinois P, 1971.

Weeks, Robert P., ed. *Hemingway: A Collection of Critical Essays*. Englewood Cliffs, NJ: Prentice Hall, 1962.

Wylder, Delbert E. *Hemingway's Heroes*. Albuquerque: U of New Mexico P, 1969.

Young, Philip. *Ernest Hemingway: A Reconsideration*. University Park: Pennsylvania State UP, 1966.

Index

About the Contributors and Editor

SUSAN F. BEEGEL, visiting scholar at the University of Idaho and editor-in-chief of *The Hemingway Review*, was co-director of the 1990 International Hemingway Conference in Boston and has published *Hemingway's Craft of Omission: Four Manuscript Examples* and *Hemingway's Neglected Short Fiction: New Perspectives*.

ROBIN GAJDUSEK has published numerous articles on Hemingway as well as two books, *Hemingway's Paris* and *Hemingway and Joyce: A Study in Debt and Payment*.

THOMAS HERMANN is an assistant at the English Seminar at the University of Zurich. His chapter is part of his Ph.D. dissertation on Hemingway and the visual arts.

ALLEN JOSEPHS, University Research Professor and Professor of Spanish at the University of West Florida, has published *White Wall of Spain*, several critical editions of Lorca's works, and (with Sandra Forman) *Only Mystery: Federico Garcia Lorca's Poetry in Word and Image*.

DONALD JUNKINS has published nine books of poetry, the most recent of which is *Playing for Keeps*. He has lectured on Hemingway in Spain, Italy, Germany and China, and he was a Fulbright lecturer at Xiamen University in 1993.

MIRIAM B. MANDEL, Professor of English Literature at Tel Aviv University, has published articles on Fitzgerald, Conrad, Jane Austen and A. E.

Houseman. Her book *Annotations to the Work of Ernest Hemingway* is forthcoming.

LARRY MERCHANT, a former columnist in New York, Philadelphia and Los Angeles and currently a television sports commentator and writer, is the author of *And Every Day You Take Another Bite, Ringside Seat At The Circus* and *The National Football Lottery*.

ERIK NAKJAVANI specializes in the aesthetics of Hemingway's fiction in its connection with literary theory and psychoanalysis. His latest publication is "Hemingway's *The Fifth Column* and the Question of Ideology" in the *North Dakota Quarterly*.

JAMES PLATH is the director of the Hemingway Days Writer's Workshop and Conference in Key West. He also edits *Clockwatch Review: A Journal of the Arts*.

ANN L. PUTNAM of the University of Puget Sound has published a short story, "The Bear" in the *South Dakota Review* and articles in *The Hemingway Review*, Susan Beegel's Hemingway collection and the *Journal of Western American Literature*.

WOLFGANG E. H. RUDAT has published two books on Hemingway, *Alchemy in "The Sun Also Rises": Hidden Gold in Hemingway's Narrative* and *A Rotten Way To Be Wounded: The Tragicomedy of "The Sun Also Rises,"* as well as articles on Hemingway and others.

FRANK SCAFELLA directed the Third International Hemingway Conference in Schruns, Austria, and has published *Hemingway: Essays of Reassessment*. His chapter is part of *Hemingway on Soul*, a book in progress.

PAUL SMITH, the founding president of the Hemingway Society, has published *A Readers Guide to the Short Stories of Ernest Hemingway* and various articles in *American Literature, Journal of Modern Literature* and *The Hemingway Review*.

MARK SPILKA, Professor of English and Comparative Literature at Brown University, is the editor and one of the founders of the journal *Novel: A Forum on Fiction*. He has published books on Lawrence, Dickens and Kafka, Woolf, and Hemingway. *Hemingway's Quarrel With Androgyny* came out in 1990.

H. R. STONEBACK, the director of English Graduate Studies at SUNY, New Paltz, has taught at the University of Paris and as a Fulbright lecturer at Peking University. He has published articles on Faulkner, Hemingway and modern fiction.

ELIZABETH DEWBERRY VAUGHN has published articles on Hemingway in *Modern Fiction Studies, The Hemingway Review* and *The Com-*

paratist. She has published a novel, *Many Things Have Happened Since He Died,* and a second novel, *Break The Heart of Me,* is forthcoming.

KENNETH ROSEN was co-founder and co-editor of *Hemingway Notes,* the first journal devoted exclusively to Hemingway studies. He has been a member of the executive board of the Hemingway Society and the first board of directors of The Ernest Hemingway Foundation. He has published articles on Hemingway and contemporary Native American literature both here and in other countries; his books *The Man To Send Rain Clouds* and *Voices of The Rainbow* are edited collections of American Indian fiction and American Indian poetry. He has twice been a Ford Foundation fellow and has taught Hemingway as a Fulbright lecturer in Greece, China and Indonesia. He is currently Professor of English at Dickinson College in Carlisle, Pennsylvania.